S0-DTB-563

TORRES

TORRES

An Intimate Portrait of the Kid who Became King

Luca Caioli

CORINTHIAN BOOKS

Published in the UK in 2009 by
Corinthian Books, an imprint of
Icon Books Ltd, Omnibus Business Centre,
39–41 North Road, London N7 9DP
email: info@iconbooks.co.uk
www.iconbooks.co.uk

Sold in the UK, Europe, South Africa and Asia
by Faber & Faber Ltd, Bloomsbury House,
74–77 Great Russell Street, London WC1B 3DA

Distributed in the UK, Europe, South Africa and Asia
by TBS Ltd, TBS Distribution Centre, Colchester Road
Frating Green, Colchester CO7 7DW

This edition published in Australia in 2009
by Allen & Unwin Pty Ltd,
PO Box 8500, 83 Alexander Street,
Crows Nest, NSW 2065

Distributed in Canada by
Penguin Books Canada,
90 Eglinton Avenue East, Suite 700,
Toronto, Ontario M4P 2YE

ISBN: 978-190685-007-4

Text copyright © 2009 Luca Caioli
Translation copyright © 2009 Geoffrey Goff
Photos © Back Page Images

The author has asserted his moral rights.

No part of this book may be reproduced in any form, or by any
means, without prior permission in writing from the publisher.

Typeset in New Baskerville by Marie Doherty

Printed and bound in the UK by
Clays of Bungay

Contents

Chapter 1

Liverpool's Number 9

Thoughts and reflections from the Kop

'I love him. He's great. For someone from Spain, he embodies everything we want from our Liverpool players. I mean, obviously, we've got Gerrard and Carra who represent the spirit of the club but he's stepped into the Liverpool history and culture like he's been there all his life.' Sarah

'He was a Red long before he played for us.' Dave

'He's basically a legend. He's such a great guy. If I could have his babies I would.' Archie

'He's the boy isn't he? Class, absolute class.' Frank

'There was scepticism about how many goals he'd score here but in his first season he got 33. He's also a very humble man so he's very popular.' Paul

'He's one of the best strikers in the world.' Ryan

'He's an English striker isn't he?' Peter

'It's not just that he's a very good striker. He works really hard, he defends from the front. He chases down a lot of defenders and *doesn't give them time on the ball which makes it easy for the rest of the team.'* James

'He's one of the best players we have. He's probably far more skilful than any goalscorer we've ever had in Owen, Rush, Fowler ...' Dennis

'His physicality is suited to the English game but it's more to do with his personality and his character for me. He's a totally great lad. He's down-to-earth, working class, same as us (from Fuenlabrada, and it's quite similar to a lot of places in Liverpool), so we've really taken to him and he's really taken to the fans as well. If you see him in the street, he's happy to talk to people.' Bessie

'He's unique. Under Benítez, he's getting into space better and found a different dimension to his game'. Neil

'He's a fantastic player – good movement, he's quick. Quick with his feet, quick with his mind. He's a great goalscorer. He's got a good empathy with the crowd. He's very well-liked.' Chris

'He's a god. It's what he brings to the team. A different dimension.' Franco

'I think he's probably the best thing since sliced bread. Absolutely amazing.' Sam

No one at Anfield refuses to answer questions about El Niño. There are still two hours to go before the match gets under way but there is already a big buzz around the historic stadium. Scarves, party hats, flags and red shirts are everywhere, with people going this way and that. A man holds his son's hand in the queue to enter the club museum and admire the Liverpool trophies. Others slip into the Reds' souvenir shop, take up positions near the main stand entrance to see the players come in, pose for a typical photo in front of the Bill Shankly statue, desperately search for a ticket to see the game (despite constant PA announcements that the match has long been sold out), wait for old friends, ask which entrance to go in by, buy last-minute match programmes and give up any hope of entering The Albert (the pub right next to The Kop, opposite the new Hillsborough Justice Campaign Shop on Walton Breck Road), a heaving mass of bodies, noise, songs and pints. Red is the overwhelming colour but rumours are that is because it's full of Norwegians and other 'out-of-towners'.

And standing in the pub doorway is Jan, a fan who has indeed come all the way from Bergen in Norway just for the game. He steps outside for a cigarette. What does he think of Torres? 'He's young, he's got the speed, the ability. He's got everything. He's popular because of his attitude, the way he presents himself. He's very young but also very mature. He shines a kind of charisma that people adore.'

An English friend, Robert, butts into the conversation to give his opinion: 'We like his humility. We like the way he loves Liverpool Football Club. He's not one of these players who just signs up for the money. He's got a genuine love of Liverpool Football Club and that's reflected in the supporters who actually love the man. You'll see Torres tattoos, Torres shirts, banners.

'Everything's for Torres because he's for the club, which this club hasn't had for a long time, since your Ian Rushes or your Kenny Dalglishes. He has his own songs. He's one of us. When he hears his name sung, his heart beats. He wants to play for the club. You don't get that very often in the modern game.'

Gus reinforces the message: 'Liverpool is very much a working-class city. A player like Torres comes along, plays the same way and connects with the fans and that ethos. The fans love him. He loves the fans. It's a match made in heaven.'

There is more in the same vein, this time from Sean: 'I think he's got a rapport with the fans. He understands them. He understands the passion. He's committed. Not only that, he's technically brilliant. He's fast. He's pacey. Whereas, at Atlético Madrid, he was struggling for goals, at Liverpool he's now the striker and we centre our game on him scoring goals and it suits him perfectly.'

Round the corner, Ian, who has a stall of fan memorabilia selling everything from badges to flags, gives his view – economically speaking – of the Torres phenomenon: 'Definitely worth the money, yes, but Gerrard's still the one.'

In the club shop, however, they think otherwise. Torres is the top shirt-seller. Inside is Callum, aged ten, closely watched over by his father, who is wearing the Number 9 shirt. They go to every home game. What does Callum think of Fernando?

'It can be frustrating at times when Rafa doesn't pick him but when he plays he's a quality player and he knows where the goal is. I like how he can dribble past a lot of players and score.'

Joanna is sitting on a low wall with some friends, eating a plate of sausage and chips with a plastic fork. She happily breaks off to say what she thinks: 'What I like about Torres is he's not just speedy. There's skill in there as well, his technique is fantastic. So he's married the two really. He's got the skill and the physicality. He's the whole package for me.'

Alexandra gives a hearty cackle before making her contribution: 'His best quality – his looks! Look at my hair!'

A quick glance is more than enough to realise that the Spanish striker is the main inspiration behind her fringe and blonde colouring. And Cecilia adds, with a cheeky grin: 'We love the Spanish in Liverpool.'

Right in front, and across the street, is The Park – another pub bursting at the seams. To get inside you have to use your elbows but at the same time try not to knock over the huge number of beers squeezed onto the tables. At the bar, waiting for a pint takes time, but conversation sparks up immediately. The only problem is making yourself heard above the songs, chatter and increasingly animated prematch chanting. It's a fun atmosphere, with the imposing structure of Anfield clearly visible through the window. When one of the throng, with his military shirt and shaved head, hears the question about Torres, he breaks into song. The scarves move, the beer glasses are held high, everyone dances and claps their hands, singing:

> *His armband proved*
> *he was a red*
> *Torres, Torres!!*
> *You'll never walk alone it said*
> *Torres, Torres!!*
> *We brought the lad from sunny Spain*
> *He gets the ball, he scores again*
> *Fernando Torres – Liverpool's Number Nine*
> *Na-Nar*
> *Na-Nar-Nar*
> *Fernando Torres – Liverpool's Number Nine.*

You have to wait a bit for the noise go down to a level where you can carry on talking. For some time, a group has been gathered round a table stacked with beers of every type. Initially, no one wants to talk, each trying to persuade the other to speak. In the end it's John, with his coloured serpent tattoos and red shirt, who begins: 'What I like about Torres is that a lot of foreign players come over to England and take some time to adjust, whereas he's got stuck in. Defenders tackle him hard, but he can still put the ball back in the net. Brilliant.'

Eventually, the others pluck up courage to join in. 'He's a very unique striker because he can score long-distance goals, tap-ins, he can do anything really. You've got to tie him up for a longer contract,' says Steve.

Joe, leaning against a doorpost, picks up the same theme, shouting to make himself heard: 'No matter what happens, he says he's staying. That's good. There are too many players these days who are looking elsewhere for clubs but Torres says that Liverpool "is in my heart".'

Chapter 2
He is a red

4 July 2007

The photo is unforgettable. On the left, Rafa Benítez, as happy as a sandboy, in dark jacket and white shirt with red stripes, holding up one end of a Liverpool scarf with the words 'You'll Never Walk Alone' written on it. On the right, holding the other end, is Fernando Torres, wearing the club's Number 9 shirt. The one that has graced legends like Ian Rush and Robbie Fowler.

The tiered seating in the stands at Anfield forms the background. It's a little after 3pm (UK time) when El Niño arrives to be presented to the media as a new player in the Merseyside squad. First, the signing of the contract that ties him to Liverpool for six years on a salary of 6.5 million Euros a season – a sum exceeded only by captain Steven Gerrard's. Then the press conference in jacket and tie with the shirt collar slightly undone. One can see that the lad from Fuenlabrada is nervous. He talks in Spanish and says straight away that 'the club is one of the best in Europe, a victorious club, its past and its present shows it. For me it was an opportunity which I couldn't miss out on.'

He looks to Benítez, always at his side, and explains:

'We didn't know each other personally but when I spoke to him for the first time … simply to know that Benítez had confidence in me is something incredible. And that a club like Liverpool, which can buy any of the best players in the world, should choose you to form part of the team comes as a surprise and fills you with pride. The fact that Liverpool are giving me the Number 9 jersey just goes to show the confidence they have placed in me, when considering those who have worn that shirt before me. But I'm not afraid of the responsibility that this brings.'

Torres knows the expectations that his transfer has created, the most expensive in Liverpool's century-old history (£26.5 million compared with the £14 million paid for French striker, Djibril Cissé, from Auxerre in July 2004). He knows that the public wants compensation in the form of goals. He hopes he can do it.

Rafa Benítez, who doesn't let him out of his sight for a second, maintains: 'We have signed a youngster with a promising future ahead of him. He is the player we needed.' There is no problem with responsibilities within the squad: 'Crouch,' he explains, 'works hard and Fernando can hold up the ball, look to get round the defence and construct moves.'

He stresses Fernando's intelligence, his ability to understand situations in a flash, and gives, as an example, the fact that the lad had immediately understood what it means to touch the badge with the words 'This is Anfield' at the entrance to the tunnel leading to the pitch – perhaps the most frequently broadcast image on the British television reports.

The Spanish manager reiterates Torres' passion and competitive abilities: 'He demonstrated these when he was only seventeen.' When asked what his goal-scoring abilities will be, he responds: 'I'm not going to put any pressure on him and say that he's going to score more than twenty goals. I prefer to have four strikers who score fifteen each.' He stresses the fact that 'Torres wanted to come. He was very clear. It would be a disappointment if he doesn't try to be a star.' He also talks of his new acquisition's feelings. Benítez has no problem in declaring them: 'His heart will stay with Atlético and that's normal. But one cannot doubt his professionalism. In his two final games with Atlético he played with an injured toe. He defended the club badge right up until the end!'

Of course, his Atlético heart ... Fernando confirmed it a few hours earlier in Madrid when, dressed in black as if at a funeral, he said goodbye to the Atlético fans in the Vicente Calderón stadium at 10.30am (9.30am UK time): 'Wherever I am, my heart will always be red and white. This isn't a goodbye, it's a "see you later". Atlético is my family. I hope to return one day, when the club is at the high level where it deserves to be,' says El Niño who, with difficulty, manages to contain his emotions. He assumes responsibility for the transfer, saying that he had asked the directors to listen to the Liverpool offer.

Taking this position goes down very well with the club, which does not want to appear as the guilty party in the departure of Torres. Enrique Cerezo, the club president – more relaxed after hearing what the blond youngster sitting at his side has said – wishes him good luck and adds: 'Atlético understands and lets you leave in the hope that you come back soon. We don't want this to be a sad farewell act but a happy one, as when people who are very close say goodbye to each other.' To explain the mutual separation after twelve years of life together, Torres adds that 'the club is more important than the individual people. And my leaving for Liverpool benefits everyone.' It benefits Atlético, which, thanks to the money from the transfer, will be able to reinforce the team. And also Fernando Torres, who takes the right European train to be nearer those goals he has always dreamed about.

But things are not so simple ... Despite the African-level heat and blistering sun, some 100 fans demonstrate outside the gates of the Calderón, shouting at the tops of their voices and holding up banners, on which is written 'Fernando, don't go!', 'We love you', 'Torres yes, management no', and then a series of strong insults aimed at the president, sporting director, secretary etc. They don't believe all the nice words. They are convinced that the people behind El Niño's exit are the Atlético top brass, together with the club's policies, the years of bad signings, the dashed hopes, one manager after another, of responsibilities never undertaken. The *colchoneros* (fans of Atlético) feel sad, despondent and angry. They forgive their captain, their emblem of recent years, who has, without doubt, been the positive image and focal point for the dreams of a club that knows what it is to suffer. And yet the *colchoneros* don't get too upset with Torres. They understand him. They understand that he wants to go from what has been his home, that the Little Prince wants to grow up. And even if El Niño says: 'Take it easy, time heals everything,' getting used to the idea is not that easy.

The news of Fernando's move to Liverpool is confirmed by Atlético at 7pm on 3 July. But it was 'Pulcinella's secret' – something everyone already knew. The Manzanares (the river of Madrid) club and the Merseyside club had reached a provisional agreement at the end of May. How did this come about? Every summer, offers for Torres arrived at Atlético from several big clubs.

In 2005, for example, there was talk of Chelsea, Newcastle, Arsenal and even Inter who, according to the press, had offered Christian Vieri plus a large transfer fee. In an interview with an English newspaper, Fernando explained:

'People always ask me about my departure. Atlético is a big club but we don't win much. Somewhere else, I would be competing for important trophies but here I have things that I wouldn't be able to have in other clubs – my family and my friends, my feeling of belonging to a humble Madrid team, the one that represents the working class. We don't have money, nor power. Very occasionally we win trophies but we exist for other reasons. We give the fans a safety valve of escape for their problems and because of that they absorb themselves into the club.'

In a few words, he explained the quasi-absurd philosophy of the *colchoneros*, the hopes of the fans and the players, which are that – one day or another – their destiny will change. Perhaps for this, after taking into account together with his representatives all the offers that arrived, he never decided to say 'Yes'. In 2006 the voices of the market became ever more insistent. Three candidates for the presidency of Real Madrid (which will be won by Ramón Calderón) have long pursued El Niño but have always received negative replies. At the end of the season, Manchester United also comes in.

In July, there is a rumour that Sir Alex Ferguson's club is about to put in, on paper, a 37-million-euro offer. Inter come back again, offering 38 million. But it doesn't stop there. The Atlético directors say that El Niño is not for sale and is too important for the club.

And in September 2006, they announce the renewal of Torres' contract until 30 June 2009, with a clause for breach of contract, which, strangely, goes from 90 to 40 million Euros. The player also improves his salary to 7 million Euros per season.

Spring 2007 – Rafa Benítez is thinking of a new striker for his team. Eto'o or Torres? The gaffer weighs up the two possibilities and, according to his custom, asks for reports covering everything under the sun. Not only about the pair's football skills, but also about their personalities, the behaviour of the Cameroon and Madrid players in their respective dressing rooms, and in their daily lives off the pitch. Scrupulous and methodical, he does not want to miss even the smallest detail. He wants to minimise the risks of the transaction. In the end, after closely studying the two options, he decides to go for Fernando – who, it seems, has triumphed in the reports.

We are in April and the negotiations between Liverpool and Atlético get under way. Acting as mediator is Manuel García Quilón, a famous football agent who, amongst other things, is also the representative of Rafa Benítez.

At the end of May, a provisional agreement between the two clubs is reached, to the point where Atlético begins to look for a substitute for El Niño. They ask Villarreal the price of the Uruguayan, Diego Forlán. Meanwhile, Rafa Benítez, after the Champions League final in Athens, which the Reds lose against the Milan of Filippo Inzaghi and Carlo Ancellotti, calls Fernando. To begin with, the Atlético player thinks it's a wind-up, some imitator who is trying to trick him. So much so that he cuts everything short and replies in monosyllables. He doesn't want to be set-up. So he calls Pepe Reina, his friend in Liverpool, to check that the number of the person who called really is that of the manager. And it is. He can now have a more relaxed conversation and listen more closely to the Madrid-born manager's offer. Benítez says to count on him, that he will do everything to bring him to England, and that he hopes he will accept. El Niño has always liked English football. He's always said that, one day, if he decided to leave, he would prefer to end up in the Premier League.

Two years previously, Liverpool got to the final of the Champions League and won. It's a club with a style and philosophy that's to his liking. Its fans are devoted to the cause, just like those of Atlético. At a stretch, the Calderón reminds one of Anfield. And also the Reds' fans have a history of being working class. For sure, it's not the Manchester of the shining stars or even the Chelsea of the Russians, but this could mean that there will be more space for him. On the positive side, there is also the fact that Reina, Xavi Alonso and Arbeloa are at Liverpool. With them, and with Cesc Fabregas, Fernando has talked many times of what it's like to live in the UK, the atmosphere and the way they play football. And he has always got positive feedback. In reality, the Spanish Liverpool could be an important factor in helping to adapt to a new football environment.

Last but not least, there is his Atlético captain's armband. For years it's carried the words 'You'll Never Walk Alone'. The story behind it began with Fernando's group of friends. They all wanted to have the same tattoo and they discovered that this expression represented exactly what was most important to them – the bond of friendship that will never be broken, wherever you are. Torres is reluctant. As captain of Atlético, it's not particularly smart to get the Liverpool motto inscribed on your arm, because maybe the papers would write about it. So, in order that he's not left out, they find the best – and the most discreet – compromise. It will be written on his captain's armband. They get it engraved and give it to him as a gift. A story that is revealed when it comes loose during a match with Real Madrid and the message is caught on camera. A sign, almost a premonition, of what, in fact, is actually happening.

But despite all that, the connection with Atlético is strong. It's an emotional and footballing way of life that he needs to put aside in order to make the big leap. But here fate steps in to help him make the final decision. It happens on 20 May 2007. Atlético Madrid v Barcelona, league match number 35, the final result 0-6. It's Atlético's worst-ever home result. A tennis score that hurts, really hurts. At the end of the match, Torres is alone in the middle of the pitch, crouched down with his head in his hands..'Never have they beaten me like that. They could have scored twenty,' the club captain commented immediately afterwards. He had said that Atlético was inferior as a team to the top four in the table, but that he had put his faith in the fact that Barça hadn't won in the Calderón since the 1999–2000 season. He also wanted to end the debate over a UEFA Cup place as soon as possible. If they had beaten Barça, they would've been halfway along the road to Europe. But instead – no. Messi, Zambrotta, Ronaldinho, Eto'o and Iniesta hit the net of the unfortunate keeper, Pichu, one after another, highlighting all the team's failings.

As if that isn't enough, the fans, who have always supported the players right up until the final whistle, this time actually want a defeat because it would mean that the eternal enemy, Real Madrid, would not win the league. It's a bad sign and demonstrates the fact that the team isn't making every effort or, almost, that it prefers to bow down to its historic opponents rather than celebrate its own victory. And that's not all. The crowd is already starting to leave the Calderón once Barcelona get their fourth. They abandon the stadium with their heads low, tired of always having their hopes dashed. The ones who stay behind whistle and shout at those on the pitch: 'Mercenaries, you're just mercenaries!'

It's the final straw. The situation that pushes Torres to take the decision he's put off so many times. He's getting out of Atlético. He's disappointed, infuriated, impotent and envious of the winning Barça players, who make up a great team capable of dominating at any ground. He also wants to savour this. He no longer wants to be like a young Atlas, carrying the weight of a 104-year-old institution on his shoulders and which, in recent years, is only able to offer disappointment to its supporters.

On 19 June 2007, the agreement between Liverpool and Atlético is signed and sealed. The only thing missing is Torres' contract with the English side. In the end, El Niño will accept a lower annual salary (but there are add-ons once certain targets are achieved) in order to be able to leave.

Sunday, 1 July: Fernando interrupts his holidays in Polynesia and returns to Madrid.

Monday, 2 July: he flies to Liverpool after a meeting with Bahia International, the agency that has represented his interests for several years. Here, he spends around 40 hours holed-up in an apartment the club keeps for such situations. It's forbidden to go outside, go for a walk, a meal, or anything. Liverpool want to keep the transfer completely secret.

Tuesday, 3 July: from the apartment Fernando goes directly to a car parked in a space below the building, and from there to undergo a medical examination. He's proclaimed fit and ready to join up. And then the last return flight between the city of the Beatles and the Spanish capital. El Niño, the most expensive signing in Liverpool's history, the most expensive transfer of a Spanish footballer abroad since Gaizka Mendieta (sold in 2001 by Valencia to Lazio for 42 million Euros) first wants to say goodbye to the people he knows in Madrid. It's only that night that a photographer gets a shot of Torres on his way to the airport …

On 4 July, the Spanish press say their farewells to Fernando. Mundo Deportivo uses the verses of The Doors song, 'The End': 'This is the end. Beautiful friend. This is the end. My only friend, the end.' A sad farewell in Spain, a welcome full of hope in England. The desire of the English media is that The Kid becomes a legend at Anfield. For Torres, it's the first day of a new life. A truly strange day. In the morning he leaves home and in the afternoon discovers his dreams have become reality.

Chapter 3

The culprit of his success

Conversation with Liverpool manager,
Rafa Benítez

The gaffer is pretty tied up with a whole pile of things on his plate. He's putting the finishing touches to the 2008–09 season, which finished a few days before, and beginning the next. As usual, he'll have a summer of hard work. And this year even more, now that – thanks to a contract until 2014 – he has complete freedom regarding the buying and selling of players and in all sporting matters. He'll have to take the right decisions and sign the right players to reinforce the Reds. To buy and sell with more than £30 million in his pocket. With this money, it's not easy to bring in the best footballing components, but Rafa is used to challenges and overcoming the odds. He wants to do it as soon as possible so that the newcomers can make themselves at home in the pre-season and get familiar with how the club plays, in order to go for the league title, which they have not won since the 1989–90 season. It will be another 'Rafalution' – the Red revolution of Rafa.

In Anfield they are used to this because, since arriving in 2004 from Valencia, the Madrid-born 49-year-old has changed Liverpool. He has brought it up to date. Over two seasons, he reorganised Melwood, changing the preparations, the training, the players' diet and the way the team plays (and whoever accuses him of being defensive, he responds by pointing to the 100-plus goals they scored last season). He has set up a scouting and talent-spotting system that enables him to keep tabs on around 14,000 players across the globe. And above all, he has returned Liverpool to the European elite, winning the Champions League and European Super Cup in 2005 and getting to another Champions League final in 2007, when they lost to Milan. 'He's demonstrated that he's hungry for success,' said Tom Hicks, one of the club's owners. Rafa is a man who lives and breathes football and works on football 24 hours a day if needed. As he's said on many occasions, he wants to help create a new chapter in the legendary history of the club. Gerrard, the captain, and Torres, El Niño, are two essential elements of his sporting project. Let's see how he came to choose Fernando ...

Why did you decide on Torres as a future signing for Liverpool?
'Fundamentally, it was based on information in our possession, thanks to the tracking we do on many players, his excellent skills and the potential he had to develop still further over the short and medium term. Thinking about the English league and his special characteristics, he seemed ideal to be the striker of a team with the philosophy of our Liverpool FC. The truth is that he hasn't let us down in any way.'

What skills did he have to be one of the Reds?
'Well, it isn't easy to summarise a sportsman, an elite player, a footballer of the highest level like Fernando. But with a bit of analytical skill we could highlight his power, his strength to withstand physical contact, to go all out – in a legitimate, sporting sense – to win a game, and with sufficient quality and skill to end up being the kind of player who can change the flow of a game.'

*Your bet (on Torres), Mr Benítez, was not an easy one, considering
the fee paid and the average goal tally of Fernando in his six
seasons with Atlético Madrid. How in the end did this bet
transform itself into a winning one?*
'Well, I think that although everyone's made an effort to
help him, the main 'culprit' for his success is him, because
of his great determination and his very hard work. Since his
arrival he pushed himself hard to improve. He was getting
more and more confident and therefore getting better day-
by-day. I think that the main guiding principles of Torres'
transformation are Fernando himself and the abilities that
he has shown since he arrived in England.'

*Did you think that Torres would get 33 goals in his first season?
How did that happen? Why has he adapted so rapidly to Liverpool,
to the club and to its playing style? Has the 'Spanish Liverpool'
helped him much?*
'To be very sincere, and in spite of all the earlier remarks
regarding his potential and attitude, the truth is that we
didn't expect so many goals in the first year. Not even the
most optimistic could have imagined it. But of course one
should also say that he deserved each and every one of
them, which were the result of his work and dedication and
his already-mentioned desire to improve. And yes, talking
of his adaptation and the ease with which he was able to
do it, it would only be right to recognise that the group of
Spanish players who have been with him at Liverpool have
helped him a lot to achieve that.'

*They say that, at Liverpool, Torres is much more relaxed, has
got rid of the responsibilities (captain, club image) that were
suffocating him at Atlético, and that this has been one of the keys
to his success. What do you think?*
'Well, one can't know that for sure from outside. I think

that's something one would have to ask him and only he could give an absolutely genuine response. In his immediate environment, we have been with him in this process and we can agree that, yes, he has been able to shed an excess of responsibility and that has helped him considerably with his bursting onto the English football scene as a player. Here in our group, our team, Fernando is important – but for what he does on the pitch, not for his image and what he represents or might represent off the pitch.'

Spanish, Italian and English managers and players all agree with the fact that you have greatly improved Fernando's game. How have you done it? What advice did you give him?
'I wouldn't want to repeat myself unduly but it's necessary to go back over parts of the previous answers. The secret is his work, his attitude, his willingness to improve every day. He has listened carefully and resolutely applied what the technical staff at Liverpool FC have taught him in training. To mention some aspects that I consider fundamental, his movement and calm finishing have been key from my point of view.'

How has Fernando reacted to your orders?
'I presume this refers to my advice, to the guidance we can give him for achieving his best possible progress. And to be very truthful, in this respect, I believe he reacts very well. He always listens and tries to apply the advice to his game in every meeting, in every training session and, finally, in every game.'

What has Torres brought to Liverpool's game?
'Once again, we'll have to summarise. But I would pick out, basically, his ability to change the course of a match, his speed on the counter-attack and the fact that he poses a

constant threat for rival defences in each and every game he plays.'

How do you explain how Torres has, over such a short time,
become one of the players best-loved by the fans, who compare him
with legendary players like Dalglish or Rush?
'It's not going to be me here and now who describes the philosophy of the Anfield terraces, the merits which the fans of Liverpool FC value most. But taking all that into account, his performance during the first year was spectacular, although in this second year, the truth is that Fernando hasn't had much luck with injuries. Besides that, one is dealing with a footballer who is humble and works hard, and all that makes our fans very enthusiastic about him and in him they recognise – let's say, they identify – yesterday's values, today's values, and the values that are always there in the 'Red' story.'

What is your assessment of his two seasons in the Number 9 shirt
of Liverpool?
'To give a brief assessment, without going into details and looking for the appropriate adjectives, I think the first campaign turned out to be excellent in every respect, as we talked about before, and the second, which has just finished, one would have to say it could have been better, although at the same time, and to be fair, you have to bear in mind the mitigating circumstances referred to earlier. Injuries have prevented any kind of continuity and that, as we all know, is fundamental for any footballer at the end of the day.'

What, for you, has been Torres' happiest, his best moment with the Reds?
'Obviously one would have to pick out some of the goals he's scored. One is talking about a striker, and in this sense he's brought a lot to the team, particularly during his first

year. But not being Fernando, it would be difficult to choose one or two. It should be him and only him who can give an opinion on this. No one knows the feelings of Fernando Torres more than Fernando Torres himself.'

What has been, and what is, your relationship with Torres?
'From my point of view, we are talking about a normal relationship, more or less like I have with the rest of the footballers. For sure, someone could probably say that I've talked more with him than some of his team-mates. But that's due exclusively to the argument that I see the potential he has, and I try to help him exploit that to the full, for his own good, although also for his contribution to the team, which is the really important thing. He's a great lad and it's not too difficult to have a good relationship with him.'

What kind of person is Torres now?
'If we have to talk about him in a personal sense, as the question requires, there probably hasn't been much change. We're talking about someone who is pretty similar to the lad that arrived just under two years ago – a bit shy, a very good team-mate, pretty humble and, above all, respectful. As you see, one can make out quite a lot of qualities in him on a human level as well.'

And finally, how do you see the future and next season for Liverpool and Fernando Torres?
'With the optimism and hope that the situation demands. I think that as long as he stays injury-free, he could have another great season if he keeps working with the same humility, dedication and attitude that he has up until now. We have great expectations for Fernando and believe that he's not going to let us down. He's working on that and doing very well. Let's hope that's how it is …

Chapter 4
A nice lad

Conversation with Spain manager,
Vicente Del Bosque

A quiet man, a coach and father-figure, who took charge of the national team following the euphoria of the victory at Euro 2008 and who knew how to bring everyone back to earth. While not denying the legacy left by his predecessor, Luis Aragonés, he has achieved the team's qualification for the 2010 South Africa World Cup well ahead of schedule.

The national team is the latest stage of a long sporting career: 'We'll see when it finishes, maybe after the World Cup, who knows … Let's hope up until the next European Championship, if things go well.' Then he will close the door on soccer, a world he first entered in 1 August 1968, when he left his home city of Salamanca to join the Real Madrid junior team.

At the club's former Ciudad Deportiva training complex, he learned the skill of being an attacking midfielder from players such as Pirri, Grosso and Velásquez. He came up through the ranks with the 'ye-ye' generation of players from the 1960s. They were dubbed the 'ye-ye' generation because of the 'Yeah, yeah, yeah' chorus in the Beatles' song, 'She Loves You', after four members of the team were photographed in Beatles wigs for sport daily, *Marca*. It was this group of players that had won the club's sixth European Cup in 1966. He also played with the *Quinta del Buitre* (or

'Vulture's Cohort' team from the 1980s, which derived its name from its top-scoring player, Emilio Butragueño). Wearing the white of Madrid between 1975 and 1984, he won five league titles and four Copas del Rey (King's Cups). He was on the losing side in the famous 1981 European Cup final against Liverpool, which affected him deeply.

But from this disappointment he recovered well when, as manager, he brought the Real Madrid of the *galácticos* (so-called because the team included world-famous star players such as Zidane, Figo and Ronaldo) two Champions League titles (2000 and 2002), a European Super Cup and an Intercontinental Cup (both also in 2002). All in four seasons – and that is without counting the titles won in Spain.

It was a managerial skill acquired under the Yugoslav schooling of Vujadin Boskov and Miljan Miljanic (two of the managers of Real Madrid between 1974 and 1982). 'Bigotón' ('big moustache'), as he was called because of the facial whiskers that give him a likeness to Inspector Maigret, knew how to manage in a calm and friendly way a dressing room where the egos of the champions were as inflated as hot-air balloons. How? Behaving 'like a good father who draws the line, sets an example, tries to convince without imposing himself and who allows a freedom within certain limits. I don't like to spend the whole day waving a stick.' Secrets? 'Don't try to be too clever or tell the players the absolute truth every day.' And now it's time for the ultimate test, and perhaps the most difficult.

Wearing the national team tracksuit, he is breakfasting in the Ciudad del Fútbol de Las Rozas training complex and chatting with his assistants. Del Bosque talks about Torres – now an essential element in the Spanish forward line – in his usual good-natured way: 'Fernando already has a brilliant career. He began very young at Atlético de Madrid, where he had been a focal figure for many years. I think that he has benefited a great deal by going to England to play football, to a well-organised club like Liverpool, where he is alongside a manager and other players with considerable experience. He's had very good runs, and in the national team as well, and he still has a great future ahead of him …'

Without further ado, he begins to talk in more depth about a youngster he's known for some time, when he was an opponent in the Madrid city derby.

What was your opinion of him when he was here at Atlético?
'Here, Torres didn't enjoy the best years of Atlético Madrid. He had too much pressure, was made captain too soon, he didn't have that space as a youngster, the time to develop without feeling under pressure or protected by more-established team-mates.'

How do you explain the fact that he has doubled his goal tally and his scoring ability since moving from Atlético to Liverpool?
'Likewise, I think it's down to the environment where he is playing his football. Atlético isn't the same as Liverpool. The environment, his team-mates and Liverpool's presence in Europe – all that has helped him.'

What role has Rafa Benítez had in Torres' development?
'Benítez is a manager he's benefited from. I'm not saying that those he had before at Atlético didn't try, but more than that, he's now getting a more comprehensive training and he has matured.'

To be alongside a midfielder like Gerrard has helped him to grow as a player?
'Yes, I think so. It's clear that Gerrard has brought a lot to his game but Torres is also giving the Reds a lot more

possibilities, particularly to the players behind him. Fernando has great value – his speed and his running off the ball give options to Liverpool's game. He's a Number 9 that any midfielder would want to have in front of him.'

What has English football brought to Torres?
'It's brought different ways of understanding the game, which is important – although now there is little 'native' football, it's more a mixture of styles. Nowadays one doesn't talk of a true English style. Arsenal, Chelsea, Manchester (United) and Liverpool themselves have lots of foreign players. Yes, I think that this coexistence between English and Spanish football has helped him in his development.'

Briefly, what are the differences between English and Spanish football?
'The two are very competitive and they are clearly dominant in Europe, at least at the moment. In any case, I don't see any great differences.'

Fernando's technical qualities?
'He's a player who has a dominant physical presence, who is very fast and a great goalscorer. He probably doesn't have a great technique but he does things that are unexpected …'

For example?
'Hitting the ball very hard, a sudden burst of speed … and then his ability to improvise in front of goal. Anything to surprise his opponent. He's not a very orthodox player technically but overall he is in excellent shape and has scored some amazing goals.'

*Since his arrival at Liverpool, do you think he has improved in
certain technical respects?*

'Undoubtedly. His time at Liverpool has enabled him to
acquire better technical skills. This improvement has been
good for him and for the other Spanish players. That speed
he has must be accompanied each day by building a better
technique and that's what Torres has done. Quality? To play
in the footballing elite where he is playing, in the team he's
playing in now, he wouldn't be doing it if he didn't have
quality.'

Human qualities?

'He's a modest lad, very normal and gets on well with his
team-mates. He's a nice lad, yes, very nice. He has a very
stable life and that's good for footballers.'

As national team manager, what advice would you give him?

'The advice one normally gives to a striker. In the national
side, Fernando has some defensive duties to fulfil because
they benefit greatly the rest of the team and then there are
the attacking duties of a player who knows how to max-
imise the possibilities for all the players behind him. His
speed, his movements, his mobility and his ability to lose
his marker are essential in order to give our midfielders the
best options.'

*Before Euro 2008, there was a lot of debate about the national
side's way of playing – lots of short, horizontal passes – and that
of Liverpool with their rapid movement of the ball from one end of
the pitch to the other. The conclusion was that Spain's slower style
would give Torres less space and therefore fewer opportunities to
score. What do you think?*

'In football there isn't just one way of doing things – it's a
mixture of everything and I believe Fernando knows how to

play in space as well as play with short passes. Fortunately, the national side mixes the two, which is the ideal.'

The role of Torres changes between Liverpool and the national side?
'No, I don't think it changes much. Our group is pretty integrated in that everyone has their role and, without doubt, Torres is one of the most important players in the national side, for sure.'

How do you remember his goal in the final of Euro 2008?
'I think it's the culmination, the final phase of a move involving the whole team. He knew how to score a quick goal and finish well in front of the keeper.'

Which player does Torres resemble?
'I don't know really. I can't think of any players who remind me of him or who resemble him. I think he has a very individual way of playing.'

From when he was very young, he's been compared to Raúl, the captain of Real Madrid, who you know very well …
'Raúl has more than 100 international caps, something which is not easy to achieve in Spain. Torres already has more than 60 and, considering his age and what remains of his football career, he could equal or surpass that. The other similar thing is the two of them come from the same junior ranks. Both are an example for younger lads.'

Torres' future … Do you think it's true that he can go on even higher?
'I think that he's at a great club and that he still has challenges to meet. Without doubt, he wants to win the English Premier League title as well as the Champions League. And

also with the national side we know there are challenges ahead.'

The most important of those is the World Cup. How do you view that?
'Well, for us it's exciting to think that we are one of the contenders to win it and that the individual talent of each team member, his reputation and his status could result in a collective victory. We know that a World Cup victory would bring much acclaim to all who take part.

Chapter 5

Fuenlabrada

Penélope Cruz, to applause from the public, goes up to the stage in the Kodak Theatre in Hollywood to accept the Oscar for the Best Supporting Actress for her role in the Woody Allen film, *Vicky Cristina Barcelona*. Kisses and hugs from Tilda Swinton, Goldie Hawn and Whoopi Goldberg, then the speech with the statuette in her hand. It won't last the normal 45 seconds, she says straight away. Visibly moved, she pays tribute to the directors, the actors and the people who've helped her become the first Spanish actress to win the Academy Award. She dedicates the award to her parents, to her brothers and sisters and to whoever isn't there. And she doesn't forget Alcobendas, the town about 9 miles from Madrid where she grew up and where she used to watch the ceremony on TV – an impossible dream.

Alcobendas is now on the map, its residents say with pride. The same thing happened to Fuenlabrada – thanks to Fernando Torres. So much so that, on 5 February 2009, the Town Hall recognises this by awarding him the 'Citizen of Fuenlabrada' medal 'in recognition of his special sporting and personal values, of his professional career, which has led him to be considered internationally as one of the most important footballers in the world, and of his commitment and loyalty to his town, for which he is an exceptional ambassador. The hope and spirit shown by the footballer is an excellent example for children and young people who, by playing sports, not only develop a physical activity but also highly important values such as knowing how to share with their team-mates the dream of achieving a common objective.' This is how the joint motion, presented by the various political groups in the municipality of Fuenlabrada, reads.

And it's here, 'in this humble neighbourhood, to the south of Madrid, that I was born,' explained the Liverpool Number 9 in an interview some time ago. Twenty-five minutes by rail from the centre of the Spanish capital. The regional *Cercanías* trains, which serve the town, are always crowded. They come from the station of Atocha, which, on the morning of 11 March 2004, was hit by the terrorist attacks that left 199 people dead, another 1,800 injured and sent shock waves across the country and the rest of Europe. A train leaves Platform Nine every fifteen minutes. Aboard are commuters, students, workers and many immigrants who live on the city limits. Orcasitas, Zarzaquemada … the stations pass by one after the other. High-rise housing projects, neglected spaces, intersecting motorways piled on top of each other, small residential houses, graffiti on abandoned walls, planes flying low as they come in to land at Barajas airport, shopping centres and some shanty towns. Leganés, Parque Polvoranca, La Serna … and then, Fuenlabrada Central.

Not far from the station exit is the Town Hall, a modern complex of steel, cement and glass, which can be identified by a series of horizontal yellow lozenge shapes in-between each floor. It looks onto an enormous square with a fountain occupying the centre, around which are seated several old people. Manolo Robles, aged 56, socialist, mayor since 2002 and local councillor since 1983, is a confirmed *madridista* (fan of Real Madrid). But he adores El Niño. He saw him play many years ago, when Fernando was just a boy and taking his first steps in the Atlético Madrid junior sides.

The mayor also has a son who, when he was that age, enjoyed playing football but hasn't become a champion like Torres.

Around that time, by chance, he bumped into Fernando's parents in the Colegio Amorós school in Carabanchel and spent some time chatting to them. He's proud that his local administration has officially recognised El Niño: 'He's the city's most important sporting figure, because he grew up here and started playing football here, because people think of him as their neighbour, even if, for some years, neither he nor his family have lived in Fuenlabrada,' says Robles in his second-floor Town Hall office. Large windows behind him depict the town he governs. 'El Niño is very much loved here and even more since his goal in Euro 2008. He's very well-known internationally and has put our town on the world map. Only the other day, I did an interview for a radio station in Guatemala. The first thing they asked me about was Fernando.' A 25-year-old, whose name the municipality will use for a new 90,000-square metre sporting complex containing football pitches, tennis courts, athletics tracks and a swimming pool. 'It will be ready in 2010 and we hope that Torres can inaugurate it,' explains the mayor.

But what was Fuenlabrada like and what is it like today?

'In 1973, it was a rural town of 7,000 inhabitants. But in the final years of the Franco dictatorship, there was a lot of property speculation. They gave thousands of permits to build and by 1979, we had a population of 57,000. The town grew chaotically without any proper urban development plan. In the 1980s, Fuenlabrada was the subject of a major internal migration process. Lots of young people came from (the Spanish regions of) Andalucía, Galicia, Extremadura and Castilla-La Mancha, looking for work and a place to live. They settled here, next to a small community of Polish immigrants.

'In 1995, we were witness to a wave of immigration from the Maghreb region and then from Latin America at the end of the 1990s. Today, Fuenlabrada has 209,102 inhabitants, 15 per cent of whom are immigrants from outside the European Union. It's the fourth biggest city in the Madrid region in terms of population. It accounts for 25 per cent of the region's industry, above all furniture-making and metallurgy. We've got 22 industrial estates and 30 per cent of the region's small and medium-sized businesses.

'In the last decade, we have greatly improved the residents' quality of life. In terms of transport and communications infrastructure, thanks to new roads, the regional *Cercanías* train network and the metro, Fuenlabrada is now closer to the capital. In terms of education and culture, we have 70 teaching centres and the Universidad Rey Juan Carlos campus, four theatres, a library for every 35,000 inhabitants, six sports centres, a basketball team playing in the ACB (the top division of Spanish basketball) and a football team in the third division.

'It's a city, and a very different one from that which Fernando knew when he was small. His neighbourhood, the Parque Granada, at that time was almost a village, where everyone knew each other and where the majority of people had arrived only a short time before. If there's something that hasn't changed, it's the fact that Fuenlabrada continues to be one of the youngest municipalities in the country.'

José Torres – Pepe to his friends – arrived in this 'dormitory city', 22 kilometres (about 14 miles) from Madrid in the 1980s from Galicia. He was born less than 20 kilometres from Santiago de Compostela, the regional capital. José is the second of nine children of Claudio Torres and Maruja. 'Our Pepe, who is now 59, began at the army barracks in Pontevedra and later joined the police. He was deputy-inspector and after two years in the Basque Country, he requested to be transferred to Madrid, to Fuenlabrada (a new station was opened in 1987). Now he's retired,' recalled Claudio Torres recently. In Madrid, he married Flori, who is from the city, and bought an apartment in the street of Calle Alemania. It's here that their three children were born and grew up. Mari Paz, the oldest and eight years Fernando's senior, has a law degree and today works for Bahía International. Israel, seven years older than Fernando, has followed in his father's footsteps. He joined the police and was assigned to the security of María Teresa Fernández de la Vega, the deputy prime minister in the socialist government of José Luis Rodríguez Zapatero.

'My parents weren't expecting me. I arrived by chance,' confessed El Niño some years ago. His brother and sister were already quite grown-up when the new arrival made his entrance. Attention centres on the little Fernando José Torres Sanz who, despite the normal petty jealousies, is welcomed by his two older siblings. In fact, Flori and José say that, with the arrival of Fernando, the older two become more settled.

The most amusing anecdote from those early years is the fright his mother gets when he throws around 80,000 pesetas (about £400 at today's values) out of the window. He was playing with a model toy in his parents' bedroom. A lorry with a big trailer. He'd filled it with banknotes he'd found in a drawer and then ... threw it out of the window. He liked to drop things to see where they ended up. Flori, working round-the-clock to look after the three children, had begun searching for the cash but couldn't find it and had run out of places to look for it. She was desperate. She only realised what had happened when the neighbours knocked on the door to ask: 'I don't suppose you've seen what's fallen out of your window?' She couldn't imagine that her little 'Fer', as his friends call him, had done such a thing. El Niño was a bit naughty both in and outside the house. So much so that José and Flori decide, in a family meeting, to impose tough measures to prevent any more such 'brilliant' ideas on Fernando's part.

Even if he is the little one of the house, he can't get away with everything. He has to be subject to the same rules as the other two. Having said that, his brother and sister still allow Fernando to get up to all sorts of mischief. Israel, his older brother, is the model, the example to follow, while Mari Paz is the older sister who indulges him in everything and who makes a fuss of him whenever she can. The friends of the family say that Fernando has his father's character, the character of the shy, almost introvert, gallegos (people from Galicia) but who are at the same time, good, responsible people and good workers. Pepe doesn't share this view and today describes his son as 'an intelligent person, with a head for taking in information and different situations, capable of withstanding difficult moments and enjoying the good ones. Apart from his physical and technical qualities, he's very strong mentally, has an absolute belief in what he can achieve, has always wanted to get on and improve and this has allowed him to get where he is.'

The youngster also shows these qualities at school. He gets on well, has good marks, behaves well, is very determined and has a great capacity for concentration. 'I remember a play we put on at the school. His part was to recite a poem about solidarity,' remembers Alicia, the language teacher at the Colegio Público Francisco de Quevedo school. 'He learned it by heart and recited it perfectly.' All in all, a clever student, but not one who's averse to a bit of cheating. Once, the teacher catches him red-handed while he's copying but doesn't punish him and doesn't pull him out of the exam. The other students are angry and protest.

'If you don't take him out, then we'll all start cheating,' they say. But it's difficult to punish that angel face, which looks as if it would never hurt a fly. His classmates remember …

The end of term and the beginning of summer. The Torres Sanz family spend the holidays in the father's home village. There are long weeks with his grandparents, uncles and aunts, his brother and sister, his friends in the village, months of adventure amongst the fields and vegetable gardens. Until his parents discover the seaside town of Cee in Galicia. It was by chance that they passed by there, they liked the place, found a small apartment on the beach and bought it. Fernando is then eight years old and for the following summers this will be his holiday destination. He makes new friends and acquaintances – and one of those will have a fundamental impact on his life. Because on this very beach, the thin, blond, shy lad falls in with a group of youngsters his own age, and meets Olalla Domínguez Liste, who is from the San Lázaro district of Santiago de Compostela and keen on figure skating. She is fifteen and he is seventeen. They meet, get to know each other, and fall in love. From then on, they are never apart. But this story is still to come. For the moment, Fernando is a lad who grows up, as his father says, in a 'normal family' surrounded by the love of his parents and paternal grandparents as well as those of his mother, Eulalio and Paz, who live not far away from Madrid in Valdeavero. A boy who grows up learning what it means to make sacrifices, to work hard, 'to appreciate the important things and to understand,' as José Torres always says, 'what are the true values of life.'

And to enjoy his football …

Chapter 6

Leader of the gang

Five or six o'clock on a Saturday afternoon – a good time for a kick-around with the usual gang. Fernán, as his friends call him, puts himself in the goal that has been created between a wall and a mound of clothes. The game is non-stop, the boys create a huge dust cloud as they tear around after each other. The rules – even for those who want to use them – are virtually ignored. Then a pass is threaded through to Alexis, who finds the ball at his feet. Without hesitating, he shoots hard, very hard. The ball catches Torres full in the face and his mouth fills with blood. He bursts into tears and the game is over. His friends gather round and take him, running, back home to his mother, Flori. It's a big shock for them all. He's missing two front teeth.

This is the point where Fernando Torres' goalkeeping career ends. His brother, Israel, and his mother ban him from playing between the posts on the cement pitch. He himself also understands that maybe it's better to try putting the ball into the net rather than trying to keep it out. And so begins the career of Fernando Torres as striker.

'Fernán loved being in goal because of his brother, Israel, who was one of the best indoor football goalkeepers I've ever seen. He wanted to be like him but after he got smashed in the face, he never went back in goal. I was responsible for what happened and I felt bad. I was scared of getting a huge telling-off from my parents and from his. But, to be honest, it upset me a lot to see him like that and

I remember going several times with him to the dentist. However, in one sense, the incident turned out well for him,' says 26-year-old Alexis Gómez, now a security guard and the person responsible for changing the role of one of the world's most famous strikers.

Fernando Torres is six years old. One of the series on TV is *Campeones: Oliver y Benji* (Champions: Oliver and Benji), the Spanish language version of a hugely popular Japanese comic-style cartoon series about the adventures of a Japanese youth football team. It features super striker Tsubasa Ozora (known in Spanish by the English-style name of Oliver Atton) and the invincible goalkeeper Genzo Wakabayashi (Benji Price in the Spanish version). It tells the story of these two friends from their childhood to becoming professional footballers and, eventually, to being called up to the Japanese national side. Their adventures take in their team-mates, the training, the matches and the tournaments, as well as spectacular moves and action that would be impossible to perform in real life. These are the words of the (Spanish) theme tune:

They go with the ball at their feet
and nobody can stop them.
The stadium vibrates with emotion
to see both of them play.

They only play to win
but always in a sporting way
and there's nobody better
for the fans.

Oliver, Benji
magicians on the ball.
Benji, Oliver,

dreams of being champions.
Benji, Oliver,
mad about football,
they have to score another goal.

Words and music that a lot of Spanish children have not forgotten. Torres was also a big fan of Oliver and Benji. He identified with the stories of the two youngsters and imagined himself being a footballer like them, a goalkeeper who let nothing past and a striker who, in the gardens around his home, was getting good at scoring against his brother Israel.

Torres first began to kick his brother's football around at just two years old. His brother was the model to follow. During the summer, the Torres Sanz family spent their holidays at Gastar (a small village about 12 miles from Santiago de Compostela), with the paternal grandparents. It's where they got used to playing football. He played in the vegetable patch together with a group of cousins and local friends. Uncle Bruno was the most enthusiastic footballing family member and he worked hard to teach them the basics of the game.

And still in Galicia, several years later, during summer holidays on the beach at Estorde, he would spend his days playing never-ending matches. 'Mini-World Cups' with everyone against each other. He gets stronger. 'He was fast, agile, versatile, with very sharp changes of pace. You didn't see great displays of quality but strength and power, yes. When he played, he had a special touch and in the sand he ran like a madman,' remembers Ramón Marcote.

At five years old, he enters his first team, Parque (Park) 84. Parque is the name of the neighbourhood and 84 the year of birth for the boys playing in the team. The shirt is red and the event is the footballing marathon that takes place at the Polideportivo (sports centre) in Fuenlabrada. It is a local trophy but a real occasion for any child. Amongst the spectators are parents, friends, colleagues and school-mates. No one is bothered that the matches take the form of piles of kids – around fifteen to twenty – all kicking the ball in whatever way they could. They have a good time and they get to feel like real soccer stars and no one minds that the team has been put together just for the event. Two days later and they all go back to playing how they'd always played.

That is, until the people from Cafetería Mario in Holanda Street decide to organise a team that will be called Mario's Holanda.

'An adult team was already in existence when we decided to create one for the youngsters. At that time in Fuenlabrada, there were a lot of young parents with lads who were really into sport. These families were a bit con-cerned about street crime, drug-taking and their kids get-ting into bad company, so we tried to get them together and keep them busy with football,' recalls Juan Gómez, now aged 55, one of the founders of that team and the coach for Torres and his mates. Today he works in the Real Casa de la Moneda (the Royal Mint).

One Friday afternoon, in the Fuenlabrada sports shop called Camacho, just 100 metres from where Fernando used to live, the ex-trainer has time to sit down with his son, Alexis, the captain of Mario's Holanda, and winger Javier Camacho, amongst the rackets, trainers, balls, bathing costumes and shirts of Real Madrid, Atlético, the Spanish national team and Liverpool. He remembers the time when the Reds' Number 9 used to run around on hard cement surfaces.

'They were a pretty good group of kids,' says Juan. 'We saw Fernando play and we thought this lad ought to be in our team. Why? Because at eight years old he had the same skills that he has now – speed and technique. Training didn't bother him but, more importantly, he never got tired of learning. I had to teach him everything from the throw-in to what it means to play in a team. We had to tell him that football is a game and that was how he should approach it. But right from that moment, I was convinced that Fernando would go far. I always said that to his father, a delightful person – like his brother and the rest of the family. They didn't believe me. Once, after a game in which he scored eight goals, I said it again and José was almost in tears. But I was absolutely sure.'

As you look at the photo of the Mario's Holanda team for the 1992–93 season, Javier Camacho, the son of the shop owner, is standing to the right of Fernando. He has a serious expression with his mouth half-open in the team's green, white and black shirt, and is looking directly at the camera. Sixteen years later, apart from a slight beard, Javier hasn't changed much. Nor has Fernando. El Niño's birthday is in March and his in July. Javier is studying in Madrid to be a surveyor but still loves playing football for the fun of it, for the team of La Moraleja De Enmedio, a village about 18 miles from Madrid, in the Segunda Regional (Second Regional) division (the leagues below the Spanish third division). And like Torres, he is a striker. He remembers well that photo, taken all those years ago at the Colegio Publico Andrés Manjón school. Without hesitation, from left to right, he reels off the names of his then team-mates:

'Juan the coach, Rubén the goalkeeper, Alexis, Fernando and I, then the really tall one in the green tracksuit, Israel – the brother of Fernando who always came to watch us and sometimes, when Juan Gómez wasn't there, would act as coach, along with Ivan, the brother of Alexis. Squatting down in front are Alejandro, Dani, Rici, Rocha and Alvarito.'

He describes Fernando at eight years old: 'Physically very thin, very blond, with loads of freckles. He looked English. As a person he was the typical leader, the leader of the gang, very mischievous and very shy.' How is it possible to be shy and a leader? 'Amongst us, he was the extrovert, he ruled the roost, he spoke for everyone else. In the park, when we all ran off because some neighbour got angry and shouted at us, he stayed behind to argue and defend our right to play there. But with people he didn't know, he put his head down and said nothing. Apart from with the girls, of course. He really had an eye for them. You'd always see him with one from school or from the local area. To be blond and have the air of a leader, the girls really liked that.' And being mischievous? 'For Fernán, like all of us in the gang – we were some twenty-odd kids with three or four years age difference between us – we liked to play jokes such as ringing the door entry phone bells on houses in the neighbourhood and then running away. Typical pranks like that.'

And football-wise?
'He was the same as he is now – a star. He was playing Number 9 and he had the ability to go past the opposition and score loads of goals in every game. When things weren't going well and we couldn't score, we'd give him the ball to sort things out. I remember once, against Colegio Valle Inclán (school), we won 24-0 with him scoring eleven on his own. Juan wanted to substitute him to give some of the others a chance but he wouldn't have any of it. He wanted to keep going and pile on the goals. That's what he liked doing.'

Juan takes up the story:
'It's true to say that if he was taken off then he would be really angry. 'I'm taking you off for being a bully,' I told

him, 'you've got eleven goals. That's enough.' Treating it as a joke like that, it worked. I remember him once leaving the field crying uncontrollable tears of happiness. And what was the problem? He'd wanted to come off because he hadn't been able to get a goal and the score was 0-0. He'd tried everything but it just wasn't possible. He was beside himself. It was the only time he asked me to substitute him. I told him to stay on and in the end he scored. In the 1992–93 season, Fernando got no less than 80 goals and during the three years he was with Mario's Holanda, we won all our league games. We were champions in everything. And everywhere we were followed by loads of people – fathers, mothers, brothers, friends. We were one big family.'

Javier elaborates:
'To tell the truth, we did in fact have two defeats but they were friendlies. The first was at Navalcarnero, just before the start of the league season and the other against a group of girls – who were bigger than our lot. They gave us a real hiding and we left the pitch in complete silence, with our pride wounded. It was the first time we'd played in a closed sports hall on a wooden parquet surface. We were used to cement. Just about all the school indoor football pitches in our area were cement. We weren't a school team though and we didn't have anywhere to train either, so we used what everyone here calls the Plaza Blanca (White Square), a hard area above a car park where, every time there was a match, we had to find something that we could use for a goal. Or sometimes we used the playing area of the Colegio Francisco de Quevedo, which was Fernando's school. We used to train one or two days a week with a match on the Saturday morning. Afterwards, all of us went to the cafetería and they invited us for Coca-Cola and crisps. We ended up

throwing everything around and then we ran outside to play football again in the Parque Granada.'

So there was a lot of football at that time, then?
'Absolutely', continues Javier. 'There was no Playstation, Nintendo, consoles, or video games – or 1,001 TV channels. So in the evening, after homework, we went outside, together with our nocilla (a hazlenut and chocolate spread) sandwich. We would sit in front of the local chemist and decide what to do – football, bottle tops, spinning tops, picture cards and marbles were our favourites. We played football in every possible space – in the Plaza Blanca, the street behind the school and between one building and another where there was a bit of actual grass. Imagine that – what a luxury! Although one should point out that the two bits of garden were separated by a cement kerb, but that didn't bother us. We used to jump over it just for the pleasure of stepping on the grass. The only two problems were Mr Miguel and the security guard. They were nightmares for us because one of the goals was just below Mr Miguel's window. He was a bit of a strong character and we were scared of him. After we'd fired off a few shots he would appear at the window and begin to shout. We got frightened and used to run off. Our other dread was the security guard who used to patrol the zone, checking everything was in order. We were scared of him as well because it was forbidden to tread on the grass and if he caught us, he would take the ball off us. So if someone warned us he was coming, we would just pretend to be sitting around, twiddling our thumbs and keep the ball hidden.

'I don't know how many times we managed to avoid getting caught by the caretaker at the Colegio Tierno Galván school. In the evening, when no one was around, we used to jump over the fence to play on the indoor football surface.

Then they put up a higher fence but we still managed to get over until one of us got stuck there. Even in the swimming pool there was a bit of grass and, secretly, we would take a few small balls in until the people who were sunbathing there started to complain.'

Alexis continues:
'Football was our obsession. One thing we really enjoyed was taking corners. We would do a throw-in from an imaginary corner flag and either shoot or head-in. Then there was the 'German goal', which you scored after keeping the ball in the air without letting it touch the ground. The winner would be the first to score 10 and for that game there was no punishment, which was not the case with 'the bottom' ...

The bottom?
'We all had to endure it from time to time. You have the ball in the air and whoever is the first to let it touch the ground has to get on top of one of the goalposts – the goal could be a bench, for example. You then have to show your bottom while the others would shoot at you from the penalty spot, trying to hit you on the er, well, you know, on the bum ...'

Haven't you forgotten about the bottle tops and the picture cards?
'You're right. Those were the other things we were crazy about at that time,' said Javier. 'Yes, the little squares in-between one building and another – today they're cement but before that there was earth. And it's there that we set up our 'stadiums' and 'cycle tracks' with Coca-Cola and beer bottle tops, which we got from the bars. We put the club colours and the player's face on them, a plastic stopper for the goalkeeper and a chickpea for the ball. In summer we changed from football to cycling, this time with bottle tops in the colours of Banesto or Kelme and faces of cyclists like

Indurain. I remember that Fernando used to love playing with the bottle tops. He was good with them, while the marbles weren't really his thing. And then there were the picture cards. At the beginning of the season, everyone went out to play with their wad of cards. When someone completed an album he could go up to the 'castle' – a place we'd built – or the window of his house and throw down the duplicate cards for the others below who would go crazy to grab them.'

Which team did Fernando support?
'At that time,' continues Javier, 'he wasn't supporting any team in particular, although he clearly loved playing football. It was only later, when he was at Atlético that he really began to follow their colours. He went to the Calderón as a ball boy while I, who'd always been a colchonero (fan of Atlético Madrid) and a milanista (fan of AC Milan), went to see the matches. Afterwards, we'd talk about the new songs, chants and dances they'd made up that Sunday. In fact, a nice little story comes to mind about Fernando when he was a player with the Atlético junior team. You should know that 14 September is the day of the fiesta of Fuenlabrada, in honour of the Cristo de la Misericordia, with celebrations going on the whole week. There are concerts, dances and around 24 hours of football, from nine in the morning to eleven at night, featuring mini-leagues, knockout games and finals in all categories. When we were small, our team always took part and we always won. This particular year, Fernán was already at the junior level with Atlético, which obviously meant that they wouldn't let him play in neighbourhood tournaments like ours. But we needed him. We had to win a match in order to get to the final. So we went to get him. He came out with a photocopy of his DNI (national identity card) and signed up. There was someone who really didn't

like him and called us cheats but thanks to him, we won the match and the tournament. It was the last time he played with us.'

Gómez senior explains:
'Torres left, while most of the local lads didn't want to go off and carried on playing as amateurs and fans of the game. It's true that various good players like Fernando Sánchez and Fernando Burgos came out of Fuenlabrada but the majority, like Israel for example, just wanted to do it for fun and stayed here or, like my son, didn't have the determination or the will to make the effort. Training didn't bother Fernando, for example. He would come out on his own with the ball under his arm. In the case of Alexis, someone had to take the ball. Torres had all the determination in the world and he wanted to get on the ladder.'

So, for the 1994–95 season, he went to AD (Asociación Deportiva) Rayo 13. The rayo (ray) was the symbol of the club, founded in 1992, and 13 was the number of the street for the team headquarters. The diagonal yellow ray was emblazoned into the badge of the club shirt, which featured vertical blue and black vertical stripes like those of Inter Milan.

'Four of us went from Mario's Holanda to Rayo: Fernán, Alejandro, Rici and me,' says Alexis. 'The change from indoor football to a team of eleven suited Torres very well, because on the bigger pitch he could make better use of his speed and his shooting skills. Fernando was already a "killer", a real assassin in the penalty area. Myself, I'd gone from left wing in indoor football to midfielder in 11-a-side. I searched him out, gave him the balls and he took his fill of goals. It was incredible – if I'm not mistaken his tally was around 55 or 60. We won the league, pretty much without a problem. I only remember one match where we had to make a real effort, against Naranjo. We were losing 2-0 but Fernando arrived and made it 2-1 and then scored again to make it a draw. Amazing.'

That's the opinion of his friend and team-mate. But what's the view of the Rayo 13 coach, Andrés Perales? Now 54, his enthusiasm for the game is as great as ever and he continues to teach young boys the art of football.

'He was a marvel and very kind-hearted but in the first few sessions it was really complicated to work with the lad. He was annoyed with his team-mates because they didn't pass the ball to him. He always wanted the ball, he always wanted to score. And he did it in every way possible, from midfield, or by outwitting the opposing players in front of him. He had quality and he was smart. Once or twice he really lost it, like with 'El Chino' ('The Chinese'), a left-footed winger, a nice lad. They got entangled and I had to go and sort them out. El Chino went home while Torres stayed. With me, there were never any problems. I was pretty strict and asked for respect and hard work from the whole team. I made him play on the right wing and then as striker.

'Anecdotes? Loads … like the time in Leganés when we were losing 3-0, he and one of the wingers, David, gave the runaround to his marker. We won 4-3, which put us in the final. Yes, Torres was a footballing machine. But I never thought he would get so far.'

But Torres did get far. And very far. What do his ex-team-mates think of him now?

'He's realised the dream we all had,' says Alexis, 'all those kids kicking a ball around the neighbourhood. We grew up together and now he's the striker who scored the goal for Spain in the final of Euro 2008. It's a pleasure to have played with him and to have him as your friend.'

The long chat is over and the train for central Madrid is leaving shortly from Fuenlabrada Central. Javier walks through the local streets to the station, pointing out the places of his childhood: the small squares, Mr Miguel's window, and the fence they jumped over. Just in front of the Mario's Holanda cafetería, which has been closed for some time, is Rubén, the goalkeeper from that team. He also continues playing football as an amateur. He starts to talk about matches, results, and coaches who were changed too quickly ... and football in the *Segunda Regional.*

Chapter 7

A born winner

'How much do we give this lad?'
'This little freckled one with the blond hair
gets 10 plus one … an 11'

The conversation takes place in June, 1995, in the Ernesto Cotorruelo sports facility in the Carabanchel district of Madrid. The protagonists: Manolo Briñas and Manolo Rangel. One is the deputy director of Atlético Madrid football school and the other is one of its coaches.

The two find themselves, one summer morning, on three hard, bare playing surfaces, lost in the middle of a huge boulevard full of cars and in front of a row of sad-looking buildings. They have to select some youngsters to form part of the junior team, which will take part that August in an international tournament at Bierbeek, in the Brabant province of Belgium, a few miles from Leuven. Briñas holds the notebook, Rangel gives the points. He gives a score for each of the would-be footballers from one to ten but when that freckled one with the blond hair appears in front of them, the guidelines disappear.

'After five minutes,' recalls Antonio Seseña, today aged 66 and retired but then director of the Atlético Madrid junior players, 'we told him, 'Go and get dressed, lad.' He looked surprised, he wanted to keep on playing, he thought he was no good, that he'd failed. He asked me, 'Am I doing something wrong?' On the contrary, he had completely won us over. We saw an intelligent lad, who moved well on the pitch, had pace and good technique as well, qualities which, at that age, really stand out.'

'Yes, Fernando Torres at eleven was a very smart kid – fast, able to lose his marker and beat his opponent. Without having participated too much in the action, I realised that he was doing everything fantastically well. And above all, he seemed to me like a kid who wanted to be a footballer,' explains Manolo Rangel, aged 55, who worked with the Atlético junior teams for twelve years.

In that June of 1995, Fernando had already passed the first selection test to enter the ranks of Atlético. Like lots of other kids of his age, he had gone to the Vicente Calderón stadium, filled in the registration forms, and had been invited – along with 200 others – to go to the ground in the Tres Cruces park between Aluche and Carabanchel. An 11-a-side match to sort out what each of them was able to do, then after that another 22 kids and so on. 'Victor Peligros, Antonio Arganda and I were there that day,' recalls Briñas in his office at the Calderón. Behind him, and framed in a glass-fronted case, is one of Fernando's shirts. It's the one he was wearing on 23 February 2008, when he got a hat-trick at Middlesborough. Alongside is a photo of an ecstatic El Niño, having just scored a goal for the Reds, and on it is written in felt-tip pen: 'For my great friend, Manolo Briñas, a heartfelt embrace in return for all the affection that you have shown and continue to show for me, Fernando Torres.' On re-reading this dedication, 77-year-old Briñas is visibly moved and points to the walls covered with cuttings describing Fernando and all the other youngsters from the Atlético junior teams who have ended up in the top division. The only exception is the Uraguayan Diego Forlán (formerly of Villarreal and Manchester United), whose impressive tally of 32 league goals last season was a huge factor in taking

Atlético into the Champions League for the second year running, as well as earning him the Spanish *Pichichi* trophy and the European Golden Boot for the player with the highest number of league goals in Spain and Europe respectively.

After this diversion, the veteran coach continues with the story of that team in the Tres Cruces park: 'From those 200 youngsters, we had to choose 40. If I remember rightly, Fernando scored four goals but the coaches didn't choose him for that. Apart from the goals, he was marked positively for his involvement in the game and for his unselfish attitude.'

In the official test notes for that day, in strict alphabetical order, one can read, alongside the name Fernando José Torres Sanz: 'Suitable (to be seen in our teams). He will be sent instructions.' To be more precise, he would go to the Cotorruelo ground, where Manolo Rangel, some time later, would give him the mark of eleven.

But why did Fernando end up taking his chances with Atlético and not Real Madrid, the city's 'first' team? It was all down to Eulalio Sanz, Fernando's maternal grandfather.

By way of a short preamble, the Torres family was not very football-oriented. It was not one of those Spanish families glued to the radio listening to live match commentaries, nor was it one of those where, when there was a big match, all the relatives and friends joined together to experience the event on television. The passion for football and particular clubs in the Torres household was pretty lukewarm. There was certainly a fondness for Deportivo La Coruña because of the father's family origins. But nothing special. The real fan was his grandfather. A lifelong *rojiblanco* (supporter of Atlético Madrid).

In the sitting room of Elulalio and Paz in Valdeavero, there was an impressive-looking ceramic plate with the

Atlético badge. It was an object that fascinated Fernando. He could remember it from when he was two or three years old. At that time he knew nothing about football matches or clubs, but his grandfather – thanks to that plate – began his 'sentimental education'. Each time the small Torres went to look at it, he repeated to him: 'When you're grown-up, you must be with Atlético.' And with the passing of the years, he began to explain the club's ideals and values. He began to explain that Real Madrid was everyone's team, the one that always won, while Atléti was the other side of the coin, where defeats had to be suffered and where being a fan required real effort.

The seed of support took hold and grew. When he was nine, Fernando's father took him to the Vicente Calderón museum, where they keep the trophies, cups, old photographs, footballs, badges and pennants – a trip that left the youngster in awe. Some years later it will be Manolo Briñas who explains to Fernando, one-to-one, the symbols and the 106-year-old history of a club founded in April 1903, which boasts nine league titles, and which, historically, comes to be considered Spain's third-best team in terms of trophies and supporters, behind Real Madrid and Barcelona. So when Fernando qualifies to join Atlético, he's hardly got home and in through the door before he's on the phone to his grandfather to tell him the great news. A grandfather who will have the greatest satisfaction, before his death on 23 February 2003, to see Fernando in the shirt of his beloved team, playing in the Vicente Calderón.

But going back to the summer of 1995 and to the first impressions of Briñas, the person who began to train him:

'Fernando was an open, amusing, happy and very responsible lad who gave everything. He wasn't the typical joker who took his attitude into the matches. He already had his head well screwed-on. And all that was due to his parents, who told him, "enjoy yourself at football but study". And he followed that to the letter. I remember once, when I went to meet him at Atocha station, he was coming back from winning a tournament. He got off the train, he had a copy of *Marca* in his hand, where it was talking about him. I thought that he would want to show it to me but no – under the newspaper he had his end-of-term reports. He proudly showed them to me, "Look Manolo, I've passed in all subjects. And I've got quite a few top grades." Yes, very often parents think they have a Maradona, they think their son can score the second goal before the first but life isn't like that. To get there, you have to make sacrifices, not leave school and move forward bit-by-bit.'

And to explain how Torres was, he remembers the away match in Belgium: 'At dinner, in the hotel, they served a vegetable soup and lots of the lads put their plates to one side without touching it, saying they found it nauseating, so much so that Rangel shouted 'You don't play if you haven't eaten everything.' It wasn't necessary to say it to Fernando. He ate anything.'

Bierbeek – the first away match, the first foreign trip, the hotel, the team-mates, the first team base, the first international tournament. A lot of excitement for Fernando in those days of August 1995. Around 30 different teams are taking part in the tournament, including Ajax, Anderlecht, Werder Bremen and Bayern Munich – clubs that boast a long tradition of bringing through new talent. Atlético, on the other hand, has only just set up its junior teams. Manolo Rangel is worried about making a bad impression because his lads don't know each other well. They haven't even had time to train together. So, in-between matches, he gives them sessions with the ball and while walking round the hotel grounds, tries to explain how they should position themselves on the pitch.

During one of these sessions, he realises that 'one of them, I think it was Fernando, had kicked a stone and unfortunately it broke a window in someone's house. The owner came out shouting and protesting, with us not being able to understand what he was saying. We went through some difficult moments before someone from the organisation came and sorted things out.' A stone that stayed in the memories of the coach and the youngsters. And it may actually have helped to unite the team because, in spite of the improvisation, they finish in sixth place. 'Fernando stood out quite well and there were a lot of positive comments about him,' adds Rangel.

It was then 1995–96, the first season in the red-and-white shirt. An important season for the club, which won a league and cup (Copa del Rey) double for the first time in its history. It broke the dominance of Real Madrid and Barcelona. A success for the team managed by Radomir Antic, whose leading players included Kiko, Pantic, Caminero and Simeone. A double that reinforced the emotional ties between Torres and Atléti. And the pride of wearing the shirt of the Spanish champions.

Fernando was doing his part in the junior divisions. He gets 67 goals and is top-scorer, the sporting leader of the team and the focal point of the group. His skills are showcased in the *Torneo de Brunete* (the Brunete Tournament), a competition in which about twenty junior teams from clubs in the Spanish first division take part and where many young Spanish champions make their early mark. The youngster is fascinated by the atmosphere, the terraces at the Estadio Los Arcos, the television cameras filming the matches, the fans and the watchful eye of the observers and trainers at the games. He scores a succession of quick-fire goals, one after the other, and runs to tell his grandfather.

The following year, the shots of him used by regional television channel, *Telemadrid*, always show him at Brunete on the pitch against Milan, tall and thin, with his blond bob haircut and the Number 9 on his back. Fernando puts away penalties that the keeper can't get hold of, dribbles past opponents even with a backheel and scores to make it 3-0 and then 4-0 in a perfect counter-attacking move going round the onrushing keeper.

'Fernando was a born winner. He also wanted to win in training. I was 39, I had to quit playing football but I was in good enough condition to run with them,' remembers Rangel, 'I enjoyed making bets with him regarding a game, penalties, or who would score the most goals from a free-kick. And Fernando was really competitive. At the end of training, he would be waiting with his sports bag to inform me, 'Coach, you owe me a Coca-Cola for what I've won from you.' He was very bright, very smart.'

And Rangel is keen to stress, like Briñas, the importance of grandfather Torres Sanz: 'A fantastic family, very close and well-balanced, which helped him enormously to be a footballer.' His parents, José and Flori, his brother Israel and Mari Paz, his sister, help him in every way. On many occasions, his father has to get permission from work to take him from Fuenlabrada to Orcasitas, where he trains. His mother waits for him in front of the school gates in the wind and the rain, goes with him on the bus or on the train to the ground, and waits for the training to end to bring him back home. And without ever insisting or demanding that he become a professional. On the contrary, she tells him many times that 'if you are tired or you don't want to play, tell me and we won't go again'. His brother and sister also assume their responsibilities for the 15-kilometre (about 10 miles) daily trip. They have to study and do their homework sitting on the terraces at the ground. Years divided between school and training, with matches at the weekend. The best thing is when Fernando joins Atlético's residential Colegio Amanecer school, just outside the centre of Madrid where, today, around 30 youngsters between the ages of fifteen and eighteen study up to the Spanish equivalent of A-levels. 'Fernando was a student who knew how to combine books with the ball,' recalls school coordinator Rafael Bravo. 'His parents wrote us a very emotive letter when Fernando got his *Bachillerato* (equivalent to A-levels).'

A good student and an excellent footballer, so much so that he regularly ends up being the youngest in each of his Atlético junior teams. He plays with youngsters who are one, two or even three years older than him. It is a way of growing up more quickly and a way of learning more rapidly the rules of football because the older ones are stronger technically and physically and better-prepared mentally. Fernando works his way up through the junior ranks. Manolo Rangel is his teacher for three seasons.

Then it is Pedro Calvo's turn to take charge of him for a year. Fernando is fourteen. How was he? 'His manner and professionalism were the same as they are now,' explains 40-year-old Calvo, enjoying a cafe *latte* in a central Madrid bar. 'He was already the team captain but the responsibilities didn't weigh him down. You would tell him that we eat at two o'clock and that everyone should come properly turned out. And ten minutes before time, he would be there with his team-mates, all properly dressed. He was always thinking about the group. He was very humble and he didn't like too much praise. He didn't get nervous, a normal thing at that age. He didn't get angry. I remember that once I blamed him for the behaviour of the team and, instead of giving me a dirty look, he thought the problem over and it never went further than the dressing room. In a footballing sense he was the same as now: rapid, sharp, skilled, very calm in front of goal and, above all, a sponge – he liked to learn.'

Calvo had in his care a line-up that, apart from Torres, could boast players like Manu Del Moral, now at Getafe, Francisco Molinero, today at Real Mallorca, Fernando Usero, now at Elche, and Sergio Torrers who will later win the Under-16 European championship with Fernando. Elements that made for a great season. The key moment is the Nike Under-14 World Club Cup, which took place in May 1999 in Reggio Emilia, Italy. The Atlético Cadete junior team has won the right to play in the prestigious European tournament after first coming through a national competition. The participants are: Real Madrid, Roma, Reggiana (Italy), Belenenses (Portugal), LASK (Austria), Amiens (France), LASK (Austria), Amiens (France), Mouscron (Belgium), B 93 (Denmark) St Joseph's Boys (Ireland), Servette (Switzerland), Symonds Green (England), KFUM Oslo (Norway), Etzella (Luxembourg), PSV (Netherlands), Hammarby (Sweden), Inter Turku (Finland), Borussia Dortmund (Germany), Heart of Midlothian (Scotland).

Before the final phase, they take part in a four-sided event with Porto, PSV and Andorra. 'Against our near-neighbours, Andorra, we won 11-1 but we played poorly, without commitment, without bite,' remembers Calvo. 'So everyone, and Fernando in particular, was read the riot act before the final against PSV. They were told that this would not do and that they had to do better. He went out onto the pitch really wanting to show me that he didn't merit what I'd said. So in one of the first moves, he swerved past five opponents, then went round the keeper, stopped the ball on the goal line, looked over to the dugout and blasted a shot into the goal.'

In the quarter-finals at the Reggio Emilia tournament, the Atlético youngsters once again come up against PSV.

The Dutch are dismissed with a decisive 3-0 scoreline. And Fernando repeated the same trick – in the first move of the match, he gets past three opponents, nutmegs the fourth and lobs the keeper to put them in the lead. The semi-final sees them up against Real Madrid, a Spanish city derby in Italy. A difficult contest against the title-holders, who had disposed of Borussia Dortmund in the quarter-finals. The 2-0 final scoreline leaves no doubts, however, as to the title pretensions of Atlético, who will now meet host side Reggiana in the final. Molinero scored in the eighth minute and it stays at 1-0 until the final whistle. It is the first important title – the first European Cup – that Fernando, the captain, holds aloft.

He is chosen as the best player of the tournament, a recognition that, together with his goals and his movement off the ball, attracts the attention of several European clubs. 'Arsenal made an offer to Fernando's father and Barcelona and Milan were also keen. So much so that the club decided to offer him his first professional contract,' explains Calvo. At fifteen years of age, Torres signs the contract. It's not worth as much as Arsenal were offering but he's happy. He is playing for the team he loves. Football, for him, begins to be more than just a hobby, even if he does not yet realise that it will be his life and his profession. That is still some years ahead.

Meanwhile, he moves up from the *Cadete* team to the *Juvenil* – another way of saying he jumped three years in one go. He meets Abraham García – the last coach he would have in the junior teams and a key figure in his career development – and Ignacio Aznar Torrente, better known as 'Nacho', with whom he formed an attacking strike duo. 'We understood each other well. We knew, without speaking, where the other was on the pitch at any given moment,' recalls Aznar, who today plays at Club Deportivos Leganés in Group II of the Spanish Second Division B. 'Fer was a model of power, ability to score with headers, movement and finishing in front of goal. We became a pair capable of scoring 70 goals a season. Abraham demanded a lot from us. He pushed us, him and me. He was never satisfied. He knew that Fernando and I could go further.'

One match that Nacho has not forgotten is the final of the international tournament, Citta di Rieti, in May 2000. Fernando says one of his legs is hurting but García knows that his presence on the pitch is important. 'Get out there and win this final. If not, you're not going to get anywhere,' he tells them. Fernando plays and scores the goal that sets them on their way. Lazio are swept aside 5-0 and Atlético win another prestigious trophy – as well as the junior league championship a few months later. But the young striker in red and white is then hit by a setback. It happens on 9 August at Boadilla, while training with a team made up of players from the Spanish third division. Fernando clashes with a central defender and collapses. Damaged knee ligaments is the grim verdict. A really bad-looking injury. After the operation, the doctors say it will be eight to 10 months before he can play again. Team-mate José Verdú Toché (now with Numancia), who suffers the same injury at the same time, returns to football eleven months later, in May 2001. Fernando Torres, on the other hand, thanks to his determination and exceptional physical condition, is already back on the pitch in December 2000.

The year to come will bring a huge amount of satisfaction as well as a major disappointment.

Chapter 8

A model footballer

Conversation with Atlético de Madrid junior team coach, Abraham García

There is more activity than usual at the Ciudad Deportiva de Majadahonda (Majadahonda Sports City) in Cerro del Espino, about twelve miles from Madrid city centre. Abel Resino, the new manager of Atlético Madrid (who replaced the Mexican, Javier Aguirre), is directing his first training session. Television crews, zoom lenses and all eyes are focused on the playing area, where the first team is being put through its paces. Journalists are commentating and taking notes on the team set-up, while fans and curious bystanders watch with interest. They are trying to work out what the ex-Atlético goalkeeper (whose European tally for clean sheets – 1,275 minutes set in 1990–91 – was beaten earlier this year by Manchester United's Edwin Van de Sar) is telling his new players.

Everyone has their back turned to the green rectangle where Atlético B is training or, to be more precise, where the junior team – made up of seventeen- to eighteen-year-olds – is playing a match. Green bibs against red vests. On the edge of the pitch is the manager, Abraham García, arms folded across his chest, watching how his charges are developing. Every now and then, he shouts an instruction to Cedric, a young midfielder born in Kinshasa, or to striker

Didí, who is from Barcelona. Ten minutes after the training is over, the youngsters all pile out. Abraham comes over to the boundary fence and arranges to meet at the dressing room exit. First, there is the customary banter with his young players and then a shower to freshen up and get warm again. Despite the spring sky, it is still cold at Cerro del Espino.

For 35-year-old Abraham, built more like a rugby prop forward than a midfielder, football runs in the family. His father, 'Juanjo' García, who died a few years ago, was manager of Castilla, Real Madrid's second team and took the side to a Copa del Rey (King's Cup) final against the Real Madrid first team. For the last eleven years he has trained junior teams, first at Atlético, then three years at Real Madrid, and is now back at the home of the red-and-white stripes. Fernando Torres always speaks of him as the most important manager of his career. Why? Abraham, who is now out of his training tracksuit and sitting at a café in front of the Ciudad Deportiva with a large glass of Coca-Cola in front of him, begins to explain: 'Fernando is very generous and recognises the work of a manager and the effort he puts in. Our relationship, which lasted two years, was more of a professional than a personal one. When I look at the great managers that he's had during his career, for him to remember me like this gives me a lot of pride and satisfaction.'

When did you begin to work with him?
'Fernando was fifteen and had just won the Nike International Cup in Reggio Emilia, Italy, where he was top scorer and been voted the player of the tournament. He was with me until 2001, when he made his debut with the first team.'

How was Fernando at fifteen?
'A player with a tremendous build, which comes from his family (his older brother, Israel, was 6ft 3ins when he was fifteen). He had the muscles of a sprinter, was fast, skilful, smart, hungry for victory and always wanting to get better. He was very professional, self-critical and never 100 per cent happy with how he was playing. He put the bar high. He had a strong personality. On a mental level, to me he always resembled Raúl for his strength of spirit. For his importance as a footballer, I would compare him to Van Basten with his elegant style of running and capacity for scoring goals. From when he was small, he was always thinking of the goal, of scoring.'

And off the field, how did he behave?
'He wasn't a docile lad. Dealing with him, sometimes, was tricky. He was quite shy and would mind his own business. From when he was a small boy, he was sheltered by his family, which knew how to keep him on the straight and narrow. I remember his father or mother always brought him to training sessions and I never saw them brag about the lad. His personality and his environment have absolutely been key to Fernando's success.'

Abraham paused a moment before reflecting on his work …
'In all the years that I've been training youngsters – and I've worked with more than 300 – only about fifteen or twenty have gone on to be professional footballers. Talent is inborn, each one (of them) has it, but to reach the top level – that's something else. You must stick to your guns. You've got to have your feet on the ground, to know what's really important in life, to earn yourself a place in the team, to fight for a position and to overcome enormous difficulties, particularly psychological ones. To put it simply, you

not only have to have the gift of being able to control a football – your mentality, desire and determination counts for a hell of a lot as well. This is the most important thing that I've tried to instil into my players, apart from obviously giving them a training in those technical skills that could be useful to them in the future.'

What exactly did you teach Fernando?
'All I did was try to tell him some things that, at a sporting and human level, could help him deal with whatever might come his way. I told him to be what he's always been, an ambitious young guy who'd be able to sort out the short-comings he had, as everyone has, and in the end his desire to do things well would overcome any criticism or difficult moments. Then, more as a joke than anything else, I told him not to worry, that if one day the football didn't work out, with his looks and general appearance, he could always earn a living in the world of fashion. And now look where he is, a star player as well as being a model in loads of adver-tising campaigns.'

What are your best memories of Fernando at that time?
'Without doubt, a fantastic goal he scored in the league against Rayo Vallecano. He got hold of the ball in the mid-dle of the pitch, he went past one, two, three, dribbling his way through the opposition midfield leaving them rooted to the spot and then scoring an amazing goal. And then after that, how can you forget the trophies we won with that team? For example, the league title, which we snatched from Real Madrid. A pity about the Cup though, Fernando was a member of the Spanish national side that had just won the European Under-16 Championship and he didn't want to miss the Cup final against Osasuna. We lost 1-0. In any case, it was another example of the desire he had to be

on the pitch and to help his team-mates win another title. He was the player everyone looked up to. He had charm and he made the difference.'

Talking of that, how did he get on with his team-mates?
'Very well. Even though some of them were two or three years older than him, he was always competing at a higher age level. I remember a team dinner after winning the league. They were all grown-up by then and everyone wanted to go out on the town. I smiled to myself at Fernando, the youngest of them and his refusal to let himself be led astray. He was very responsible and knew how to behave – both at a party like that and in the dressing room. He didn't put on any airs. He was always talking about the team and encouraging the others. He was very humble but at the same time very mature for his age. He would listen when you explained something to him or commented on something he was doing wrong that he should improve.'

He didn't want to put on any airs but he was captain of Atlético at just eighteen years of age …
That's true. But you have to remember when he joined the first team. He came on the scene at a time when the team wasn't doing well. He was a lad who came from the junior Spanish national side, which had won the Under-19 European Championship, who brought a breath of fresh air to the squad and who, in a few years, had transformed himself into the public face of the club.'

With all the criticism that brought with it …
'They criticised him for the results, for the missed goals, for the side's bad run but also for his technique – his poor left leg, his lack of control and inability to lose his marker.'

And what does his former coach say now? Has he improved?
'Now he plays much better off the ball, he knows how to lose his marker and when he gets going, he's unstoppable. He's a modern striker in the true meaning of the word. He's complete, fast, can apply pressure and is a good finisher. He can use both his legs and his head. He doesn't have the class of Van Basten, the technique of Ronaldo, or the elegance of Ibrahimovic, nor is he unbalanced like Messi, but he scores a lot of goals – and really good ones too. He works for the team and has a drive to be the best, which takes him where he has to be. He knew how to overcome his limitations using character and nerve.'

And the human side? Has that changed?
'No. He's still the lad I knew here in Atlético. Last year, I met him in Liverpool, where I'd gone to see Rafa Benítez, and he was as warm and generous as he he'd always been. There was none of the 'I'm a star' who's forgotten his friends or a junior trainer like me.'

Chapter 9
The Torres generation

'Vamos a quemar el pueblo.' ('We're going to paint the town red.') Wrapped in the Spanish flag, a seventeen-year-old youth is threatening to disturb the peace of Sunderland's 177,000 inhabitants. And team-mates, parents and Spanish fans are ready to join him. The youngster has just won the Under-16 European Championship, he is on a high and wants to party. It is the afternoon of 6 May 2001, and Fernando Torres is leaving the main gate at Sunderland's Stadium of Light, where Spain has beaten France in the final. There are celebrations everywhere, on the pitch, in the stands and in the dressing room. The youngsters are in a daze as they pass round the cup presented to them by UEFA President Lennart Johansson. They aren't sure what to do. One of them runs wildly round the pitch with a pirate-style headband, another uses the Spanish flag as a kind of cape in front of an imaginary bull, while several others leap over the edge of the pitch in tears to embrace mothers and fathers who have come for the occasion. Training staff, players, parents and friends join together to form a giant human fir cone. They all shout: 'Campeones!!! Campeones!!!' ('Champions!!! Champions!!!') over and over again until they're hoarse. Torres the goalscorer, still can't take in the fact that it is all really happening. He shouts: 'We are the champions!'

It's his first trophy with the national team, an adventure that began on 5 April 2000, in Badajoz (south-west Spain), when he wore the shirt of the Spanish Under-15 side. It was a friendly against Belgium, which they win 4-1, including Torres' first goal in the red of Spain. A knee injury had stopped him playing in the preliminary rounds of the tournament but on 24 February 2001, he took to the field with the Under-16s in the Algarve Tournament. The opponents were England, Finland and Portugal. Spain notched up two wins and a draw against the hosts with a four-goal booty for the lad from Atlético Madrid's junior team – the best score of the tournament. Not bad for someone coming back from an important injury, which had put into doubt his future career. It was the test that Under-16 coach, Juan Santisteban, and Iñaki Sáez, the coordinator of all the junior sides, had needed. Soon afterwards came the naming of the national side for the European championship, which would take place in England from April to May.

Durham is the team's base, where the youngsters lead a cloistered existence: training followed by a siesta from 3.30 to 6pm, homework with private teachers (because when many of them get back to Spain, they will have to take school exams) followed by more study and videos, this time of their next tournament opponents – a strict regime. Spain is placed in Group A, which journalists and commentators name the 'group of death', with Romania, Belgium and Germany the teams they have to beat to get to the quarter-finals. The aim is to repeat the performance that saw them win the title in 1999. The first match is on 24 April against Romania and the result is 3-0 to Spain with Torres, wearing Number 14, scoring his first goal on English soil. Who knows, maybe a premonition of what would happen six years and a few months later ...

After this game, the side is top of the group on goal difference. They play their next match against Belgium who, surprisingly, have beaten the Germans 2-1. It finishes as few were expecting, with a 5-0 scoreline in favour of Spain, including a double from El Niño, although no one yet calls him that. The last group game against Germany is to be played at Durham. For the boys in red, a victory or draw would see them through, although even a defeat would be enough because they have a three-point lead over their German rivals. The result is a bad 0-2 defeat but it's enough for them to progress. However, Santisteban's youngsters lose playmaker Andrés Iniesta through injury.

The quarter-finals are against the Italian side of Paolo Berrettini. It's a difficult encounter against an experienced team with good players like Giampaolo Pazzini (today a leading goal-scorer with Sampdoria), Alberto Aquilani (now in the Roma midfield) and Giorgio Chiellini (a defender with Juventus). In the 26th minute, a Torres penalty gives Spain the lead, but on 54 minutes Mauro Bellotti heads in an Italy free-kick. The scoreline is still the same at full-time and qualification for the semis will be decided from the penalty-spot. Juan Santisteban can't bear to watch this Russian roulette and takes refuge in the dugout. But the Spaniards are unforgiving. Fernando Torres, Senel, Carlos and Melli all score, while the Italians slip up. Their first hits the post and the fourth is saved by Miguel Ángel Moya. This time luck goes their way, unlike on the previous five occasions. Santisteban is finally able to open his eyes and runs to embrace his team. It's a story that will be repeated in another European tournament, the big one, that of 2008. A coincidence, of course …

The last hurdle before the final is Croatia, a match that takes place in Middlesborough on 3 May. Torres opens and closes the scoring (with a goal from Senel in-between) and even allows himself the luxury of a chip from the edge of the area, in very little space, which crashes against the angle of crossbar and post. 'We had a great second half, really impressive. We got ourselves to 3-0 and after that we just kept on moving it around, playing football, which is what we like,' explains the lad from Fuenlabrada.

France, the overwhelming favourites, are waiting in the final, having scored a tournament tally of seventeen without conceding any – a track record of impressive proportions. In order of matches played, they had dispatched Scotland (3-0), Croatia (3-0), Finland (5-0), Russia (2-0) and England (4-0) in the semi-final. 'They're a footballing machine but we will try to give them a game,' says Santisteban. Much more optimistic is Fernando: 'Of course they are an amazing team but if we get on with playing football, we will win.' In their Durham base the day before the match, they follow a similar routine to that of previous days, apart from the presence of the senior national team coach, José Antonio Camacho. Then lunch, siesta, homework with a private teacher and, before going to bed, videos for everyone. The France-England game makes the youngsters realise that *Les Bleus* are a tough, physical, tactical and technical outfit. The game proves it. In the second minute, in front of the French keeper, Torres has a good chance but the shot goes just outside the left post. It is an open match and even if the Spanish manage at times to impose their game during the second half, it is the French pair, Le Tallec and Sinama, who get closest to scoring. But just when the 20,000-strong crowd inside the Stadium of Light are almost resigned to the prospect of extra-time, English referee Andrew D'Urso blows his whistle and awards a penalty following a tackle in the area by France's Colombo. The decision is hotly contested by the French players but a spot-kick it is.

It is minute 36 of the second half with just four more remaining (junior matches are 80 minutes). Fernando Torres moves towards the penalty area. He has already taken two from the spot in this tournament and converted them both. No one has any doubts about how he is going to hit it – hard and towards the left post, like the other two. There is no reason to change, given that the other two have been so successful. He takes a short run-up and shoots hard. Keeper Chaigneau guesses right but the angle of the shot is too much and he can't reach it. It is the winning goal and the Atlético player cries out like a man obsessed, lifting his shirt to reveal a message to Andrés Iniesta and thereby keep the promise he made to dedicate his goal to his injured team-mate. Then the youngsters' exuberant celebrations – first in the Stadium of Light and then, that evening, at the Newcastle ground, St James' Park, where the gala dinner is being held with officials from UEFA, the Spanish Football Federation and their opponents. From shorts to jacket and tie, handshakes, friendly chat, dancing, polite laughter and toasts with Coca-Cola. It's all done very seriously 'because then,' explained one of the team, 'they cannot say that we don't know how to behave ourselves in society.' The partying relocates in the early morning to Durham, the team base. The Under-16s have, for once, got permission to stay out until the small hours. It is, after all, their big day and the technical staff say they deserve it. As indeed they deserve the full attention of the media, which, during the previous week, has discovered what it was already describing as 'the Torres Generation'. The reason is quickly apparent: Fernando is the slayer of France with seven goals, the top goalscorer and the best player of the tournament. It's Fernando who comes to symbolise a national side made up of Iniesta, Gavilán, Melli and Diego León.

This is a generation the commentators hope will continue in the same vein, will make the senior national side and win those trophies that have eluded them so long. Meanwhile, the stories of who these seventeen-year-olds are, and where they come from – especially Torres – are being uncovered.

The first background articles appear in the press on the lad from Fuenlabrada, whose physique and strength someone compares to a sabre, with others recalling idol, Marco Van Basten, his favourite singers (Andrés Calamaro) and films (Roberto Benigni's *La Vita è Bella*).

A little more than a year later, the Torres Generation will repeat the celebrations in Norway. In-between, there was the black hole of the Under-17 World Cup, which took place in September 2001 in Trinidad & Tobago. Spain arrived, fresh from their European triumph, but two bad defeats against Burkina Faso (0-1) and Argentina (2-4) left them in third place in their group and they did not make the quarter-finals. Fernando got just one goal – in the first half of the match against Oman. But he came back with a vengeance in July in the second leg of the Under-19 Euro qualifying tie against Macedonia. He scored two goals to qualify the side for the finals in Norway from 21–27 July 2002.

José Camacho, the manager of the senior national side, decided to quit after Spain's exit from the 2002 World Cup in South Korea and Japan (at the hands of joint host South Korea, managed by Guus Hiddink). On 2 July, the Spanish Football Federation appointed Iñaki Sáez as his successor, but before getting down to work with the grown-ups, he wanted to finish the job with the juniors: 'I had taken them through to qualification, so I wanted to go with them to the finals,' he says, now retired from the Federation. After a long round of golf and a restorative shower in his holiday home in Tenerife, he talked with pleasure about that July in Norway and Fernando Torres: 'The year before, he had made his debut with Atlético Madrid's first team and with Luis Aragonés as manager. That season, he had been important for getting the team promoted to the Primera División. He was very good and stood out because of his speed and strength, qualities which, at that age, always create problems for opponents. He was full of promise – a youngster who'd always scored a lot of goals in all the leagues he'd played in. One could see that he had a lot of potential and that there was still room to improve various aspects of his game. Our objective, as coaches of the national team, was to improve how he received the ball with his back to his opponent and to play it as quickly as possible. In other words, that he would be able to use to the full the enormous skills that he had. In the dressing room, he was a very cheerful lad, an important person. He symbolised the attack and his team-mates had confidence in him because he always got them out of trouble. He got on tremendously well with Iniesta and you could see this on the pitch. And I saw it in the final.'

But staying in chronological order, there were three more matches to play before arriving at the final. The first, a Group A tie against the Czech Republic, finished 1-1. Fernando is not on the score-sheet. In the second, Iñaki's youngsters find themselves up against the hosts – a straightforward game because the Norwegians, apart from honest effort, commitment and a competitive spirit, don't put up much resistance. The first goal comes in the 22nd minute, when the keeper can only parry Torres' rocket of a shot and José Antonio Reyes (later of Arsenal) is on hand to pick up the loose ball and score. Nine minutes after the restart, Iniesta feeds Fernando, who beats Larsen to make it 2-0, with Reyes scoring again in the 68th minute to close the proceedings at 3-0. In the last match they meet Slovakia, who had put five past the Czech Republic and scored another five against Norway to give them a maximum six points and make them the highest-scoring team in the tournament. The only result that will see Spain through to the final is a win.

However, things start going wrong almost immediately. A free-kick on the edge of the area and Cech finds the back of the net off the left-hand post: 1-0. Then, just before the interval, Sergio equalises, thanks to a calamitous error by Konecny, one of the opposing defenders who fails to clear. Then, in the second half, Torres takes to the stage and, in injury time, diverts a superb cross from Carmelo into the net to make the final score 3-1 to Spain, who make the final. There they will meet Germany, managed by Uli Stielike – someone who knows Spanish football well. During the 1977–78 season, after spending four years at Borussia Mönchengladbach, he joined Real Madrid to become a pivotal figure in the midfield, remaining there for eight seasons. The Spaniards hold him in high regard and he has much respect for his opponents.

He recognises that Spain has players with better technical skills than his, and the trio of Torres, Iniesta and Reyes give him concern: 'They are very good from the midfield to the front line and very skilful on the ball,' he explains. Iñaki's assistant, Santisteban, picks out the same players: 'Iniesta directs the play as if he has had years of experience, Reyes creates all sorts of problems, and Torres? Well, I think he's amazing, He can cover a huge amount of ground, he's courageous, smart with the ball at his feet, skilful and ready to create space between defenders and not be afraid. If he gets a kick he gives three back and won't give way. He's not frightened of physical contact, is always willing to have a go and has a winner's mentality. He knows he's good, what he can achieve, and that conviction makes him similar to players like Raúl – strong characters who don't give up.'

Santisteban, also an ex-Real Madrid player, is confident about the result of the final because 'the lads have talent, class and self-discipline'. The match takes place on 28 July in Oslo's Ullevaal Stadium in front of a sold-out crowd, 16,000-strong.

This was what the Spanish newspaper *El Mundo* had to say the day after the encounter: 'Germany had to face the facts and admit defeat when confronted with the generation of Fernando Torres, icon and beacon of the Spanish side, the star emerging from his shell, who intimidates his opponents and achieves success every time he plays. He was top-scorer in the European Under-16 championship-winning side and a year later repeated the trick with the Under-19s. He already looks mature enough to forget playing with the kids and take on the challenges of the grown-ups.'

Another newspaper, *ABC*, had the headline: 'Torres runs riot against Germany' and wrote 'Crone and Volz (two of the German defenders) couldn't avoid him. They were met by El Niño in every Spanish attack and couldn't catch him. Fernando had already destroyed them in the first minute. He got himself in front of Haas and shot wide after running six metres held by Fathi, who gave away a penalty, which referee Ceferen did not give. From that moment on, Fathi didn't want to know about Torres. Torres, though, definitely did want to know all about being crowned Under-19 champions and had another penalty shout – Crone tackled him as he entered the penalty area – but the referee didn't agree with that one either. Third time lucky. The crafty Reyes took a quick free-kick and the Atlético Madrid player took the opportunity once more to escape the weak opposition defence and shoot, forcing Haas into the first of a series of impressive saves and in turn making himself Spain's principal problem.'

But in the 55th minute, even Haas had to admit he was beaten: 'It was a very similar move to that which won Euro 2008 for the national side also, as it happens, against Germany,' recalled Iñaki Sáez, 'Reyes, in our half of the pitch, passes to Iniesta almost on the halfway line. Andrés sees Torres and makes one of his trademark deep passes.

Fernando wins the race for the ball with Crone and has just the German keeper to beat but fluffs the shot. The ball goes loose. Crone and Haas look at each other and don't react. Torres sticks out his boot and nicks the goal. He knew how to keep going until the end. He knew how to keep on fighting until the end. That goal, exactly like the one last year against Germany, perfectly demonstrates his style,' explained Saéz, 'a striker who finishes the move with speed, force and intelligence.'

'Torres … y Reyes' read the red and black front page of Spanish sport daily, *Marca,* the next day, the first of many with El Niño centre stage (the headline played on the name *Reyes,* which also means 'Kings'. The headline could therefore be read: 'Torres … and we are Kings'). But Fernando, although excited by the two titles already won, doesn't let it all go to his head and is already thinking of the next Under-20 World Cup. He's hungry for victory. And this is how he responds to the praise he receives from Stielike after the match: 'It's always good to receive praise from one of the best managers in Europe but I still have to work on my game and improve so that this doesn't turn into criticism.'

Another example of the young man's desire, commitment and determination.

Chapter 10
A special dedication

Conversation with Barcelona and Spain midfielder, Andrés Iniesta

An injury is keeping him out of the Barcelona team ahead of the final of Spain's Copa del Rey (King's Cup) against Atlético Bilbao. His side relies on the 'hero of Stamford Bridge' (where he scored the winning goal in stoppage time against Chelsea in the Champions League semi-final) because of his qualities as a 'total footballer'. He can play in midfield or on the wing. His dribbling skills and vision of the game have made him a key player. But this time Iniesta will not be there. It will be several days before the Barcelona midfielder can run out onto a pitch again, but he is expecting to be fit for Rome in the Champions League final against Manchester United. Instead, he's here at the Ciutat Esportiva Joan Gamper (a complex situated about 3 miles from Barcelona's Camp Nou stadium, which hosts training sessions from junior teams as well as the Barça first team) in the hands of the physiotherapists. The treatment is taking a while and in the meantime, the words of his manager, Pep Guardiola, come to mind:

'He's an example to everyone and above all for the next generation. I always tell them to look at him because he doesn't wear earrings, he doesn't change the colour of his hair and he doesn't have any tattoos. But they all know he's the best. He plays wherever you put him and he never complains, not even when he's on the pitch for only twenty minutes. And he always trains well. Iniesta is priceless, tremendous.'

In the beginning the Spanish press christened him *Andresito* because of his small size. Now he's become *Don Andrés* and 'The Sweet', after ex-Barça manager Frank Rjikaard said 'on the pitch he gives out sweets' to describe his way of playing. They've called him 'The Philosopher's Stone' of Barcelona. Opposing managers and team-mates consider him a player capable of deciding a match but he himself shuns praise. The physiotherapy session over, he arrives pale-faced and wearing a white jacket, accompanied by Sergi Noguera, the club press officer and introduces himself as follows:

'I was born in Fuentealbilla, a small village in La Mancha, about 25 miles from Albacete. My father, José, was a building worker and my mother worked in a bar with my grandparents. I come from a modest family. I started to play for Albacete and came to Barcelona when I was twelve. In 2003, my parents and my sister moved here too. I consider myself a very normal and straightforward person. I like to do my work well and try to enjoy football.'

His voice is frail, as is his general appearance, and his shyness is obvious. Andrés Iniesta Luján is not one for long chats. He does, though, gently begin to open up.

Let's go back to April 2001 and the Under-16 European championship and – I'm sorry to remind you of this – another injury …
'It was against Germany. For them it was a must-win game and they came at us full-on. My marker was Mair, a huge, blond midfielder. They wanted to get the ball off us. In the end I had to leave the pitch. These things happen. Nothing more than that. The doctors suspected ruptured knee

ligaments but luckily it was only a bruised shin bone and a sprained lateral ligament inside the knee. But my European championship finished there and I came home.'

You left and your team-mates promised to dedicate the goals in the semi-final against Croatia to you.
'Yes, Diego León (then in the Real Madrid youth team and now playing for English Championship side, Barnsley) called me the day before the match. He had replaced me and promised that both he and Torres would be wearing my shirt, the Number 8, under their national shirts. I was zapping between the channels at home in Barcelona but couldn't find any station that was showing the match. I didn't know that it wasn't being broadcast in Spain, which was only showing the other semi-final between France and England. I switched off the TV but after the game, my team-mates called from the dressing room so I could share the win with them. I was touched by that and felt that they were really fond of me. They were a fantastic group of players who deserved to get to the final. They told me that Fernando, after scoring the first goal, went past everyone looking for the cameras to show me his dedication. He didn't know that here (in Spain) I couldn't see him. In any case, he told me not to worry because he would wear (the shirt) again in the final against France.

And did you get to see the dedication this time?
'Yes, of course. Fernando scored the penalty, lifted his shirt and underneath he was wearing a white T-shirt with the words: 'Para tí, Andrés' ('For you, Andrés'). He dedicated the winning goal to me, he dedicated it only to me.' (Iniesta repeats it over and over again, as if the words bring back the emotional power of that day.)

Why was there this very special relationship?
'From when we were sixteen, when we came together in
that team, we got on really well. For me, Torres has always
been a team-mate with whom I've had a great understanding. Each of us has been in our own particular (club) teams
and got on with our lives but when we come together in
the national side we've always understood each other perfectly. Above all on the pitch, because Fernando has always
been a player who gets away from his marker well, who has
speed. And from my position in the midfield, I've tried to
take advantage of his skills to get the ball to him.'

As you did for him in the Under-19 final in Oslo?
'Yes, in Norway, I passed the ball to him but it was he who
made the goal. Fernando did the difficult part.' Modest as
ever, Don Andrés.

*Iñaki Sáez, the manager of that Under-19 side said that you were
the one who best understood Fernando?*
'Well, in a team there are always some footballers who
understand each other better than others and that was the
case then. But I have to say that for a midfielder to have a
striker with Fernando's qualities is fantastic. It makes everything so much easier.'

What are Fernando's skills?
'He gets away from his marker very well, he sees space, he
has a lot of strength and uses this strength so that when he
comes to shoot, he does it coolly, with the certainty that he
will score a lot of goals.'

Which player does he most resemble?
'Ronaldo, because of his strength, his bursts of power and
for the finishing which Fernando has and which, in his day,

Ronnie had too. Aside from that, each of them is different technically but in those specific respects, Fernando reminds me of him a lot.'

And do you remember that, at that time, Fernando never stopped talking about Van Basten?
'That's right, Marco Van Basten was one of his idols but I didn't get many opportunities to see him play and I never came across him on the pitch.'

Which is not the case with Torres, who's also been your opponent?
'Yes, we have come up against each other and with every kind of outcome. There've been matches that his team has won, matches that my team has won, and matches where he's scored against us. He's always a really difficult striker to keep under control.'

Let's move on from confrontations to the national side. How would you describe the experience of winning the Euro 2008 tournament playing in the same team? And how did you both get on together?
'We got on really well and with all the others in the team. It was the same group of players that had won the qualifying matches. We experienced everything. We were criticised after the games with Ireland and Sweden but it could be that the hard time we had in qualifying actually worked in our favour to make us stronger. Once we got to Austria, we were really motivated as well as committed and united as a team. When you have that kind of combination, it brings victory a bit closer.'

How did you feel when Fernando got the goal against Germany?
'Completely elated, really happy. To have scored and to have scored in such an important final and to have put us

ahead of Germany is no easy feat. We were then in reach of the title.'

What do you talk about now when you meet up in the national side?
'About everything really but especially how each of us is doing in our respective teams.'

And what has Fernando told you about Liverpool?
'He told me that to begin with it was a really big change and that there's a huge passion for football over there. For a player, it's really important to feel the support of the fans. I have to say that, at Anfield, where I've played, it's incredible. It's wonderful that the crowd is always 100 per cent behind their team and that makes it really difficult for any opponent to win there.'

What do you think of the change he's undergone since going to Liverpool?
'It's been hugely important. The Premier League is very different from La Liga and I think that the way of playing in England and, in particular, the style of Liverpool, is perfect for someone with Fernando's skills. Also, one mustn't forget that Torres had always been identified with Atléti. He had all that weight, being promoted to the first team at seventeen and having to keep going despite everything that piled up on top of him. There's no doubt that was really hard. At Liverpool he doesn't have any of that baggage.'

And what do you think about the success he's enjoying in England?
'I think he deserves it. Fernando's always had these qualities but with time he's matured and acquired much more

experience as well as improving his technique and now he's one of the best strikers in the world. No doubt about it'

And finally, do you see yourself lifting the World Cup with Fernando?
'I really, really hope that we can get to that point and succeed in such an important tournament, one that Spain has never won. It'll be very difficult but we'll fight to reach the final and then see what happens.'

Chapter 11
A fairy tale

Years later, remembering those days, he can't think of any words to describe it other than 'it seemed like a fairy tale'. It was hard to believe, 'Because everything happened in such a short time, everything went so quickly, it was difficult to take in,' says Fernando Torres. And he's right: On 6 May 2001, he was proclaimed Under-16 European champion and on 27 May, exactly three weeks later, at just seventeen, he realised his dream, making his debut with the Atlético Madrid first team at the Vicente Calderón stadium. On 3 June, he scored his first goal for the senior team. And that's not all, because in-between there was the call-up from Iñaki Sáez to the Under-18 national team, the final of the Spanish Under-19 league and even the news that he'd been sold to Valencia. Unbelievable indeed.

Let's take it from the beginning …

Right after the success with the national side in Europe, it occurs to the Atlético directors that it would be a good idea to include the lad from Fuenlabrada in the first team. The day after the defeat against Murcia the atmosphere is noticeably tense. Hopes of immediately going back up to the first division following relegation are fading. The fans have had enough of everyone – the president, the club, the manager and the players. There are even some attacks against the perceived 'culprits'. Maybe the Golden Boy of Spanish football, as he has been labelled after the European victory, is just what's needed.

Jesús Gil, the club president, thinks Torres could be used to calm the waters of a fan-base on the edge of a nervous breakdown. But he can't do it straight away. Torres is committed to Iñaki's Under-18 side. On 16 May, at Vila Real in the Portuguese region of Algarve, Spain play Portugal in the Under-18 European championship. The result is a 1-3 victory with a goal for Fernando Torres. Two weeks later it is possible. Paolo Futre, the Portuguese ex-Number 10, the striker who played seven seasons (1987–93 and then again in 1997–98 after a year with West Ham) in the red and white of Atlético before moving into the club offices as sporting director, picks up the phone. He calls Torres at home and asks the youngster to join up with the first team. The idea is that he should start to get himself used to the dressing room of the senior players, seeing that he will be with them for the 2001–02 pre-season. Torres, having finished his commitments with the national and junior teams, is preparing to go on holiday. At first, he doesn't understand why Futre is calling him and can hardly believe the sporting director's words. But he doesn't let himself get carried away. On the contrary, he replies that if it's just for training, he would prefer to go on holiday because after the injury and national team duty he hasn't been able to rest even for a single day. Futre then lets drop the fleeting possibility of being on the bench and Fernando replies immediately with an enthusiastic 'Yes'.

On Wednesday, 23 May, Fernando trains with the first team, scores five goals and Futre tells Carlos García Cantarero – the manager who replaced Marcos Alonso for the last seven games of the season – to call him up for the next match. So, on Saturday, 26 May, the youngster went off with his idols. Those who, a week before, he had seen on the pitch from the stands at the Calderón, those whose autographs he had asked for, and those who were now alongside him as his team-mates. The youngster is a bundle of nerves. The atmosphere isn't hostile but many look sceptically at the new arrival. 'In the coach, they were making jokes about him. It was the way the squad welcomed him to the group and they were telling him, "you are a boy but one of ours"', recalls Cantarero.

Sunday 27 May is the big day. Unforgettable. The heat is unbearable, Atléti are playing at home against Leganés and drawing, with 35,000 in the Calderón whistling and bawling at the players who are seemingly incapable of getting a vital home win. Cantarero raises his hand towards the subs who are exercising to the side of the pitch. He indicates to Fernando José Torres Sanz. The lad runs towards his manager and gets himself changed in a flash. Meanwhile, on the pitch, Luque scores from outside the area to make it 1-0. It is the 54th minute. Cantarero sends Torres to warm-up along the edge of the pitch. His debut seems to have been postponed. But the manager knows that the fans want to see him on the pitch. All the papers have been talking about him, praising the new red-and-white hope. For several days the talk about the team's fragile state or its endless economic problems stopped in order to concentrate on the lad from the junior team.

In the 65th minute, Cantarero brings off Luque, the author of the goal and sends on the Number 35, Fernando Torres. The fans, placated by a positive scoreline, give him a warm welcome. In the minutes that remain, there is nothing special to report, but he's made his debut. A member of the opposing team wants to exchange his shirt but he refuses. That shirt's very important – he's promised it to his brother, Israel, and it'll be the only one like it being worn at the Estadio Carlos Belmonte the following Sunday, 3 June 2001.

Atlético have to win if they are going to keep alive their hopes of promotion but, against Albacete Balompié, things aren't going well. Atléti are playing badly. An ugly game, marked by tension. Fear of losing haunts Cantarero's men. The defence is fragile and exposed to the counter-attacking of their opponents. In attack, there are fleeting glimpses of Kiko, who has returned to the team, and of Cubillo. With seventeen minutes remaining, it's a miracle the Madrid side isn't losing. They create three half-chances on goal with Luque and Correa, while Albacete go close on several occasions. Cantarero plays the one card he has left at his disposal – the youngster. 'We needed a goal. That's why I put Fernando on,' the manager will say later, rubbing his hands with glee for making the right move. Yes, because El Niño, cheered on by 5,000 Atlético fans who have gone down to Albacete to support the team, has just five minutes to change things round. He comes on in place of Kiko and goes immediately to take up his place in the attack. The first time he touches the ball, he is knocked flat by Arias, who earns a red card and a dismissal.

In the second move, a long cross from Iván Amaya comes into the area from left to right. Fernando pretends to go one way, then the other, gains ground on the central defenders and gets behind them. It seems the cross will end up being too long, but the youngster moves rapidly without taking his eyes off the ball falling out of the sky. He stretches out his neck, hitting the ball decisively, accurately and power- fully, directing it towards the opposite post. He fears that it's hit the post and gone out of play. But no, it rebounds into the net. The keeper looks at his defence with disgust while Fernando runs towards the goal line and, beside himself with joy, embraces Aguilera and Hernández – men almost twice his age. It is his first goal at national club level and a happy ending of the fairy tale for him and the team, which, with those three points, can continue to dream of promotion. The referee blows his whistle to end the encounter and El Niño succeeds in getting his hands on the ball that marked his first goal. He wants to keep it as a souvenir of his fledgling career. But then he changes his mind and kicks it hard and high towards the south end, where the Atléti fans are concentrated.

Meanwhile, on the pitch, around twenty journalists are following him, microphones at the ready, to interview him and hear his first impressions. Hernández and the others lift him up and take him to the dressing room.

After the shower and celebrations, there is time for comments, thanks and dedications. 'Very emotional. I feel very emotional,' is the first thing he says. Then he explains: 'It was what all my family were waiting for, it's what I wanted, to score such an important goal as this for Atlético to return to its natural home, which is La Primera División (the first division). We're a little nearer thanks to this victory. I dedicate it to all the members of the *Frente Atlético* (the group of fans with whom Fernando usually watches the matches in the Calderón. He also gave them the match shirt) who have come here to cheer us on. They are fantastic and it's worth battling on in order to get them the promotion.' He also has words of thanks for his team-mates: 'They've helped me so much and have accepted me into the squad. Without them, the goal would not have been possible.' He's in Seventh Heaven and you can understand why. But he wasn't the only one jumping with joy. Paolo Futre declares: 'Torres is a star player, a phenomenon who will bring a lot of joy to the fans of Atlético and will be fundamental to the future of Spanish football.' And Cantarero adds: 'Fernando is going to be this week's leading figure. He deserves it and let's hope he's going to be the leading figure for the next few years.'

There is no mistaking the following day's headlines, all
of them about him: 'A Magical Apparition in Albacete,' said
El Mundo, while *El País* screams: 'Fernando Torres Saves
Atlético.' The TV channels call him into the studio to comment on his goal, to talk about himself, the two remaining
matches of the league season and the chances for his team.
From that Sunday on, little-by-little his life changes. From
Albacete he gets to Fuenlabrada around two in the morning
and, as his parents remember, 'he went into his room and
about five minutes later he was sleeping. But the morning
after and for the following two days, his usual wolf-like hun-
ger at breakfast disappears. His stomach shrinks due to the
effects of all the emotion and his new-found fame. But the
youngster gets over it easily enough.

What's nothing like as easy to get over is the huge disappointment at Getafe two weeks later. In the Coliseo Alfonso
Pérez (Getafe's stadium, to the south of Madrid city centre), Fernando starts in the team for the first time and is
the principal figure for the first 45 minutes. He has only
matches behind him but he shows a maturity and coolness
that some of his team-mates, with much more experience
than him, do not display on this occasion. In spite of the
numerous errors in front of Atlético's goal, they chalk up a
1-0 victory but at the end of the match, there aren't the celebrations many were hoping for. Everyone is quiet on the
pitch, in the dugout and in the stands. The news from the
radio has already reached the players, technical staff and
the 10,000 Atléti supporters that Betis and Tenerife have
won, which means Atlético will remain in the second division solely because of an inferior goal difference with the
Canary Island team. The fans slowly slip away with heads
bowed. Some vent their anger against the stadium, ripping
out seats and throwing them towards the pitch. The police
escort Jesús Gil and his wife out of the ground. Around 50

of the radical *ultra* fans call for heads to roll, shouting: 'Gil, you bastard, get out of the Calderón!' Paolo Futre kicks the wall and throws his ever-present cigarette into the far distance, muttering: 'It's been a huge disappointment but this pain is over. We've lost the battle.' Cantarero declares: 'We're distraught. I've seen a lot of sad things in football but this has been the worst.' The players depart in silence. It's a big blow for everyone. And for Fernando Torres in particular. He's shattered. He just wants things to move on as quickly as possible. He just wants to forget. He is experiencing the disappointment more as a fan than as a player. And it's massive. What had been a dream has now turned into a nightmare. That night he takes refuge in his room in Fuenlabrada but this time he can't sleep. He is inconsolable because of all the missed opportunities and the promotion that has now disappeared. The next year Atlético will have to start all over again in the second division. But first, Fernando still has to resolve, once-and-for-all, the strange matter of his phantom transfer.

It hits the headlines on 11 May. 'We were coming back in the coach from Sevilla where we had lost the final of the Copa del Rey (King's Cup). It was night-time and we were about 7 miles from Madrid. Someone was listening to the radio when suddenly one of the sports programmes on the *Cadena Ser* station announced that Valencia had signed Fernando. He knew absolutely nothing about it. No one knew anything about it. It seemed very strange to us given that Jesús Gil had been in the dressing room with the lads before the game and, as always, had sung along with us 'Atlético 1-2-3 Go get 'em.' It seemed impossible that they would have sold El Niño but the news spread like wildfire and when we eventually arrived at the Calderón there were loads of media there, all waiting for Fernando but he had got off outside Madrid at the Hotel Los Olivos. Recalling how it all started is Miguel Ángel Gómez Gonzalez, aged 45 and known to everyone as 'Cirilo'.

At that time he was the Atlético kit man and had followed Torres' progress step-by-step through the junior ranks. The news on *Cadena Ser* is like a bomb going off. It turns out that on 15 March 2001, the Madrid club had received 400 million pesetas (about £2 million), which, including VAT, became 464 million, from Valencia Football Club to deal with a liquidity problem – and the Atlético directors had put up the rights of their 'golden boy' as guarantee. If they didn't pay the debt within the time stipulated (by 25 June), then Fernando Torres would become a Valencia player on 1 July. It was an operation that provoked a huge row, stirred up the anger of the fans and ended up being the subject of a legal investigation. Miguel Ángel Gil, director general of Atlético Madrid, maintained that it was 'a usual thing between clubs, to use players' transfers to disguise loans'. The professional league said that it had never seen anything like it before. Torres denied having signed a contract which obliged him to leave and denied absolutely having any preferred option for that club. His representatives talked of compensation of 2,600 million pesetas (about £13 million) if Atlético did not pay up and Torres was forced to leave for Valencia. It wasn't the case. The debt was paid off. El Niño's adventure in Atlético Madrid continued.

Chapter 12
Yogurt

*Conversation with former Atlético de Madrid
striker, Francisco Miguel Narváez Machón,
better known as 'Kiko'*

A baseball cap above his black curly hair, wearing a leather jacket, coloured jersey and a weary look is how Kiko appears in the hotel bar at Madrid's *Ciudad de la Imagen*. He has just emerged, battle-scarred and breathless, from a game of indoor football, during which he has scored the equaliser, but which has left him completely drained. In little more than an hour, he will be on television commentating for the Spanish channel, *Sexta*, on the Copa del Rey (King's Cup) tie between Atlético Bilbao and Sevilla (Seville).

Born in Jerez de la Frontera, Andalusia and now aged 37, Kiko has a long career behind him. After three years in the Cadiz team and a gold medal with the Spanish national side at the 1992 Barcelona Olympics, he became the figurehead player at Atlético Madrid. Chalking up eight seasons (from 1993 to 2001), 278 appearances and 64 goals, he played a key role in the squad, which, with the Serbian ex-Luton Town (1980–84) player Radomir Antic as manager, captured a league and cup double in the 1995–96 season – the last silverware won by the club.

Tall (1.89m/6ft 2ins) and rangy, he was in a class of his own, a striker but not in the classic sense of the word. He played behind the main striker, combining great imagination and vision with decisive assists and scoring many goals of his own. He was Fernando Torres' hero.

Kiko takes a long drink of water to rehydrate himself before recalling the end of May 2001 – the debut of El Niño.

'The team was in the Second Division and the situation wasn't good. Results were mixed and we weren't playing well. To sum it up, we had a lot of problems. At the beginning of the season, we'd been hovering above the relegation zone and getting promotion was looking unlikely. To raise the fans' hopes, they decided to give a debut to El Niño, a true *atlético*, someone with whom the fans could identify. It was a marketing exercise, something which would divert the public's attention from the day-to-day happenings at the club.'

And how did the dressing room view him?
'We thought we'd have to have some kind of arrangement with a children's nursery. What was a kid of seventeen doing in a team of experienced professionals? And above all, we were suddenly being asked to look after this youngster when we were right in the middle of our final, crucial matches. I remember the first day he introduced himself to me in the dressing room. He was thin, freckled, with an extremely slight build and very shy. As he went to shake my hand, he was very emotional. I was the team captain and his idol.'

Why was that?
'I was tall, like him and, like him a forward, although Fernando is more powerful and more direct. I played in a different style. I'd won the Cup and League title just when a young boy begins to idolise footballers and to admire a player who plays in his position. I was a committed *atlético*,

like him. It's normal if you come from the junior team to have someone as an example, a role model. Raúl in (Real) Madrid had El Buitre (Emilio Butragueño, a goal-scorer for Real Madrid during the 1980s), Fernando identified with me.'

So much so that Fernando, to pay homage to you, celebrated some of his goals by posing as an archer, an unusual celebration which you yourself made famous.
'Yes, that's true – him and Dani Güiza. They repeated it. I really appreciate that.'

And some people say that Fernando, during the 2006–07 season against Real Madrid, repeated the goal that you scored in the Champions League ten years earlier?
'Yes, the two are very alike. In that match against Ajax, Caminero, playing deep, began the move for Aguilera on the right wing continuing up towards the goal line before passing the ball backwards. It came to me just in front of the penalty area and, half-turning, I shot towards the far post and it went in. I remember Fernando's goal perfectly well because I was in the Calderón (Atlético Madrid's stadium, the Estadio Vicente Calderón) as a TV commentator and because it's the only goal that El Niño has scored at (Real) Madrid. Fernando got hold of the ball before passing it to Galletti who went down the right wing, putting a cross into the centre, where Torres controlled it skilfully with his best leg, the right, on the outside of his foot, and shot towards the post to the right of (Iker) Casillas (the Real Madrid goalkeeper) who could do absolutely nothing. Two important goals, especially El Niño's. Real (Madrid) was his obsession.'

Can we go back to Fernando's debut in the Calderón?

'That day I wasn't in the team. I was having problems with the club – and with my ankles. They weren't calling me up for home matches. But Fernando had already taken everyone by surprise, with his personality, self-confidence and willingness to learn plus his professional qualities and maturity. No, he certainly wasn't a kid you had to look after. In training, he came up against defenders like 'Super-López' (Juan Manuel López Martínez, an Atlético stalwart who spent ten years at the club) and Hernández (Jean François, a Frenchman who had joined from Rayo Vallecano) and he didn't give an inch. He was strong and determined to show what he could do.'

And he showed what he could do at Albacete, in his second game with the first team.

'Yes, at Albacete I was in the team. When Torres scored I thought 'Bloody hell, why didn't they take me off half an hour earlier!' That was because he came on as a substitute for me. I had told him something like, 'Good luck, come on kid, you can do it,' and five minutes later he scored the winning goal with a superb header. What a kid ...'

In the pictures of that match, one can see you alongside the subs' bench smiling and kissing the badge.

'I was very happy to pass the baton to El Niño. It was rewarding for a true *atlético* to see that, after you, there was someone you could have confidence in. I could see myself reflected in him and his happiness. We've all been junior players – our dream was to get into the first team and score a goal wearing the shirt. Fernando achieved that.

That goal was the subject of much celebration both in the stands and on the pitch.

'That's right. It gave us an important victory. It kept our promotion hopes alive. The fans came onto the pitch and we had our own celebrations in the dressing room. Fernando came and asked me if I would give him the captain's armband as a present. I told him not be so silly, that it was covered in dirt and worn out, but he insisted so much that in the end I gave in and handed it over. Someone had got hold of some bottles of champagne, which we opened to toast our win. I offered a glass to Fernando and realised he was only seventeen and wasn't able to drink alcohol and neither did he want to. So we rummaged around in the bag of a team-mate who'd brought in some things to eat – some sandwiches – and we came across a yogurt carton. I opened it and told him 'You, lad, can make the toast with yogurt.' And, with plastic carton in hand, that was how he celebrated his first goal!'

But at the end of the season, the celebrations weren't repeated.

'We stayed in the Second Division and I left the club – with a lot of problems and a particular thorn in my side: I never managed to play in a match with Fernando. In training, we understood each other well. Once I gave him two goal-scoring passes and he beamed at me, saying, 'Let's see if we can repeat this on the pitch.' It wasn't possible. A real shame.'

Eight years have gone by since then. How do you view Fernando now?

'Now I see him as the finished article. Going to Liverpool meant he could take three steps up in one. He's more relaxed, more himself, without the suffocating responsibilities and the mental wear and tear that were crushing him at Atlético. He didn't have time properly to evolve. At just eighteen, he had to take up the baton and be the flag bearer. In footballing terms, he has seen a lot in a very short space of time. But he's an intelligent lad, who, thanks to his family and the right kind of environment – without any false praise where people always tell you you're great when you're not – hasn't lost his way, as has happened to other youngsters. No, he's gone in the right direction. In Liverpool, he's made his match.'

What do you mean?
'That he's found the right kind of environment. Reina, Aberloa, Xabi Alonso have taken him under their wing. Steve Gerrard and Jamie Carragher have been able to guide him. Benítez, who is a perfectionist with great attention to detail, has helped him to iron out those imperfections his critics have always accused him of, like his passing and moving, his finishing, his ability to lose his marker, his shooting … Before, his shooting wasn't so good, now it is. And then you have to recognise that English football, with its end-to-end games and spaces in which to run, is ideal for someone with Fernando's qualities. Yes, without doubt, Liverpool has given him a big step up.'

Did you think it would all happen so quickly?
'When he scored the first goal against Chelsea, I saw that as the turning point, I saw a player who had been liberated. From there on in, he had a marvellous season. And now he's Number 3 in the world (in the FIFA World Player of the Year 2008 results).

It's also thanks to the goal in the final of Euro 2008.
'Without doubt. That match made his name. The injury to Villa was fortunate for Fernando because he's a footballer who needs space, who needs to be able to run across the line

of attack from one side to the other. And he showed that he is a man who doesn't let one down on the big occasions.'

The conversation is interrupted. Patxi Alonso, sports presenter at *Sexta* arrives for a coffee. Between smiles and jokes, the talk comes back to that demanding match of indoor football, the result and the remaining ties up to the final. A glance at the watch means that it is time to head for the TV. A good piece of programming.

Chapter 13
In El Niño's hands

There are 20,000 of them in and around the Neptune fountain in central Madrid. *¡Adiós a Segunda, adiós! ¡Adiós a Segunda, adiós!'* – 'Farewell to the Second Division, Farewell!' they shout. After 721 days in purgatory, Atlético are back in the First Division. On 27 April 2002, in the Calderón, a victory against Gimnàstic de Tarragona would have given them the mathematical certainty of promotion but on 90 minutes Ángel Cuellar equalises for 'Nastic' to make it 3-3 and the torment goes on. But only for a few hours. Thanks to a chance set of favourable results they can celebrate the next day. Not since 1996 – the year in which Atlético won the league and the Copa del Rey – have the fans had a reason to get together around the fountain dedicated to the god of the sea, their 'temple', their altar for club celebrations. They do it in style. They jump with joy, sing, wave flags, light flares, throw bangers, mock Real Madrid, their eternal rivals, block the traffic in one of the main thoroughfares of the city, and even clash with the police. The most repeated songs and chants praise manager Luis Aragonés, who has achieved the miracle, and Fernando Torres.

El Niño heard the good news about the return to the first division in the drawing room of his home. Following a frantic round of calls between team-mates, the idea was to go up to the Neptune fountain to join the celebrations. But Paolo Futre, the sporting director, thinks it's better to wait. They opt for an informal dinner in a city centre restaurant.

It's not until the early hours that the players arrive in the presence of the god with the trident in his hand, in the Piazza Cánovas del Castillo, not far from the buildings of the Spanish Parliament. Diego Alonso climbs the statue and shouts 'Atléti, *volvemos a primera*.' ('Atléti, we're coming back to the first division.')

Fernando Torres, in jean jacket and red-and-white scarf, is grinning from ear-to-ear. Finally, a real pleasure. Because even if lots of people that night can be seen wearing shirts with his name on, it hasn't all been good during his second year with the senior team. Far from it.

At the beginning of the season, at just seventeen years of age, 'they made me into an idol and now they are trying to knock down the tower that they created. The manager told me: "The higher they put you, the harder you fall." That's to say, try to learn to be like one of the others,' he confesses in an interview and adds: 'In any case, I've been at a much lower level than I thought, I've not had the season that I was hoping for. I've encountered more difficulties than I thought I would.'

What difficulties has the young promise of Spanish football encountered? A lot, beginning with the manager. Luis Aragonés, an Atlético midfielder in the 1960s and 70s with 123 goals to his name, a legend to the fans, has returned for the fifth time as manager to take the team back to the first division. But the *Sabio de Hortaleza* (Wise Man of Hortaleza), as they call him, doesn't have much faith in the youngster. As often as not, he sends him directly to the stand or leaves him for entire matches to warm the substitutes' bench. On the rare occasions he does start a match, he is substituted without fail. Changes that drive El Niño crazy even if, after thinking things over, he ends up admitting the gruff manager was right. The Wise Man corrects him continuously: 'Torres, not like that!' 'Torres, do it well, not beautifully, well!' Torres this, Torres that. He takes him off the pitch to put on a defender or the Uruguayan, Diego Alonso, an honest worker of the ball. With the lad from Fuenlabrada, he uses all the old football conventions. Or to be more exact, the brilliant, celebrated youngster must be treated harshly – he needs to be taught how to behave on the pitch and in the dressing room. He must be the first to arrive and the last to leave, to talk little and listen a lot, to be humble, he must never get cocky, he must respect his team-mates and not dare to contradict the gaffer. Training – or rather, commandments – that years later Torres will consider valuable, but at seventeen, leave him baffled.

The continuous put-downs and the constant substitutions to a competitive and fiercely proud young man like Fernando, do him damage. And there's also the fact that Luis cannot stomach the youngster's media exposure. The more they talk about him in the press, the less he plays. A popularity that even attracts the jealousy of his team-mates, who, in some cases, are twelve years older than him, and who find this callow youth hogging the headlines hard to handle. So much fame also brings with it a special attention on the part of opposing defenders. 'I can confirm that if they think you are a "name", it's worse. You have to suffer much more marking,' comments Torres.

The truth is that, on many occasions, in order to respect the famous conventions of football, his rivals gave him a rough time. As do the press. Many had given him their backing and feel betrayed by a performance that is not up to expectations. They talk of the crisis in his second year, of how the Under-17 World Cup at the beginning of the season didn't allow him to start the league campaign on a good footing, pointing to his goal tally (only six) as evidence of this.

The only thing in his defence: he plays some really tremendous games. But they don't count for much, seeing that even he comes to doubt the faith placed in him. Fernando's reply, or rather revenge, comes first with the victory in the Under-19 European championship in Norway and then in the first division.

He makes his top-flight debut on 1 September 2002 in the Camp Nou against Louis Van Gaal's Barcelona. Ten months after he's scored thirteen goals in the championship and one in the Copa del Rey. He has become the star of the side – one that everyone expects to see shining. He has assumed big responsibilities and has become, without doubt, one of the best in the team. On two occasions he brought the entire Vicente Calderón stadium to its feet.

On 12 January 2003, against Deportivo La Coruña, he creates two spectacular moves. The first, he controls in the penalty area using his chest, gets round defender Noureddine Nybet with a lob and does a half-turn to score with a devastating left-foot shot. The second, he nutmegs Nybet, which dumbfounds Donato, leaving him to make a winning assist for Correa to score. The crowd gives him an ovation and his name rings out across the nearby Manzanares river and echoes through the surrounding neighbourhood.

On 24 May, in the same stadium, he puts on another show. It's the last minute of the second half when Torres begins warming up on the edge of the pitch. The fans have been demanding his appearance for some time and Atlético is losing 1-2 against Villarreal. Only he can save the situation. It's true.

On 70 minutes he shoots from outside the area, the ball just inside the angle between post and crossbar. Four minutes later, he scores the winning goal, a great left-foot shot, after a pass from Luis Garcia (who moved to Liverpool in 2004, returning to Atlético in 2007, the same year that

Fernando went in the opposite direction). Poor Pepe Reina, then keeper with Villarreal and a future team-mate of his at Liverpool, has one of the worst afternoons of his career. 'Imposing', 'formidable', 'marvellous', are just some of the adjectives used to describe the 19-year-old's display. They talk of the emergence in *La Liga* of a shining young talent. They cannot recall anything of its kind since the arrival of Raúl at Real Madrid. But El Niño has learned from Aragonés to avoid any kind of vanity like the plague, replying to all the praise saying:

'People get carried away making comparisons but that's a waste of time. I don't know how one gets to be a star. But however one does, I still need to do it. I've only just started and we'll see where I am when, like Raúl, I am 26 and playing international matches.'

But the positive opinions don't only come from the public. They are also being voiced by his team-mates. Demetrio Albertini, the midfielder who, with the Milan of Arrigo Sacchi and Fabio Capello, has won everything and more, explains: 'He's still a boy and has to mature, but he has talent. He's going to be very big. In Italy he's liked by Milan and Juventus. They talk a lot about him.' And Fernando talks a lot with Demetrio, Atlético's new signing: 'He was talking about Milan, about Marco van Basten, who was my idol, he lent me tapes to watch him in action to explain to me his style of playing. And he always recommended me to learn everything I could before leaving.'

The year 2003 is Atlético's centenary. On 26 April 1903, a group of Basque students at a mine engineering college in Madrid founded a new football club as a branch of the Basque side, Atlético Bilbao. They initially played in blue and white strips, similar to those of Blackburn Rovers. But eight years later the main team in Bilbao and the Madrid branch had changed to red and white (similar to

Southampton), one theory being that the new colours were cheaper because this combination was used to make mattresses and the leftovers could be converted into football shirts. It also helps explain why the club became known as *los colchoneros* (the mattress-makers). It's those same stripes that earn an entry in the Guinness book of records when a flag measuring about 1 mile long by 8 yards wide is paraded through the streets of Madrid from the Neptune fountain to the Vicente Calderón stadium. It's the main party for the centenary with lots of paella, fireworks and skydivers, together with leading local figures and even royalty in the form of Prince Felipe, the heir to the Spanish throne. It's a pity that Atlético then go and lose 0-1 against Osasuna.

Fernando, who comes 19th in a supporters' survey to choose the best players in the club's history, is not on the pitch. He's taking part in the celebrations of a proud Atlético as an ordinary fan. 'I have come up through the ranks, I know what it is to wear the red and white, what it means to be in this team,' he says. Unfortunately, a tear in the fibres of a leg muscle is keeping him off the pitch for around a month.

When he comes back, the club's situation has changed and become even more difficult. Jesús Gil, the godfather figure of Atlético, resigns as president after sixteen years. During his time in charge, the club has had 31 managers, almost double what Liverpool or Manchester United have had in 100 years. With Gil, Atlético have one league title and three Copas del Rey and finished in the second division for two years. With Gil, the ex-mayor of Marbella, the club has often teetered on the edge of bankruptcy and been the focus of numerous legal investigations. Gil ends up in prison. When he leaves, fed up with being insulted and accused of being the one responsible for all the club's failings, he hands over the reins to his son, Miguel Ángel

Gil Marín and film producer Enrique Cerezo ... The club shares held by Jesús Gil are seized in connection with an investigation into fraud and falsification. Financially, the club is in ruins but he does not want to be singled out as the president who sells Fernando Torres or the Calderón to put things right.

Jesús Gil had been like a father to El Niño: 'I remember him with affection, his family treated me as if I was one of their own.' Gil, who died on 14 May 2004, goes and so does Luis Aragonés. Just six matches from the end of the league, he says he can't work as he would like to and has no intention of respecting his contract, which expires at the end of the season. Before going, has he changed his opinion of El Niño? Not at all: 'Fernando Torres could be a very good footballer, who still has to correct some flaws,' he says in the club magazine. 'Right now, he's performing well in the Primera Liga but, paradoxically, in almost all the matches where he hasn't played, we've won. Irreplaceable? It's very difficult for a player in a team to be like that but Fernando is certainly a very important element in front of the opposition goal.' The warring between the two continues and it will resurface some years later in the national side.

Gregorio Manzano arrives for the 2003–04 season from Mallorca, where he won the Copa del Rey. He declares immediately that he wants to put his priorities into the attack because that's what the fans are demanding. He counts on a midfield notable for the presence of Cholo Simeone, who, after several years in Italy (Inter and Lazio), returns to Atlético, and on a left wing, where Musampa is expected to perform well. In attack, to support El Niño, there is the Greek, Nikolaidis:

'Our objective was to consolidate our status and after that, fight to get as high up the table as possible. We had a good season and we surpassed our initial expectations, relative to our sporting and economic resources. The only thing that was missing was Europe. In the last game against Zaragoza, the team couldn't manage a win and we missed out on the UEFA Cup through a lower goal average than Sevilla,' as Gregorio Manzano, or 'The Teacher' as he was known, recalls today. He boasts ten years of Spanish first division management with more than 300 matches under his belt. Manzano, now back with Mallorca, hasn't forgotten that year in Atlético, just as he hasn't forgotten Fernando, with whom he maintains good relations.

Going back to the beginning of that season, one should say that Torres avoided a goalscoring crisis thanks, above all, to the confidence of the manager, who has given him a starting place when neither his dribbling nor his shooting is working. It's a situation from which he escapes only at the end of October. Against Manzano's former side, El Niño finally unleashes himself and doesn't stop hitting the net – so much so that halfway through the season, he is the first division's top goalscorer with eleven goals. And at the end of the season – won by the Valencia of Rafa Benítez – Torres is the club's top-scorer, only four less than league top-scorer Ronaldo.

One of those goals is a masterpiece: 'It is without a shadow of a doubt that great goal at Betis that gave us our 1-2 victory,' explains Manzano. A move worth a slow-motion replay. It's 2 November 2003 in the old Benito Villamarín stadium in the 40th minute. Atlético midfielder Jorge crosses the ball towards the centre. Torres, in a yellow 'away' strip, runs, loses his marker, neutralises the defender and lets fly. It's an artistic action, harmonious and elegant, filled more with agility than energy. It compares to a cat lazily stretching its paws one in front of the other, like an exhibition performance of karate. Thanks to his soaring leap, Fernando touches the ball with the tip of his foot and directs it between the opposite post and crossbar. A goal of cinematic quality.

Unfortunately, in February 2004, El Niño is again injured and the second part of the season isn't as productive as the first.

Meanwhile, Torres has extended his contract up until the end of 2008. It's somewhat less than what the board had wanted. It would have liked to renew it up until 2010 or even 2014. El Niño is one of the team captains: 'It was difficult because of his age and because there were other players older than him in the dressing room but they helped him to be a good captain. They respected him and everyone listened to what he thought. He was the emblematic player and symbol of Atléti but he still didn't consider himself a star and nor was he,' recalls Manzano. 'He was beginning to grow and mature a lot during the season. He's always been someone who's open to everything with an extraordinary human quality. If you had to pick out some things, I would choose his ability to surmount difficulties, his humility, his unselfishness and his ambition. The only bad point was his lack of experience and not pacing himself during matches.'

Despite the good results, Gregorio Manzano lasted for just one season and in 2004–05, César Ferrando arrives. The manager changes but the club's institutional crisis means there is no money to reinforce the squad. The key element in all this for Atlético is, once more, Fernando, who is twenty and a star. He is one of the most sought-after Number 9s in Europe and the idol of teenagers, mothers, and of the younger fans, who believe he will be bigger than all the club's previous glories. He is a marketing man's dream, selling everything from watches to footwear, from video games to beer, from breakfast cereals to jeans. One example is Pepe Jeans. Thanks to the Torres effect – charismatic, charming and dynamic – it increased its Spanish sales by 25 per cent. Torres is a model for fashion and women's magazines. The rates for use of his image rise 75 per cent in three years.

And he is the driving force behind Atlético's commercial operations – 70 per cent of the replica shirts sold have his name on them. He earns 3½ million Euros a year, drives a metallic grey Porsche Carrera 4S (his first capricious buy) and is superstitious – so much so that every time things don't go well, he changes his hairstyle. He goes to Olman, his hairdresser, who invents a style. From shaved head to punk look-alike, from spikey to coloured highlights. He likes to dress up in the latest fashions and, sometimes, when he can, he even goes to watch a fashion show. An elegant champion who does good business with his image to such an extent that they've started comparing him to David Beckham, the football pop star who arrived in 2004 on the other side of Madrid. But he wants to clarify that 'Beckham sells a huge amount all over the world but if he stopped playing, his advertising income would also go down. Basically, the image of a footballer is built up starting with what he does on the pitch. For this reason, I would never not go to a training session because of a photographic shoot.'

He doesn't like politics but is fascinated by the people who go out into the street to protest against the war in Iraq or to condemn the Atocha bombings of 11 March 2004. He hopes they succeed in changing things. He's a modern type, who believes in God but sees no problem with homosexual marriages, which the Spanish church vehemently condemns. As an adult, if he wasn't a footballer he would have liked to be the singer of a rock group: 'Someone capable of moving a lot of people, like footballers, only a rock star doesn't have opponents.'

In an interview with the Italian newspaper, *Corriere della Sera*, he even describes how he doesn't like football: 'I say it in all seriousness. It bores me to watch a match on TV. I've never seen one all the way through. I like to play. I love the match and the fans but everything that goes on behind the scenes – from the little I know about it – I don't want to know. The television companies, which impose their own rules and economic interests, which overload the (sporting) calendar. At the end of the day, it's only business and nothing to do with watching sport.' A surprising response for someone who lives thanks to football and who enjoys a huge popularity.

Fame continues to surprise him. 'All the time. Above all, outside Spain. But football is now almost like a worldwide commercial.' Difficult to live with? 'At first I found it difficult. I was shy, I was embarrassed. I was blushing. Now, a little at a time, I'm getting used to it even if it's difficult. I miss the times when I was able to go for a walk with my dog without anyone stopping me in the street. But that's the price you have to pay.' What does he make of the millions he's earned? 'The first thing I did was buy a house for my parents, a car for my father and my sister and help my brother Israel with his mortgage. I've become what I am thanks to them. I will never forget that if it wasn't for my mother (several times she arrived late at work to take me to training sessions) I would not be here. It seems right and proper to give back to them everything that they've given me.'

A good lad who still lives with his parents: 'My mother is a great cook. Her pasta with cream and ham is streets ahead of anything you get on training camps. And of course they know me well. If I got big-headed, they would let me know about it.'

Even his manager says so: 'The success hasn't gone to his head.' In spite of this, the sports journalists dedicate their front pages to him after he puts two goals past Barcelona in the Camp Nou on 6 February 2005. 'He trains just the same as any of the others because he is very competitive and a very good team-mate. He never tires of learning. These things outside of sport don't affect him.' Another thing that pleasantly surprises manager César Ferrando is the 'leadership ability of Torres. He has taken the bull by the horns and said this is down to me, I will be pulling my own weight.' Come May, though, because he has been pulling his own weight, El Niño is worn out. In-between the league, the Cup, the Intertoto and the national side, he's the player who's played the most minutes in Spain. He can't go on, he hasn't scored in more than a month and Atlético have come to a halt. They no longer have any options in the league and they've been knocked out of the Cup. They will finish 12th, a long way off the champions, Barcelona. His own account, however, is positive: sixteen league goals and two in the Cup.

In 2005–06 he begins another season and in the dugout there's a new manager. This time, it's the Argentinian, Carlos Bianchi. He has an impressive CV, which includes Boca, Velez and Roma, the backing of the directors and major reinforcements on the pitch – Mateja Kezman (signed from Chelsea), Martin Petrov (now with Manchester City) and the Argentinians, Maxi Rodríguez, and Luciano Galletti. On paper it's a strong and winning squad. There's hope of qualifying for the Champions League. The new gaffer starts well, Torres playing his part, scoring as he knows how and ending up surrounded by controversy because of a very unusual celebration.

In October, in the Rosaleda stadium against Malaga, he scores a penalty – his third goal of the season – then sticks out his tongue and puts his fingers in his ears while running down the pitch. The crowd don't like it and take it very badly, perceiving it as an insult, while in fact, it's a birthday dedication to his friend Jorge Larena who plays for Celta.

A juvenile joke between the two that becomes a hot media topic. But that's nothing compared with what happens some time later.

By the 18th match of the season, Atlético are floundering in the lower reaches of the league, raising once again the possibility of ending up in the second division. Carlos Bianchi packs his bags. Four years later, Torres will say: 'He had very good ideas but the players didn't understand him.' In his place, comes Pepe Murcia, who begins in style. He wins five matches on the trot and brings the team back from the depths to end up just four points off a position that would have finally seen them playing in Europe. It's fourteen years since Atlético has achieved anything like that and the fans had their hopes high. But as always disappointment is just around the corner. Atlético once again finish empty-handed, in 10th position, and Europe remains a mirage. It's necessary to start all over again.

The next season – El Niño's last – begins in the company of Mexican manager, Javier Aguirre and 'Kun' Sergio Agüero, the young Argentinian phenomenon who's being compared to Maradona and Romario. He's the most expensive signing in Atlético's history. He has come from Independiente at a cost of 20 million Euros. He should be the perfect support for Torres, who, in the Germany World Cup, described him as a great striker. The ingredients for success, this time, really do all seem to be there. Atlético, together with Barcelona, are the teams generating most expectations. Instead, it's Fabio Capello's Real Madrid that wins the league on the last day of the season. El Niño has already decided to leave. In seven seasons without winning a single trophy, he has scored 82 goals and seven in the Copa del Rey. He was the icon and standard-bearer of the team who, at seventeen, 'knew how to take on the starring role and keep alive the hopes of an institution in its darkest hour. The administration', writes Manolete-Manuel Esteban – journalist of sport daily newspaper, *AS*, and one of Atlético's best-known supporters – 'was dominated and hounded by the courts. The club's enemies were taking advantage and no one gave any importance to what was happening on the pitch. His appearance on the scene led to an explosion and a breath of fresh air. He didn't have any doubts about putting his professional future at risk, even when the directors asked him to help underwrite and ease the financial difficulties. He knew how to raise the hopes of the fans and declare that he would never wear the white of Real Madrid. His years were always presided over by performances of a high calibre and, above all, by being a kind of Robin Hood figure, who was trying to take a part of the popularity from the big clubs and give it to the less fortunate ones. In the end he needed a change of scenery to make his wishes come true.'

Chapter 14
He's earned it the hard way

Conversation with Mexico and former Atlético de Madrid manager, Javier Aguirre

Following an afternoon in Madrid's Las Ventas bullring to see his fellow countryman and bullfighter, 'El Payo', in action, followed by some *tapas* with friends, 'El Vasco' ('The Basque') Aguirre has a few moments to chat. It is almost midnight and he still has his case to pack. In the morning, he leaves for Mexico City, where, in a few days, he will be in the dugout for his first match in charge of the Mexico national team. On 3 April 2009, the Mexican Football Federation appointed him to succeed ex-England and Manchester City manager, Sven-Göran Eriksson. It is his second spell as manager of the national team. The first began in 2001 and ended after the side's exit at the hands of the US from the 2002 South Korea and Japan World Cup after reaching the last sixteen. For the seven years in-between he lived his big Spanish adventure.

It started in Pamplona with Osasuna, the team where Aguirre played briefly in 1986 before a broken leg put a premature end to his Spanish playing career. Returning as manager in 2002, over the next four seasons he took Osasuna to a Copa del Rey final and classification for the UEFA Cup. In 2006, thanks to a fourth place in the league, they qualified for the Champions League for the first time in the club's history. An achievement that earned him a one-year contract with Atlético Madrid. 'El Vasco' Aguirre took up the challenge of returning the club to the upper reaches of *La Liga* and a place in Europe. He says of Fernando: 'Any manager in the world would want Torres in his team. Who wouldn't? Fernando is the standard-bearer of the team.'

On 3 February 2009, when El Niño had been with Liverpool for almost two years, Aguirre was sacked after the club suffered a bad run of results. Fernando gave an interview in which he spoke positively of his former manager: 'He's probably been the team's best manager in recent years, getting them into the Champions League, and no one can take that away from him. That's why he was hired and that's what he achieved. I don't think he is the real culprit of this situation. That's how football is.'

Now it is his turn to talk about Fernando. With the Atlético uproar now in the past and with the relative calmness his experience and new post allows him, he recalls in measured tones El Niño's final year in the red and white of Atlético Madrid.

What do you think now of Fernando?
'I think he deserves all the good things that have happened to him. And when I say that, I'm referring to the advertising contracts, to playing in the Champions League, to battling on right until the end of the English season. He deserves it all because life hasn't done him any favours. In the year that I was with him, I realised that he was a lad who was trying to improve himself every day. What he has, he's earned it the hard way.'

But that 2006–07 pre-season didn't begin well. You declared that you could not guarantee Torres his place in the team. The newspapers were saying that Manchester United were ready to pay 37 million Euros for El Niño.

'I don't remember making any declaration, either me or Fernando. What I remember is that when I arrived at Atlético, we talked with Fernando about the fact that the club needed to be in Europe because a lot of years had gone by since that had last happened. Fernando had never played in a European competition with Atlético. I do remember discussing this objective and him welcoming me as captain and he said that this was his objective as well.'

How did Torres get on with you and with the dressing room in general?

'Very well. Fernando was a lad who was very straight with everyone. He was born in the club and grew up in the club. In the dressing room, he gave the impression of being shy, quiet, and it's true he didn't say much, but when he spoke one heard him. He was a natural leader. I remember that people looked up to him with a lot of respect. The club administration and directors used him at all the club events. He was the image of Atlético Madrid. There was an event for sick children and Fernando went, there was an event in the prison and Fernando went, there was a meeting of supporters' groups and Fernando went. He was always available, always saying 'yes' to anyone who asked for an autograph or a photo. He was a man who knew what he wanted and we always had a great relationship. He always treated me well and was very respectful of my decisions. He always did his best for the team, and as captain he would always be prepared to take the flak.'

What struck you about Torres?

'The person. I never saw that lad pull a long face, I never saw a rude gesture, he always had a smile for everyone. This is the best side of him because as a footballer he now has it all. He is complete, you can't single out anything. As a person, he's much better.'

And what was good about Fernando as a footballer?

'What was good was that he knew that he had to improve lots of things. He had it all, he really did, to be a top star player. He was that already but he knew that there was room to improve still further. And because of that, Fernando wanted more training every day. Every day he studied the details of every move. He was the first to arrive and the last to leave. He is a true professional. Technically, his left side required a bit more effort as well as his guidance of the ball – he would suddenly rush forward too much. There were little details that he polished up and improved considerably. But I remember telling my defenders, Perea and Pablo, not to try to play the ball, clear it long and hard, without looking, send it right upfront and this lad will use it to his advantage. And it was true. Fernando was capable of controlling the ball perfectly, of running between three opposition defenders and scoring goals. There were moves where he kept it really simple, getting hold of a loose ball and going out to the wing – or from one of those unusual clearances – and turning it into a goal.'

Why did he leave at the end of the season? Did you know about his agreement with Liverpool?

'At this point I have to explain a very odd thing that happened to me – I didn't know that he was leaving.' Aguirre laughed bitterly. 'I assumed he was going to stay. I say this because in the last league game of the season, we were in Pamplona playing against Osasuna, and for a UEFA Cup place we needed favourable results from the matches involving Sevilla and Zaragoza. With five minutes to go, we were winning 2-1, Sevilla were winning and Zaragoza were losing. In the dugout, I called Torres over and told him, 'We are in Europe, we're going to Europe, Fernando,' and he looked at me and smiled. In that moment I didn't know it but afterwards I realised what he was thinking, which was that "Yes, I will be in Europe – with Liverpool." He already had an agreement and his departure was certain. The truth is that I knew nothing. In fact, I went on holiday to Mexico and it's there that I found out, from the press, that Fernando was leaving for Liverpool. My surprise was all the greater because nobody had consulted me. It was a done deal. But really it wasn't so strange because the Reds are a team, a big team, and Atlético at that time, were an uncertainty. We went into the Intertoto, after that to the UEFA Cup and then into the Champions League. We'd have liked to have had Fernando with us. In fact, we came together again in the Champions League (Group Stage), when we drew with Liverpool here and away. It was good for us to meet up. It was a pity that he couldn't be on the pitch. In both games, he was injured and saw the game from the stand.'

The pressure at Atlético was too much for him?
'Yes, and I'll say something else. When I arrived at Atlético, I asked him if he would like to continue being captain. I said to him "Look, if you want to leave it, go and relax, enjoy yourself and just be one of the team." He replied in the negative because he felt involved, because he loved Atlético so much and he wanted to grow with the team, but I could see that the lad was suffering – he had too many things weighing down on him. Here he had responsibility for the dressing room, the administration, the fans and the press. For better or for worse, he had to be involved with everyone and everything, whereas in Liverpool he is just one more person. There are three or four who are also important and Fernando is part of that group but he is not the captain. Anfield brings out the best in him because now he doesn't have all those responsibilities.'

Yes, but the change has been impressive ...

'That doesn't surprise me at all, In the physical tests, for resistance, for strength, in the day-to-day work, one saw that he had a huge potential. But I repeat, I think the great secret of his success has been that in Liverpool he's not the captain and he dedicates himself solely to play the 90 minutes, while at Atlético he dedicated himself to a lot of things, the poor lad – interviews, sponsors, junior team, supporter groups, the social work of the Foundation. He was very involved and stressed out. Now he can relax and enjoy himself and he's had two spectacular years with Liverpool and the national team. In Euro 2008 he was completely in tune with the Spanish team, he was finishing the moves made by the midfield and scored a great goal in the final, very much in the Torres style, overcoming the German defender when he was at a disadvantage, always with that strength and that desire to score goals. His success at Euro 2008 doesn't surprise me. Luis Aragonés, the manager, knows him very well and got the best possible performance out of him.'

The best moment, the fondest memory?

'Fernando always left us some small gift, always gave us a smile – he has a big heart. The best memory that I have was when, after a big match and without being asked for it, he signed the shirt for my three sons, Ander, Mikel and Iñaki, who are big football fans.'

Would it worry you to encounter him again with Mexico?

'It would give me a huge amount of pleasure because that would mean that we had qualified for the 2010 World Cup in South Africa. Let's hope so, let's hope so. I would love to greet Fernando Torres because he is a good friend.'

Chapter 15

Real hope

Conversation with Sid Lowe and
Guillem Balagué

An Englishman who lives in Spain, a Spaniard who lives in England. Sid Lowe, aged 32, left London for Madrid in 2001 with the aim of finishing his PhD thesis on the Spanish Civil War, entitled 'La Juventud de Acción Popular en España 1932–1937'. But the enormous media interest generated by the arrival of David Beckham at Real Madrid overtook him and converted him from football fan into football writer. He is a correspondent for the *Guardian* and *World Soccer*.

Guillem Balagué was born 40 years ago in Barcelona and has lived in England since 1991. He is the UK correspondent for the Madrid-based sport daily, *AS*, and a Spanish football specialist for Sky Sports. His website (www.guillembalague.com) features information on Spanish football and footballers including rumours, interviews and comment and even a section on Spanish wine. Two journalists, therefore, who know Fernando Torres well, talk about how he is portrayed in the media and explain the reasons for his success from two different perspectives – Britain and continental Europe.

How was Torres viewed when he was in Spain?
SL: 'The Spaniards knew that Fernando Torres was very good and a talented player, but didn't think he was as

good as he has since demonstrated at Liverpool and in the European championships, scoring the winning goal. The main reason, maybe, is the fact that he played for Atlético Madrid. Fernando Torres was the captain, he was the standard-bearer and, to some extent, he was Atlético Madrid. There was a feeling that Atlético Madrid's underachieving, or their failures, were somehow Fernando Torres' failures. He was judged according to his team and not according to his own ability. The other reason, the key reason is that Spain – and Spain's media – are dominated by two clubs, Real Madrid and Barcelona. And that means that a player who has three good games for Real Madrid is a *crack*, he's the best player in the world, he's unbelievably good. Wesley Sneijder came to Real Madrid and played three games and they were saying he was as good as Di Stefano, better than Beckham. You don't get the same respect as an Atlético Madrid player. And if you asked Torres – he would never admit this publicly – I think privately that he knows that one of his problems was the media was always criticising him.'

GB: 'The image of Torres, before he went to Liverpool was that of a player-leader of Atlético Madrid and, like Atlético as a whole, inconsistent. He was far from perfect and still needed to improve a lot to reach the level he'd been promising since the age of fourteen. Atlético was a huge weight on his shoulders.'

What kind of criticism did the Spanish media make?
SL: 'The message was that Fernando Torres is an Atlético Madrid player, therefore the Madrid media – the Real Madrid media, because it's a Real Madrid media in truth not a Madrid city media – quite enjoyed laughing at Fernando Torres, making fun of him. "Oh he's never going to beat Real Madrid" – "he's a comedy character" – "we know he's talented but ha, ha, ha, he's never going to score". Torres'

big problem in Spain was that he played for the wrong club and we've seen that to some extent with the Spanish national team. That's because the Spanish national team, in theory, is everybody's team, but in reality the judgement is still coloured by which team the papers support. So you've got *Marca* (a Spanish sport daily), which says it's "all for *la selección*" (the national team), but it's "all for the *Real Madrid* players in *la selección*". So Torres plays in the national team: "He's not as good as Raúl" – Raúl doesn't play in the national team: "It's a disgrace".'

GB: 'He was criticised because he wasn't finishing well, he was criticised because he was failing to round off movements, he was criticised because his first touch wasn't good and he was criticised because, sometimes, he kept hold of the ball too long. But there were also critics making the same kind of comments about Atlético Madrid, that the club never built a good enough team in which Torres could improve. First, there was criticism of the club, which failed to instil any kind of stability while Torres was there, and then of the team. There were a lot of players who avoided their responsibilities and passed them on to Torres instead. And finally, there was criticism of Fernando, above all at the end, when his body language said he was tired and fed up of being there. And he'd been like that for a long time.'

And how is the image of Torres now in the Spanish media?
SL: 'The image now is that Torres is a wonderful player. Torres is now "our boy" doing wonders over there. He's "our ambassador". The Spanish are a very proud nation. They are very aware of their own identity and when a Spanish player goes abroad – let's take Torres – he becomes "Spain's Fernando Torres". On top of that, you've got the fact that Fernando Torres scored the winning goal in the European championships, the most important goal in 44 years in

Spain. That helps … Suddenly, people in Madrid respect him in a way they didn't respect him before. Now the media is allowed to like him, but he will always have that barrier and that barrier will be "he's not Real Madrid". And I think that's really important when it comes to judging how the media and some of the public see him.'

GB: 'Now it's that of a player who has exceeded even the most optimistic of predictions. He's turned himself into a global personality, much more than the Spanish national side, a top player and one of the biggest stars in world football.'

A lot of commentators, not only in the English but also the Spanish media, had doubts about Torres' chances of success at Liverpool …

SL: 'Definitely. Fernando Torres had a very good record at Atlético Madrid, top scorer in every season, but not the record of a guaranteed success. People say that Rafa Benítez bought an obvious player. It wasn't that obvious. Sir Alex Ferguson didn't buy him, he wasn't sure. Fernando Torres had never scored twenty league goals. He hadn't led a team to huge success. I think Rafa Benítez would be entitled to believe that Fernando Torres' problem would be Atlético Madrid. And it was right.'

GB: 'Well, there were doubts that were justified because the level at which he was playing at Atlético Madrid was average. But there were also doubts in the minds of the people who signed him. He was never the first option for Liverpool – that was Samuel Eto'o. And the actual player harboured doubts as well. He didn't know if he was able to achieve success straightaway. He knew he could go all the way but he thought it would take a bit longer. The English media weren't convinced either because they could point to the examples of Spanish players who'd arrived in England and failed, like Fernando Morientes or José Antonio Reyes. Until the arrival of Torres, Spanish strikers hadn't made much of a case for themselves. In any case, the national media had doubts. However, the Liverpool media and the team's fans were more open-minded. They went on to embrace him as a big star. "Torres has arrived" they said. They'd seen how he scored goals against Barcelona, they'd seen his speed and the Liverpool supporters, who are very committed to the club, were the ones who had the least worries. But, yes, it's true that neither the Spanish nor the English press saw the situation very clearly.'

Why was there this big change between Atlético Madrid and Liverpool?

SL: 'Well … maybe, the change is not quite as incredible as it looks. Maybe the change is just from a team that finishes eighth to a team that finishes second, a team that doesn't play in the Champions League to a team that does. It's just a little bit more. But I agree with you, I think there is a big change. At Liverpool, he doesn't have the responsibility. He doesn't have the pressure. He plays with better players. Steven Gerrard is playing behind him. English football suits him, there's more space. The game is more physical, it suits Torres' style, it's more direct and that game is better for him. The first goal against Real Madrid is almost the perfect portrait of what Fernando Torres has become. Aggressive, strong, powerful, quick – and those are things that people in Spain don't value and in England we value them very highly.'

GB : 'Well, I have my theories on that. One: that he really wanted to leave Atlético and he fancied going to England. The previous summer, before he signed for Liverpool, there were meetings between his representatives and Sir Alex Ferguson but nothing materialised. The following summer,

Fernando was absolutely clear in his own mind that he wanted to go to Liverpool. He did everything possible – and impossible – to try to convince Benítez. His representatives, his agent and his friends talked to Rafa and in the end an agreement was reached. Two: that English centre-backs and defences in general – compared with Spanish or Italian – are bad, leaving too much space, and a player who has speed can have a field day. It's also evident that Torres has improved not only his first touch but also his movement and ability to run with the ball, as well as choosing his moments during a match. And all that comes from working with the best manager in the world.'

How important is Rafa Benítez in this change?
SL: 'Rafa is very important. If you listen to Torres talk, he will tell you that Rafa Benítez is the best coach he's ever had. And it's not just because he likes him. It's because Benítez as a coach is a perfectionist. A lot of coaches are not coaches, they're the people who put players on the pitch. Benítez is a teacher, he's explained to Fernando Torres how to make the right moves, how to fit the system of the team, how to play defenders, make the run left, the next time right. You also have to remember that part of Benítez's success is because of Torres. He's very receptive to ideas, he listens and he's intelligent. He's got a player who thinks about the game.'

GB: 'Very important, because Benítez is a real pain. He succeeds in improving a player through a regimen of repetition, repetition, repetition – of ideas and exercises. Torres is absolutely clear on this. He recognises the tremendous work of his manager. For sure, Luis Aragonés had more influence on his career and taught him a lot when he was young but it's much more difficult to learn when you're already an international and been captain of your team. It's really hard to learn at this stage – at least if you haven't come across Benítez.'

And he's also done good psychological work with him …
SL: 'Without any doubt. Fernando Torres at Liverpool is a different psychological player to the one he was at Atlético Madrid. Torres felt that at Madrid all the pressure, all the blame and all the responsibility was his. At Liverpool, other players have it. El Niño has become an idol at Liverpool and the fans really love him. But they don't expect him to do everything on his own. At Atlético Madrid, the fans expected that. And also at Atlético Madrid, there is fatalism while at Liverpool there's hope.'

GB: 'I don't think psychology is Benítez's greatest strength. Psychology comes from confidence and confidence from improvement. No, Benítez isn't a manager who tells Torres every day that 'you are the best', but Torres sees it and Torres isn't someone who lacks confidence. He finds himself in a style of football that suits him perfectly, with a team that's ready to play for him, with long balls, taking advantage of his speed and getting behind the defence. The psychology comes of its own accord.'

What about the image of Fernando in the English media?
SL: 'Right now, the image is of a player who is possibly the best striker in Europe, a phenomenally good footballer. He's an athlete. He's fast, he's strong, he's powerful. He looks like a baby in his face but he's a really strong man. An aspect that people don't talk about often enough is his intelligence. He's very bright, he's willing to learn, he listens to Rafa Benítez, he listens to his coaches, he does what he's told to do and he's very committed. He is much more humble than people sometimes think. He's a very sensible, intelligent individual. His defects? Right now I don't think

he has a defect. OK, he needs to be better with his left foot, he needs fewer injuries, but maybe we are asking too much. What we're seeing now at Liverpool is that Torres is the perfect player for the perfect team. For example, Fernando Torres at Barcelona would not be the same player because Fernando Torres wants space in front of him, he wants to be able to run into gaps. If you play with a team like Barcelona – touch-touch, pass-pass – it's intricate, it's clever, it's angles. It's much harder for Torres. Even when there are criticisms, they are positive as well. One criticism of Liverpool is that they need more players like Fernando Torres.'

GB: 'In England, you don't have to do very much to be a big star. If you have something that others don't, then you're big. For example, Cesc (Fabregas) is young – in the Arsenal team he's a leader, he knows what to do with the ball, he's the player who controls the midfield, who makes the perfect pass and he's a star. The same thing's happened to Torres. He scores, he begins to notch up goals one after the other, and now he's the best striker in the world. But in reality, he isn't. With all respect and the great affection I have for him – I've also talked about it with him – he is one of the greatest but he still has to improve. The truth is that in England they know very well how to sell their own, or rather, how to sell the players that play in their league. If Torres had the same statistics in La Liga in Spain, he wouldn't be the best in the world. No, here they're very good at selling. And they're amazed when Cesc isn't playing for the Spanish national side. "Come on, that can't be right," they tell you in England. With this in mind, it's interesting the interpretation that the English media put on the Euro 2008 final when, because of Villa's misfortune, Cesc was selected and Torres scored the winning goal. Here, they say they won because these two were selected and because they were playing in their favourite positions.'

*What does Fernando Torres now represent in English football and
at Liverpool in particular?*

SL: 'In a way, Torres represents the supremacy of English
football, as Cristiano Ronaldo does, but Torres more so. We
are the league that gets the best players. The Spanish league
is strong but we took Torres from the Spanish league and we
brought him to England. Cristiano Ronaldo is different. He
might be the best player in the world but Cristiano Ronaldo
went to Manchester United very young. Torres is a demonstration of the fact that the English league can attract the
best players. Now I know we said that at Atlético Madrid
maybe he wasn't the best player but he was a big star.

'Torres demonstrates the strength of the English league
and the fact that young, talented players at the top of their
game will come to England. He's shown us that we can
develop a more European style – even though I think his
style is quite English. We are showing we can bring these
players in and we can have success with them. There was a
time when we felt in England we would buy a good player,
he would come to England and he wouldn't succeed. Now
we're seeing that we're buying good players and they succeed because they adapt to us but also the English league is
adapting to European football.

'Torres is an indication of the fact that the English league
can create loyalty – not have loyalty, create loyalty. You've
got a player there who's come to Liverpool and he feels
like a Liverpool player now. I think that happens maybe
more than it does in Spain and that brings us to what he
means for Liverpool. Torres is the nearest thing to Kenny
Dalglish because Liverpool has had some brilliant players
in their time. They've also bought some brilliant players –
John Barnes, Peter Beardsley, John Aldridge. But it's a long
time since Liverpool bought a player who the fans think is
amazing.

'If you look at Liverpool's favourite players over the last ten years – Michael Owen, from Liverpool; Robbie Fowler, from Liverpool; Steve McManaman, from Liverpool; Steven Gerrard, Jamie Carragher, from Liverpool. Fernando Torres is probably the first player for a decade that has been brought to Liverpool and everyone has gone, "Bloody hell, this guy is brilliant." It's important because it shows Liverpool fans they can bring in great players, they can make great players work and they can start having faith in buying footballers. Kenny Dalglish, although he came from Scotland, was still a bought player. He was the player who was supposed to replace Kevin Keegan and went on to be probably the greatest-ever Liverpool player. Now Liverpool fans won't say Torres is the best player who's ever played for them. There's Steven Gerrard, Graeme Souness, possibly Robbie Fowler because of what he represents, Kenny Dalglish and so on. But I think Torres is possibly the best player Liverpool has bought in ten or fifteen years.

'I think Torres has known how to embrace Liverpool as a club. I did an interview with him not long ago and he said to me that when he turned up he watched videos of Liverpool's history. He read books about Liverpool's history and the fans really appreciate that. They appreciate someone who cares, not just someone who plays. I think Fernando Torres has had the intelligence, the decency and the commitment to take Liverpool to heart. Obviously, if he'd gone to Manchester United, he might have done the same but Liverpool fans don't care about that – he came to Liverpool and he's done all of that. One of the reasons he's done that is Rafa Benítez understands what Liverpool is, Xabi Alonso understands what Liverpool is. Rafa Benítez and Xabi Alonso have very intelligent advisers who are Liverpool fans, and who have been able to explain the

Liverpool process, and Fernando Torres has built on that and learned from them.

'So Fernando Torres represents for Liverpool, in one word, hope. Torres has brought real hope to Liverpool fans, probably more hope than they've had for a long, long time.'

GB: 'Torres is the leap forward that the people of Liverpool think will enable them to win everything. Before, they had Gerrard – one of the best midfielders in the world – Hyppia, Skrtel, Xabi Alonso – all top-level players. But with Torres they think he has brought them that extra touch. They have the goalscorer who makes them candidates for everything. He represents the hope, but, more objectively, the possibility of winning, of making all those dreams they've had for so many years come true.'

Now, the future. Someone said he's still got a lot more improving to do.
SL: 'I think sometimes we talk about improvement and we're wrong. Sometimes we talk about improvement as if this player will get better and better and better. It's not a question of getting better, it's a question of repeating the same thing. For example, when Ryan Giggs started with Manchester United at eighteen years old – brilliant. When he was 25, people said, yes, he's good, he's OK. Why? Because when he was eighteen, they thought he would keep getting better. But he just carried on being the same. That was still brilliant but people expected too much. The expectation was more than the player could give.

'Fernando Torres is 25. He's in a team that's been to a European Cup semi-final. He's on course maybe to do it again. He's in a team challenging for the league and he's scored the most important goal in Spanish football history. In another ten years time, if he wins another European championship with Spain, or a World Cup, or a European Cup with Liverpool – that's not really improving, it's just repeating the same thing – then he will be a true great.

'It's not really that he's going to get better, it's that he has the attitude and the mentality to maintain what's already a fantastically good level. It's like Leo Messi. Everyone says he's going to get better. No he's not. But it doesn't matter because he's already absolutely brilliant.'

GB: 'He's seven out of 10. On a psychological level, confidence helps him a lot. He controls the ball well but he has to improve because he won't have that speed all his life. He must perfect his first touch and finishing. His future? Fernando won't leave Liverpool until they've won a league title – he's very aware that it's fundamental for the fans. Then after that he'll want another and a Champions League. At Liverpool, they like him a lot and he likes Liverpool a lot. He's immersed himself in the club philosophy and the city. I lived in Liverpool for eight years and it's a mesmerising city. Once you enter its atmosphere it makes you want to stay. It's also true that Liverpool is not Atlético Madrid, the team of his life, but we'll see. Now, in England, Torres has very clear objectives.'

Chapter 16
Liverpool 1 Chelsea 1

19 August 2007

Sixteen minutes to become a hero. Steven Gerrard, in the midfield circle, looks up. To his left, he sees Fernando, ready to pounce. A long diagonal pass with the outside of the foot. Perfect, as on so many previous occasions. On the move, Torres is unstoppable, his counter-attacking is lethal but he has to prove it at Anfield, his new home. He gets to the ball without difficulty, even though it was a bit long. He moves onto it with speed, then holds it up briefly on the white line of the opposing penalty area, strokes it with his right foot and takes on the Chelsea defender, Tal Ben Haim. In a flash, a change of pace and he's off. Petr Cech tries to close down the space but can't do anything, his white-gloved hand touches only grass. El Niño's shot is aimed just inside the opposite post. Precise, surgical and exact, like a mathematical formula. For the ex-Atlético Madrid player, it just remains for him to turn and slide along the turf, arms open wide, to offer himself to the terraces, for them to embrace what he has kept on doing since the first minute, to receive his deserved tribute.

It's not only a goal, it's love at first sight between the young lad from Fuenlabrada and the residents of the Kop. Now they've found their very own *matador*, the clinical finisher they were looking for. In just a few seconds, Torres has demonstrated his qualities – speed, power, precision and class finishing in front of goal. No, he's not the dud signing that some were afraid he might be. No, he's not the other Fernando (Morientes) who arrived from 'sunny Spain' generating huge expectations and then didn't perform as he should have done. Right from the first moment, this Number 9 seems something else altogether.

The plaudits from the press flood in. So it's a pity then that the match ends in a draw after conceding a penalty that the 45,000 present would swear they hadn't seen. But it doesn't matter. For the new arrival it's a great day. He couldn't imagine a better debut – scoring a great goal against opponents like Chelsea and then getting applauded with an ovation. So many times, old and new team-mates have told him what it means to play at Anfield. The atmosphere, the fans, the emotion you feel when you come on to the pitch, the songs, 'You'll Never Walk Alone'.

But in the end they had said it was something that was difficult to explain, and that you had to feel it on your own skin. And it's true that the sensations Fernando feels, coming down the steps, touching the club badge and standing on the green rectangle, are absolutely unique. He doesn't know how to express himself. He's happy but he doesn't allow himself to get euphoric. 'The goals are going to give me confidence, which will help me to adapt, but I still have more to do. I've only just arrived and the way of playing is very different. With goals, there's much less pressure and I hope that they keep coming, but there's still an awful lot more for me to do to be at the level of some of my team-mates and to adapt myself to the Premier League,' he declares. He claims he doesn't feel the pressure of being the most expensive signing in the club's history, people have given him a warm welcome but he has to work, 'because when you work, things happen.'

Better to tread carefully at Liverpool, having been there a little over a month. His first training session at Melwood with his new classmates is on 11 July. He gets changed in-between Gerrard and Voronin and realises that it's true, he's actually a Liverpool player, and that this will be his dressing room for the next few years. By the end of the first day, he's discovered a lot. The media are not allowed into Melwood. In Spain, they call it training 'behind closed doors' and when Fabio Capello, then with Real Madrid, introduced it, he was flooded with criticism. Here it's normal and the new arrival likes it because one can train in complete tranquillity, practise the game plan and the technical moves without a photographer trying to immortalise you in a fleeting moment, without some little problem ending up on the front page.

And then there is the important, necessary and intense physical work under the guidance of Paco, who never tires of repeating it over and over again. And the manager's technical lessons. At Melwood, they all have lunch together and very often players and technical staff stop to eat, a good way to check on what they're eating – the gaffer is very strict regarding fats – but they are also moments for getting to know each other better. Rafa Benítez explains to Fernando his new role. He wants him to play in a different way to what he was doing at Atlético. More direct moves up the pitch, operating more deeply with fast movement to take advantage of his running. He doesn't want him to drop too often to the wings or backtrack to create an attacking move. To provide him with playable balls, they think of Gerrard, Xabi Alonso and even Pepe Reina with his superlong deliveries. Rafa wants him to be the ultimate Number 9, like Ronaldo or Van Nistelrooy, always inside the opponents' penalty area and not a second striker, which is how other managers like Luis Aragonés wanted to use him. He wants him to exploit the spaces that are created when a team advances and for him to get behind the opposing team's defenders.

It's no easy thing to absorb all the tuition in one go, in the same way that it's not easy to adapt oneself to the club, to the fans, to football 'across the Channel', to speaking English, to the city, to a new country, to the food and even to driving on the left. Fernando Torres applies himself with determination and commitment. When he arrived, they gave him a pile of DVDs and books about the story, the traditions and the great champions of the Reds. Among them there is even one about the Kop. And some time later, he admits that he has kept it and read it. He researched in depth because he himself grew up in Atlético and, as captain, he had the task of explaining the values of the club to every newcomer who had to understand the origins, the passion for the club colours, to know the famous champions of the past, so that they have the necessary reference points to avoid feeling like a fish out of water.

While studying, he realises that he's arrived at a club that is even bigger and more important than he imagined. A club which functions well, where everyone has a clear role, where no one sticks their nose into other people's work, as happened at Atlético. English? Ah yes, English – or rather the scouse dialect – is a big problem. Even if, right from the first day, the club has put Rob, a private teacher and fanatical supporter, at his side, even if he has lessons every time he has a moment to breathe. He reads what Rob suggests to him and even watches *Friends* in the original English language version (he already knew the dialogue in Spanish and some of the easier bits), which requires time and patience. During the first few days he admits to understanding absolutely nothing. The people of Liverpool speak at an incredible speed and their accent is an enigma, even for some English people. But he wants to learn so that he can understand and be understood by his team-mates on the pitch, to be able to talk with the fans, to be able to give a press conference without having to resort to the transla- tor. To be sure of saying what he really wants to say. He's already set the target of the end of the year, or at most, the first months of the next, to make his debut in front of the media. 'Man on' and 'Time' are the first words of the football vocabulary that he learns. Essentials in order not to let your opponent get the better of you and why the man- ager's technical explanations are in English. In the dress- ing room, Rafa makes it clear that the only language to be spoken is that of William Shakespeare. There's trouble if he sees Torres whispering in Spanish to Pepe Reina. Just like at school, he sends one to one side of the room and the other to the other. And he repeats patiently, 'English, please.' Of course, if there's a need for a personal explanation, the gaf- fer is happy to relent and does it in Spanish. Like Pepe, who, in terms of helping him adapt to the club and the city, its customs and practices, has been fundamental – even if, later, when Fernando begins to speak in English in pub- lic, he doesn't hold back from taking the mickey, as is his custom.

Fernando goes to live in Woolton in a house with a gar- den where, a few months later, his two boxer dogs, Pomo and Llanta can amuse themselves. It's a small detached house, which has been left empty by former Liverpool player, Boudewijn Zenden. He likes the area and it also has the advantage of being about 50 metres from the home of Pepe Reina and his wife, Yolanda. A few months later, Olalla will join Fernando and the two couples will become firm friends. Meanwhile, Fernando also has to adapt himself to a city so different from Madrid, which he knew like the back of his hand, where he knew all the routes almost automati- cally, and his family was nearby. On the few times Fernando has been out and about in his Audi Q7, going very slowly and carefully because of the right-hand drive (the first few trips were very hard and he went the whole time down the middle of the road), he discovers Liverpool to be a friendly, quiet city, where, finally, he can lead a normal life. Where, after training, he can go to eat in the centre with Pepe Reina without anyone bothering him. He can walk into a shopping centre like the Met Quarter or the Trafford Centre, outside Manchester, without being mobbed by supporters. A pleasure and a novelty for a footballer, who, in a now distant 2003, was walking in the La Vaguada shopping centre in Madrid with the aim of buying a pair of shoes and ended up being surrounded by so many fans that the security staff had to close all the entrances so that he could get out safely. But in Liverpool the supporters are polite and prepared to wait hours for a photo or an autograph. 'It's a city', explains The Kid, 'where, if you give them what they want, they give you everything, and not only on the pitch.' Indeed, on the pitch. He has to get the measure of the fast, powerful and physical football in England, with its high rhythm, where you can't take a breather even for a minute, where each time your defenders get the ball you're in front of your opponents' goal within three passes and in with a chance to create something. Different from the slower Spanish football, where the little touches are important, where the possession of the ball, for many teams, is an absolute imperative. Fernando had always said the English style was something he could get his teeth into. Now he's seeing whether it really is to his liking.

It's Tuesday, 17 July, when he wears the Liverpool shirt on a pitch for the first time. Incidentally, the one he wore at his presentation was put up for auction to raise funds for cancer research. The winning bidder was an Irish businessman, a die-hard fan of the club, who paid 7,300 Euros (just over £6,000). Coming back to the long-awaited debut, it's the third friendly of the pre-season against the German side, Werder Bremen. Fernando comes on in the 64th minute in place of Andriy Voronin, who has scored the first and third goals for the Reds (the final score will be 3-2 for Benítez's side). He plays for 26 minutes, despite a slight ankle problem. He has two good opportunities – one, when he gets the ball at his feet after a short kick by the keeper, but in the end shoots it straight back to the goalie, and the other when a long shot skims the bar. The friendlies continue in the Far East. From 24–27 July, Liverpool takes part in the Barclays Asia Trophy in Hong Kong, where they play against South China. This is not a good moment for Fernando. Actually to see him score, you need to go to the Port of Rotterdam Tournament on 3 August. He comes on in place of Jermaine Pennant and scores against Shanghai Shenhua. It's a friendly of little value, the eighth of the pre-season, but a goal always goes down well. As Benítez says: 'It'll give him a lot of confidence with respect to the new season,' and to those who harbour doubts about his new acquisition, he replies: 'It reminds me of when Crouch signed for us. Everyone was asking when he would score his first goal. Now Torres has done it and he's got rid of that pressure.' The Premier League begins on 11 August.

The first match is away at Aston Villa. The Kid is nervous and excited. He wants to make a good impression, he wants to score but fails. On seventeen minutes, a great left-foot shot goes high. In the 31st minute, he seems made. He picks up a loose ball on the edge of the area, goes round his marker and has only keeper Stuart Taylor to beat. He tries a shot with his left but it's parried by the keeper. With the ball still in play, Dirk Kuyt gets halfway there before the defender and Villa captain, Martin Laursen, puts it into his own net: 1-0. Torres will reflect on that one. Then the captain takes

Mario's Holanda team for the 1992–3 season. From left to right: Juan the coach, Rubén, Alexis, Fernando Torres, Javier and Israel, Fernando's brother. Squatting down: Alejandro, Dani, Rici, Rocha and Alvarito.

Captaining Atlético Madrid against Valencia in La Liga, September 2006.

Play-fighting with his friend, Pepe Reina, during training in October 2007.

Tussling with Rio Ferdinand in a friendly at the Bernabéu back in 2004.

Scoring the only goal in the Euro 2008 final at Vienna's Ernst Happel stadium.

Raising the European Championship trophy following victory over Germany.

Torres and Gerrard at Stamford Bridge in 2008. The two have formed a formidable partnership on the pitch for Liverpool that shows no signs of abating.

Beating Fabio Cannavaro to the ball before going on to score the opening goal in Liverpool's 4–0 win over Real Madrid at Anfield in March 2009.

In the stands at Anfield with his childhood sweetheart, Olalla Domínguez. The couple have since married, and had their first child, Nora, in July 2009.

Celebrating scoring the opening goal in a 4–1 win over FC Porto at Anfield in the Champions League in 2007

care of things with a penalty to close the account on 1-2. A safe victory, Torres has been able to show his colours and show that he has learned the signals of the gaffer, who declares: 'I'm very satisfied with the way that Fernando has played his first match against Aston Villa. Normally, players take their time to get established but it looks like he has adapted very well.'

But there's a snag that has to be overcome – a goal. The drought continues on Wednesday, 15 August, in France in the Champions League qualifying round game against Toulouse. Fernando only plays the last twelve minutes, coming on for Voronin. He makes his big entry. After six years of futile attempts, he's in the top European club competition. But he doesn't score. And the old, old ghost that's pursued him for a long time (that of making too many mistakes) reappears. Four days later it disappears. Despite John Terry giving him a hard time and being determined to make Torres understand exactly what kind of footballing world he's entered, The Kid can open his arms to the goal. And it's only the first of an endless sequence.

Chapter 17

A perfect marriage

Conversation with former Liverpool player,
Michael Robinson

The background of his iPhone screen is red. The image shows a figure wearing a Number 9 shirt, with blond hair and arms raised – Fernando Torres in front of the Liverpool badge. Smiling, Michael Robinson displays his mobile phone. He has been a fan of The Reds for as long as he can remember. 'I was born in Leicester but a few years later my parents, for business reasons, moved to Blackpool, about 30 minutes from Anfield. Right from when I was a small boy I never missed a match in the Kop. I dreamed one day of being one of those players in the red shirt.' A dream that became reality in 1983, when Liverpool paid £250,000 to Brighton and Hove Albion for the striker who had so impressed at Wembley in the FA Cup Final against Manchester United.

Robinson spent just one season (1983–84) with the Reds, mostly as a reserve striker, trying to create a space for himself in-between Kenny Dalglish and Ian Rush. But for him and the club it was a glorious year, winning the old First Division title, the FA Cup and the European Cup. In December 1994, he left for Queen's Park Rangers, spending two seasons there before moving to Spain, playing for Osasuna (in Pamplona).

'I arrived the day of Reyes (the day in Spain for giving Christmas presents), 6 January 1987, so now I've been living here for 22 years!' That's right, because after retiring from football in 1989, 'The Cat' – as he was called by his friend, the Liverpool captain, Graeme Souness – has transformed himself into one of the best-known faces and voices on Spanish television and radio. 'I am', he says, 'the only English footballer on Spanish TV. I'm still alone on the podium.' He has commentated on both rugby and football matches, taken part in countless panel discussions, all in his unmistakable English accent, dubbed the voice of the ugly sister in the *Shrek 2 & 3* films and had the honour of being represented in the Spanish equivalent of *Spitting Image* on the *Canal+* television channel, with his puppet figure taking the role of programme presenter, no less. On *Canal+* as always, he now presents *Informe Robinson* (Robinson Report), a series looking at all aspects of the world of sport. To talk with him and listen to his everlasting stories is a pleasure. He knows Liverpool very well, a city and club close to his heart, as well as Fernando Torres, who was the subject of one of his programmes.

How did he seem to you when you went to film at Anfield?
'He surprised me a lot. In a short space of time, he'd learned what Anfield means, the badge, the fans, the value of the shirt, the power of "You'll Never Walk Alone". Straight away, he realised what it means to play for Liverpool. And what it means is: to play for the people. And remember that there's no code of conduct or style book – this isn't something you study, it's something you feel. When I was there, I remember that just before going out on to the pitch, Sam, who was in charge of the dressing room, would call us and open the door just as "You'll Never Walk Alone" was reaching its climax. And the manager, Joe Fagan, would tell us, as in *Hill Street Blues* (the US police TV series of the 1980s), when Captain Furillo was giving his advice before going out on

patrol, "Don't forget these people, we are always in their debt." And that's because the people of Liverpool give you everything they have. They have an amazing generosity and you have to give everything you have. You have to be on their level. At Anfield, the fans blow at you. It's like a wind that pushes you towards the opponents' goal.

'And it doesn't only happen at home games. I remember the Champions League final in Istanbul against Milan. At half-time I was completely disheartened. I was hoping that the punishment wouldn't be any greater than the 3-0 that Ancelotti's players had inflicted on us. But from the stands where the Reds were in the majority, they started to sing "You'll Never Walk Alone". Stevie (Gerrard) told me later that he'd heard it in the dressing room and that it gave everyone encouragement, it made them feel that they couldn't betray those people. They had to give it everything. At Liverpool, you have to feel the shirt. Bill Shankly said it was no accident that the strip was red. Liverpool was a working-class city, with strong trade unions, where there was a lot of poverty. The people didn't have money but what they did have was dignity and a creed and Anfield and Goodison Park were their temples, where they went to sing their songs, where they went to live a dream. And Liverpool, one mustn't forget, has always been the team of the people, a different value and a very strong one. The footballer, as Shankly used to say, had to bring happiness back to the people of Liverpool. And you couldn't show off or flaunt your wealth. When Robbie Fowler bought a yellow Ferrari, the manager took him to one side and said he'd made a double-error: that the Ferrari should be red and that no Liverpool player could drive around the city in such a flash car. He was forced to take it back. It's just an anecdote but it shows the spirit of the club. Ah, another example of what Liverpool is occurs to me … [*Pauses to light cigarette*]

'… We were coming back from Bucharest after beating Dynamo. The other semi-final was Dundee United v Roma. Back then they didn't play all the matches at the same time like they do now in the Champions League. When we were in the plane, we got Barry, our pilot – we always had the same crew and even though some of the cabin staff had retired, they didn't want to miss any of our trips – to tell us how the other game had ended up. When he said that Roma had won, the whole plane erupted into celebration. I was a bit puzzled because it seemed to me it would be better to play against Dundee. So I turned to Souness and asked him: "Do you think that's good? Wouldn't it be better if Dundee had won?" And he replied "No, because to play against Dundee would have been more of a British game. We're going to Rome, to the Olympic Stadium, to win the European Cup final, and do it in their home. We're going to make history." And I said "And what if we don't win?" He gave me a strange look and replied "How are we not going to win when we are the best team in the world?" No one had even considered the idea of losing.'

Nice story. Having seen what Liverpool is and what it represents, did you think that Fernando would have such a tremendous first season?

'I was absolutely convinced he'd be a success at Liverpool. When I saw him play for the first time in Spain, having just celebrated his 17th birthday, I thought he could be another Van Basten – and I don't say that lightly. It's correct to say that he had seasons where his form took a dip but he had the whole team's responsibilities on his shoulders and it was him who had to take the consequences. And talking in footballing terms, a good ball came his way about once every full moon. Two opportunities a match on goal was as good as it got and if he missed them and Atlético lost the game, then it was his fault. To put it simply, he was under huge pressure. At Liverpool it's not the same and he's surrounded by great players – no disrespect, of course, to his ex-Atlético team-mates – and the Benítez system suits him.'

In what way?
'When Liverpool get the ball they open things up, create space. Fernando has fantastic pace and knows how to lose his marker, turn him and finish off the move – that's his style. With Stevie (Gerrard) he's formed a footballing partnership that works perfectly. To put it another way, the virtues of Fernando+Benítez's system is 2+2 = 4 plus VAT.'

OK, tell me the truth. Do you like this Liverpool team?
'I like Liverpool when I get the sensation that the batteries on Benítez's remote have run out and the team is doing it's own thing or is a bit angry. I like football less when it looks like a game of chess. But you have to recognise that Rafa is a maestro in knowing how to read a game and that his solid commitment to Torres has paid off.'

According to a survey in The Times, *El Niño is Number 50 in the list of the best players in the history of Liverpool. What do you think?*
'Fernando is a true idol. He has the capabilities to be another Ian Rush or Kenny Dalglish. I'm certain that with his qualities, and if he stays at the same level, he is going to write a really important chapter in the history of Liverpool. He's not a scouser like Gerrard or Carragher, he hasn't emerged from the Merseyside soil, but he's not a foreigner either, because he wears the red shirt. He's another example of the type of fans Liverpool has – a club where the manager, five players and six members of the technical staff are Spanish. And one has to say that between Torres and the

Anfield fans, the marriage is perfect. We have a Number 9 who scores goals and wins matches in the last minute. If he's injured – ooooh! – we begin to get worried. At the moment, Liverpool is Torres, Gerrard and nine others.'

It's now lunchtime and afterwards, Michael Robinson has to return to the studio to edit the latest edition of his *Informe* programme, which, in this case, is a day spent talking football with Johan Cruyff, discussing everything from a pressing game to the speed of play – concepts that remind 'The Cat' of endlessly hearing the manager in his sleep telling him, 'Get it, give it, go!' And that prompts the final anecdote before he leaves. 'We were going to play against Tottenham. In the coach, the manager asks me, 'Michael, do you hunt?' 'No, I don't like hunting,' I replied. 'Well, it doesn't matter. Imagine that we are going to go hunting for hares and we come across one motionless in its burrow. We could kill it. But if it runs, and runs rapidly, it'll be very difficult. The ball is the same. If it runs rapidly, it's difficult to catch.'

Thank you, Mr Robinson.

Chapter 18

Liverpool 4 West Ham 0

5 March 2008

It's a nice gesture by the captain. After the final whistle, he walks up to the referee, asks him for the ball, goes across the field and offers it, as if it was a bunch of roses to Fernando Torres on the bench. El Niño accepts it from Stevie with a big smile. It's the third ball that he's taken from an English ground and his third hat-trick of the season. In six long years at Atlético he never scored three in one game. In England, it's become a habit. The first time was on 25 September, in the Carling Cup against Reading at the Madejski Stadium. The second, on 23 February, in the league and the latest against the Hammers. Luckily – for West Ham – he hit the post in the 67th minute, otherwise it would have been 4. Not only is he exceeding his personal boundaries but also those of Liverpool. It's the first time in 60 years that a player in the red strip has scored a hat-trick in two consecutive matches at Anfield. Never before had a single striker scored in seven consecutive home games – but it happened a short time later. And not since 2003 (Michael Owen) had a Liverpool player racked up more than twenty goals in a season.

Talking of records, before he finishes the 2007–08 season, he will break several. But first a look in the rear-view mirror. In three months, from July to September, the striker from Spain has become important, very important – for everyone. Midfield organiser, Xabi Alonso, acknowledges it in a declaration to the club website: 'Torres is demonstrating that he's not afraid of the physical contact that exists here, with defenders who will try to bring him down. His rivals realise that Fernando isn't afraid of them and that's an extra motivation for him.'

When the new acquisition is on the bench, as happened against Portsmouth, or when he's seen warming up on the edge of the pitch, as on 22 September at home against Birmingham, the fans and the media get restless. Especially when, three days later in the Carling Cup against Reading, he nets three. They always want to see him in the starting line-up and make fun of Rafa Benítez's rotation policy. Take the *Daily Mirror* headline for its analysis of the situation: 'Why Mrs Benítez would be happy if Rafa even rotated her rotisserie'. A discussion that begins with an imaginary dialogue between Rafa and Montse at breakfast time on the usefulness of rotating the various electrical appliances to make toast. It's worth another look:

> Rafa: Take the bread from the toaster, dear. Today we use the oven grill.
>
> Montse: But the toaster's quicker.
>
> Rafa: If you say to me, the toaster is best, I say OK. But I have three machines for browning bread and I must use them all.
>
> Montse: But it'll make the kids late for school.
>
> Rafa: We are a few weeks into the school year. If you want the toaster performing at a good level next June, then OK, you must rest it now.
>
> Montse: Right. Oven it is. Can I use the toaster tomorrow?
>
> Rafa: Who knows? I have to consider the George Foreman Grill also.

The main target of this ribaldry defends himself to the hilt, maintaining that, for sure, 'Fernando can play twenty or thirty matches on the trot without any problem. But if he was to do that, he wouldn't be capable of playing at the same level for the remaining fifteen games during which we are fighting for trophies.' The gaffer's global perspective is understandable, the decision to be sparing with his new millionaire purchase, to protect him, to ensure that he is fresh for when the games get harder, but it turns out, in fact, that El Niño ruins all the plans. He is too important for the team, both in the league and in the Champions League.

In early December, in spite of the injury, he's already scored twelve goals in all competitions. And three of them are heavyweight ones in the Champions League. They also serve to give new vigour to a manager under pressure from criticism, a lot of bad results and his dispute with the club's American bosses, Tom Hicks and George Gillett. Heavyweight goals that have helped the numerous protests in support of Rafa that are seen on the streets of Liverpool at the end of November – Reds fans with his image on posters saying 'Keep Rafa' and even '*No pasarán*' ('They shall not pass' – a famous rallying-call from the Republican side in the Spanish Civil War to rally resistance against the fascist Franco uprising). The stormy waters grow calm and the debate goes back to concentrating on football. In the English papers, a photomontage of Fernando appears with a sharpened nose and a pencil moustache, all underlined with a quote from Steven Gerrard: 'He reminds me of Rush.' Yes, the Welshman and the lad from Fuenlabrada hold each other in high regard. In just a few months, a mutual respect has been formed. Perhaps because both of them took on a lot of responsibilities early, both of them are shy, speak little, do not brag and eschew glamour in favour of old friends and family life. Torres says of Gerrard: 'He is the best, or one of the best, in the world. Never I play with a footballer of his level. It's a pleasure to do so. It's not only the interaction that works between us. Gerrard is able to give you the ball where you want it. He allows you to exploit to the full his qualities while improving your own game.' Gerrard says simply of Torres: 'I wouldn't change him for any other striker in the world.' A very special chemistry, which Ian Rush speaks of as well: 'This interaction between Torres and Gerrard – the same thing happened between me and Kenny Dalglish. It's almost telepathic. Torres makes the defenders work, he keeps them pinned back and he doesn't hide like other foreign players. He's strong and has adapted quickly. Drogba and Henry needed a whole season. If he can get twenty or twenty-five goals, we can win the Premier League.'

The dream of the Liverpool ex-Number 9 is the same as all the side's supporters – to win the league, which for nineteen years has escaped them. The idea is simple: getting a striker that they've not seen the likes of since the time of Michael Owen or better, Robbie Fowler, means the unattainable goal becomes possible. It's a pity that, in the end, Torres surpasses all the predictions but Liverpool end up fourth in the league.

Putting that to one side, one can see the progress of the youngster who has so impressed everyone through his ability to adapt in comparison with the strikers who, as Rush says, have taken a season to understand how things work. After the Christmas holidays that Fernando spends with his family, who have come over from Spain loaded with products from his home country, including everything from ham to olive oil (this The Kid is not giving up), a new crown arrives in early January. In a poll on the club website, the fans of Liverpool elect him as the Best Young Footballer under 23 years of age in Rafa Benítez's 2007 squad. And some days later there's also the nomination of Best Player of the Team in the month of December. It's the third time that Fernando wins it, after first securing it in August and September, before ceding it to Steven Gerrard in October and November. Recognition of his achievements arrives not only from the fans. He is a member of the 'Ideal Eleven' chosen by various European sports magazines.

February – an incredible month. He gets injured during the international friendly with France but returns in time for the last sixteen away leg of the Champions League against Inter Milan to bamboozle Marco Materazzi, the Inter and Italy defender also known for being on the receiving end of Zinedine Zidane's headbutt in the final of the Germany World Cup. He gets his second hat-trick, swelling his quota to 21 goals (fifteen in the league). In the Premier League classification for effectiveness, he is in third position, with a goal every 118 minutes played. Numbers and results that also bring him the Barclays prize for the best player of the month. But the most sought-after tribute, the most affectionate, the most unforgettable, the one that endorses once and for all, the special relationship with the fans, comes from the Kop. A song specially for him, like the greats of the past and present have had. At Anfield they start to sing the Armband song. They dug up the story of the Atlético captain's armband and made it their own. A song that makes Fernando emotional – as his playing makes his teammates emotional. The Dutchman, Dirk Kuyt, declares: 'It's incredible to have scored so many goals in his first season in England. He's getting them in the league and in Europe and is doing a great job for the team. The rest of the players think that he's going to score in every match and the way things are going, one gets the impression that's what is going to happen.'

In March, another hat-trick and one of those goals that one doesn't forget easily. In the San Siro, against Inter, he receives a deep pass from Fabio Aurelio in the 64th minute, controls the ball, then, with a half-turn on the edge of the area, fires it inside the near post, where, despite a desperate final stretch, Inter keeper Julio Cesar cannot reach it. It seals the team's passage through to the quarter-finals. It's a trademark goal. Control, half-turn, shoot and goal. El Niño will repeat the same move against Arsenal in April to ensure Liverpool reach the Champions League semi-finals. 'He turned with the speed of a reptile to deal Almunia a venomous blow,' writes *La Gazzetta dello Sport*. And *Corriere della Sera* adds: 'He created a work of art, leaving Frenchman Gallas dumbfounded like an absolute novice.' Two goals, one more attractive than the other. Difficult to choose which is the best. The *Guardian,* simply suggests watching them a million times over.

And just before the double encounter with Arsenal, Torres goes through his first test in English. He'd promised he would, months before, and keeps to his word. He was being a bit ambitious to try it even in the corridors of Anfield, one to one with a British journalist, but to take on an important press conference organised by UEFA in the full public eye is not an everyday event for anyone. However, the youngster proves he's on the ball. He doesn't speak BBC English but he holds his own. This time the translator is there just to help him with the harder questions. Rafa Benítez is at his side and looks on proudly like the father of a boy who has just got the best report in his class. 'Twenty-eight goals scored … a target to reach before the end of the season?' they ask him. He replies: 'Is my best season. I'm scoring a lot of goals, my target is score goals but I don't have one number of goals. I want to help my team-mate to win trophies but scoring goals is the job of the striker. I'm only doing my job.'

It's that simple, he's only doing his job. Even if nothing takes away the fact that the first person to be surprised by the statistics of his first season at Liverpool is himself. He confesses as much, shrugging his shoulders almost to excuse himself, like a child whose mother has caught him sticking his hand in a jar of jam. Torres is humble but in the meantime the recognitions pour in. He is amongst the candidates for the PFA Players' Player of the Year award. A title that goes to Cristiano Ronaldo. But it's interesting to hear what Gordon Taylor, PFA Chief Executive, has to say about Torres: 'There have been many great Number 9s in Liverpool and this season he has followed in that tradition, responding brilliantly to what was a great challenge, which speaks clearly of his strength of character and skill.'

In May, by then out of the Champions League – despite his away leg semi-final goal in the match against Chelsea – there is still the Premier League to finish off. The last game is at White Hart Lane, then the home of manager, Juande Ramos, the Spaniard who had won the Carling Cup against Chelsea and thereby taken the team into Europe. The match doesn't feature much of interest, Benítez's side win 0-2 and Torres scores league goal Number 24. He becomes the foreign player with the highest number of goals scored in his debut season. He beats the record of Ruud van Nistelrooy. The Dutchman had set the mark with 23 goals (including four penalties) in 32 games during the 2001–02 season on his debut with Manchester United. Ruud, whose arrival from PSV Eindhoven was an inspired gamble by Sir Alex Ferguson, in spite of a knee problem, demonstrated his class in the first of five seasons with the Red Devils before leaving for Real Madrid. Benítez's gamble also pays off with 33 goals across all competitions. Third place in the Premier League top-scorer list behind Cristiano Ronaldo (31) and Emmanuel Adebayor (24).

Then comes the prize for the Reds' best player and best striker, chosen by the supporters. And, in Madrid, they give him the Man of the Year award, which is received in his absence by José, his father. In-between all these honours there is also the Nike TV commercial, which lights up Liverpool with the colours of Spain. The Osborne bull dominates the motorway exit, ships on the Mersey fly the red and yellow flag, students are learning Spanish, the fish and chip shops offer 'All Day Tapas', giant paella pans are on sale, flamenco is the dance schools' favourite, The Cavern becomes The Caverna and youngsters playing football in the park offer their thanks to Torres with a '*Gracias*, mate.' Fernando, in red jacket with his boxer dog on a leash, goes off smiling and looking pleased with himself. That's how he appears in a commercial but it's also the reality. At Liverpool, the lad who has come from Madrid is happy. He says so and repeats it in many interviews. With the Reds, he's enjoying his football like never before. In the city of the Beatles, he's discovered a winning mentality. He speaks of how his team-mates 'do not go out on to the pitch hoping that they'll win or praying for victory. They really expect to win. They have so much faith in their ability that they simply don't consider the possibility of any other result.'

Something new for him. Just as the football experience in England is enjoyable and new: 'The fans are with your team to the death, win or lose. They are always behind their side and at away games as well. Normally in Spain, when you are substituted there is a huge amount of whistling yet here the crowd stand up and applaud you!' And then there is Benítez, the manager who pampers him and teaches him new things each day, and there is the captain who is showing him what it means to be the team leader at a great club.

To sum up, he is enthusiastic about the choice he has made. Because at Liverpool, freed from the game he played at Atlético, he doesn't feel like a star who has to deal with everything – the good and the bad – but just an important player along with lots of others. The only regret is that he's had to leave his country, because in Spain they realised what he was worth. A month later, the fresh respect of the Spaniards will become devotion and eternal gratitude.

Chapter 19
He's going to stay

Conversation with former Liverpool player and manager, Kenny Dalglish

He hasn't lost his Scottish accent. It's hard and dry, while at the same time, takes on a brusque tone. Apart from that, 'The King' or 'The Legend' as everyone calls him, is a normal person – pleasant, informal, very gracious and a bit shy. He's not a great one for talking but when he does, it's on an informed, friendly and helpful basis. He shuns high-sounding words and concepts and prefers to call a spade a spade to explain how he sees things. And at the time of writing, it has been announced that he is returning to be a part of Rafa Benítez's technical team in an advisory capacity, developing young players and sporting reports. News which all of Anfield would welcome with enormous pleasure. Because Kenneth Mathieson Dalglish, who was 58 in March and born in Dalmarnock, Glasgow, is top of the list of 100 Players Who Shook The Kop. Between 1977 and 1991, with the Reds, he won the unimaginable as both player and player-manager. He scored a fantastic 173 goals (added to the 112 he scored between 1969 and 1977 wearing the green and white of Celtic).

He was also witness to the most tragic moments of modern football: on 29 May 1985 the final against the Juventus of Michel Platini, with 39 bodies on the field of play, and on 15 April 1989, the Hillsborough disaster, with its burden of 96 dead. He has brought excitement to crowds across Europe. Apart from Liverpool, he has managed Blackburn Rovers, Newcastle United and Celtic. But he maintains that he has never felt himself to be a legend and that it's others who create legends. He has similar biographical details to Fernando. As a small boy at school, he began playing in goal, he was also a striker, his sign of the Zodiac is also Pisces, and he was also the Reds' most expensive signing. But for King Kenny, all this is just coincidence. What is certain is that he gave his blessing to Torres immediately after his second hat-trick. 'This boy,' he said, 'is the best buy that any club in Europe has made this season.'

And what does he think now? What's the best match that
Fernando Torres has had during his two years at Liverpool?
'There's not really one game for me, it's just what Fernando is. He seems very mature for his age. He seems someone that a lot of Spanish players will look up to as a leader. On the football pitch, for Liverpool, he's certainly made a massive contribution. He's just scored his 50th goal for Liverpool in 85 games, which is as good as anyone ever got in getting 50 goals. It's a fantastic achievement. He's the right man for Liverpool. He has committed himself to the way of life in Liverpool. He's learned the language very quickly. He seems very settled and he's very happy with life at the moment and his football as well,'

Have their been any games that have really showcased his
particular talents?
'He did very well at Manchester United this year, when Liverpool won 4-1, and he made a valuable contribution with his playing. He gave Vidic (Manchester United defender, Nemanja Vidic), who had played a very, very good season up until then, a really tough time. Also in the previous year,

when he scored his goal against Chelsea in the first half. He took it brilliantly. I think he's had many good games but Manchester United would be the pick of it because of the close rivalry. He also scored and done well against Everton in the league match when he played with Robbie Keane upfront. There'll be a lot of games he can look back on and be very satisfied with what he's done. But one of the big problems is going to be trying to keep him fit because both Spain and Liverpool want to play as many matches as they possibly can and it's not always possible.'

How has he managed to adapt so quickly to the history of the club and to the way Liverpool play?
'Yes, he's done it very quickly and it's a great compliment to him. It's helped that the manager's Spanish and there are some other Spanish players in the squad. It's always nice to see a face that you know when you arrive at a football club and it's nice to know that the manager is of the same nationality. Fernando has settled in magnificently well and he's been fantastic for Liverpool. The unfortunate thing this season is that he was injured for a few games and that's been a wee problem for him this season. It's been a problem for Liverpool and then he's got to go to the Federations Cup, which is a competition about nothing and there won't be too many managers who'll be happy that they (Spain) will be playing that. It's a meaningless competition and it's only a reflection of them having won the European Championship last year. That was a fantastic achievement for Spain and Fernando played his part in that but the players need a rest. This'll be three years on the road now, that they have been playing football.'

What are the main differences and similarities between Liverpool when you were a player and the Liverpool today of Rafa Benítez and Fernando?

'Liverpool, for all their history, have always had the same philosophy about how they want to play football. I don't think that's changed. I don't think there is a huge difference. Nowadays, there's much greater competition because there are a lot more clubs who are able to compete financially than there were when we were playing. I think it's always difficult to go back and compare what happened in the past. I think you just analyse what's happening in the present time and I think this year that Liverpool have improved with what they've achieved this year and if they continue the improvement then they'll go even closer next year to winning the Premier League.'

Having met Fernando on two or three occasions, what is he like?

'He's a very mature young lad and very respectful. He understands the tradition of Liverpool Football Club and he respects the people that come along and support him. He's one of the favourites of the fans but he doesn't take it for granted and they really respect him. So I would think that if he was your son, you'd be very proud of him as a person and a footballer. He's a fantastic footballer.'

What are the similarities between you and Fernando?

'Maybe we've got the same colour of hair – that's about all!'

Which Liverpool player from the past most resembles Torres?

'There's nobody similar. I think you're your own person. I don't think any two footballers are the same. I think he's his own person but it's inevitable that people draw comparisons with previous Liverpool players, but he's Fernando

Torres and that's all he's got to be. He's got to be himself. He compares favourably with anything that anyone else has done for this football club as regards goals, so to me he's done tremendously well, but I wouldn't say he was similar to any of the players that I've seen.

What does Liverpool need to do to get to the same level as Manchester United and to win the Premier League?
'Well, they're getting better and they've got closer this year than they've ever been before, so I'm sure this summer that Rafa will be busy trying to identify what he thinks he can do to improve the team to go that one step further than they went this year. But to go from two to one is a big, big step and although it doesn't seem much, it's a huge, huge step to take forward. But the best person to know and the person that everyone is going to trust to find it out is Rafa Benítez. So I'm sure Rafa will get in a couple of players who he thinks are going to be of benefit to the club and we'll have to wait until next season to find out if that's the case.'

How do you see the future of Fernando Torres in Liverpool?
'The future's very bright for Fernando Torres at Liverpool. I'm sure he's going to stay here.'

You were at Anfield for the 20th anniversary of Hillsborough. You saw Fernando and all the team – it's a special day for Liverpool, no?
'Hillsborough is a very special event for us, the people of Liverpool, because it's twenty years this year. But also it's very much a part of the history of Liverpool Football Club, the same as any cup success would be. It's there in the history, it's there in the memory and it will never be forgotten, the families will never be forgotten. It's very important to the people in Liverpool that they understand that and

that the people who come and play for Liverpool understand it. I don't think there's much more you can add to Hillsborough than for me to say that.'

Having been a manager of Liverpool yourself, what suggestions can you give to Fernando Torres?
'I would just say to Fernando Torres: Continue what you've done because you've done it very well. Enjoy yourself and we'll all keep our fingers crossed that we're going to get the prize that everybody would love them to get and that's more success.'

Chapter 20

Spain 4 Russia 1

10 June 2008

A striker is selfish by definition. He only sees the space marked out by two posts, eight feet high and an 8-yard crossbar. He doesn't look around him, he doesn't look for the unmarked team-mate. He doesn't have time because he's looking for the goal. His only thought is to get the ball over that goddamned white line. In whatever way possible. He only thinks of scoring. And his skill is what everyone – manager, team-mates, fans and commentators – wants from him. It's his obsession because he knows that whatever marvels he's able to perform on the pitch, however many opponents he can get past, however many miles he runs, however much work he does for the team, in the end he'll be judged on the number of goals scored. And he'll leave the pitch with a bad taste in his mouth if he hasn't put away at least one.

But, occasionally, he understands that rules get broken, that the Number 9 looks up and sees a friendly shirt he can trust and instead of finishing off a move, instead of being selfish, he chooses to be generous or, better still, takes the correct and easiest option, the most direct route to goal, the action that benefits the side and makes all the team into winners.

And this is what he understands in the 20th minute of Spain's debut in Euro 2008 as Luis Aragonés' team take on the Russia of Guus Hiddink in Innsbruck's Neu Tivoli stadium in Austria. A long ball and Fernando Torres uses his pace to unsettle Kolodin. The Russian defender no longer knows what to do, loses his head, is not able to deal with the red lightning at his side and gives the ball away to El Niño. With some metres still to run, goalkeeper Akinfeez comes out of his goal and throws himself to the ground but doesn't get to the ball. Fernando sees that David Villa, the Valencia striker and his international team-mate, has been following the play. A textbook cut-back and there's nothing more that Spain's Number 7 has to do other than put the ball into an empty goal. And then the celebration. The two strikers embrace, Villa beckons to Torres, they end up on the ground while their team-mates arrive and pile on top. So much celebration in fact that Villa injures the index finger on his right hand, a hairline crack that puts his participation in the following match in doubt.

Freeze frame: the ball, fired in by Villa, still hasn't hit the back of the net, two disorientated Russian defenders watch the action while El Niño is already smiling. Happy with what he's done. The rapport between the two is repeated a little later but Villa can't beat the opposing keeper – the shot is too forced because of tight marking. And it doesn't end there. On 44 minutes, Villa latches onto a magnificent through-ball from Iniesta to make it 2-0. When 'El Guaje' ('The Kid', or 'El Niño' in the language of Villa's native Asturias) scores the third of his hat-trick, the other *Niño* is no longer on the field. The manager has taken him off in the 54th minute to send on a midfielder, Arsenal's Cesc Fabregas. It's a substitution the Number 9 doesn't like at all and which generates a long drawn-out debate. But there is a gesture from Villa to remember – after scoring the third goal of his hat-trick, he runs towards the bench to embrace Torres and dedicates the goal to him.

'I embraced Fernando because people are talking a lot about him, that he's not feeling good, that he doesn't feel a part of things, that it's difficult for him. I dedicated it to him because I scored but it was Torres who found the way in. I took all the praise for finishing off the moves but the first two goals were only possible through his help. In the first, the pass was his and in the second he opened up the spaces so that Iniesta could make the final pass. He's had a really important game. He did great work – all the "dirty work", that allowed me to do the beautiful bit. I've benefited from him and wanted to thank him for it. I wanted to dedicate it to him so that he would be happy,' said David Villa at the time. A demonstration of friendship that put an end to a long month of controversy.

Voices in the dressing room were saying that the two were incompatible, they didn't understand each other, they weren't talking and they were constantly in competition with each other. What's more, many were putting forward the following theory: if Torres is playing, Villa is on the bench and vice versa. But Innsbruck proved the opposite. 'In the end, we finished up playing together,' added Villa, 'and I have to say that, with him, I felt very good. He's an exceptional footballer, who can drop to the wing and who works hard for whoever plays alongside him. He's wonderful.'

The match finishes 4-1 with a final headed goal from Fabregas but there's no doubting that the hero of the game is El Guaje. A quick glance at the Spanish press headlines confirms it. 'Illa Illa Illa ¡Villa Maravilla!' (Marvellous Villa) is the front page headline of *Marca*, the Madrid sport daily. 'Villa, the Number 7 of Spain', shouts *ABC*, while *El Mundo* booms 'Lethal Villa, Lethal Spain'. The last Spaniard to score three goals in the finals of a European Championship was Michel.

Next up was Sweden. Villa has already caught up with Alfonso at the top of the table of Spanish goalscorers in European championship finals. As is to be expected, there is much praise for the lad who comes from the Asturias region of Spain and who grew up in a family of miners. For Torres, the critics are also positive. They say that he's been rapid, lively, dangerous, demonstrated his class and formed a deadly partnership with Villa. He's not been seen very much, almost a spectator when the national side was playing the short passing game, but decisive on the counter-attack when he had space to run, like he does at Liverpool. A pity, they say, that he's on the pitch so little.

'Torres has come from a long, hard season and he is very important for us. I had to take him off to give strength to the midfield,' explains Aragonés at the end of the match. He minimises the fact that the Number 9 hadn't scored: 'The next day Torres could put away three goals just like Villa.'

What's certain is that after the first match and the first overwhelming success against a rival that, on paper, seemed a hard nut to crack, the euphoria in Spain is widespread. And it's also important to point out that this is the seventh consecutive victory for Aragonés' men in a run of seventeen matches without defeat. But nobody trusts first impressions. Starting with Fernando: 'We've played at a good pace and we've been lucky. It's very important to start like this but we haven't done anything. Don't forget what happened to us in the Germany World Cup.' Yes, Torres knows the failures of the national side all too well, having been a regular participant in recent years. Against Russia he celebrated a Golden Wedding with the side. A round figure of 50 matches and fourteen goals scored (three penalties), the numbers of a story that begins on 6 September 2003 at Guimares in Portugal.

He's called up for the first time with the senior side by Iñaki Sáez, already his mentor from the junior teams. 'He was the first that I called out of all those lads that I'd known and trained in the Under-16s and Under-19s. A fantastic group that brought us a lot of pleasure. Fernando was the most ready, physically, and he already had a lot of experience – two years in the first team at Atlético. His qualities? A speed and movement bonus, plus a lot of goals. He also had some weak spots to clear up, like receiving the ball with his back to the defender, one-on-ones with the keeper, coordination. But I had to put him on, I had to put on the best,' remembers Iñaki with pleasure.

For Fernando it's a dream that is becoming reality. For some time, there'd been talk about his possible call-up but the gaffer hadn't wanted to give in to those temptations. This time things seem to be different, so during the week before the announcement of the squad for the friendly against Portugal, the Atlético Number 9 is beside himself with excitement. He wants to be part of the 'club', to see the national team from the inside, the atmosphere within the group, the training sessions, the prematch preparations. He wants to play with the 'grown-ups', and he is fed up of being the lad destined for the Under-21s. He feels that this is the moment. The anticipation is intermittent until the great day finally arrives. He's in a car with a friend when he learns the good news on the radio. Amongst the 22, his name is included. It's the moment he's been anticipating 'for a long time. Since last season, when I was dreaming so much about being able to join the side,' he declares in an interview. 'It's not that you expect it but it's more when everyone talks about the same thing, you begin to get worked up about it. But I wasn't getting down. I knew that one day it would have to be. With each list the debate began but I was apart from all that. I said that I wasn't in a hurry, that it wasn't a priority. I never understood all that expectation. They wanted to see me in the national side. Now it's up to me to show they weren't mistaken.'

It's up to him to show them he is at the same level of the greats of Spain – the Raúls, the Valeróns, the Tristáns. He knows that they are putting him under the spotlight but he's used to it. At Atlético he is the first to be praised and the first to be subjected to scrutiny. The national side, however, is going through a bad phase. During qualification for Euro 2004, Spain suffers two bad setbacks against Greece and Northern Ireland. They couldn't make any more mistakes and above all they couldn't make them against Ukraine the following Wednesday. It will be a crucial encounter in which Torres will start. In short, the game against Portugal – although a friendly that comes at a bad time (a very bad time, four days before a must-win tie) – it's a key test for the nineteen who are in the national side for the first time. Iñaki's idea is to put him in the front line of attack, 'so that he can run and fight for the ball' with Raúl behind. The manager hopes it will work so that he can do it again. Torres, for his part, yearns for a good game, a goal and a win.

It's a clear 0-3 victory but in the Alfonso Henriques stadium (which had just been refurbished for the following year's Euro 2004) the reality doesn't match up to earlier expectations. Meira and Couto, the two Portuguese defenders, give him such a kicking that he has to receive medical treatment just before the end of the first half. In the 36th minute, Fernando Meira tackles him from behind, crashing into his left ankle and leaving him limping. Fernando Manuel Silva Couto completes the job in the 43rd minute with a ferocious kick. Raúl, captain of Real Madrid and the national side, comments: 'I warned him it was going to be a very difficult match. He was in front of some hard defenders who were going to give him a tough time but it's the route he's got to follow. Torres is the future of Spanish football.' Torres himself is also aware that these are the risks of the trade. 'What do you want? That they don't give me a hard time?' he asks at the end of the match, putting an end to any argument over the blows he has received. And he adds that he's as happy as a sandboy because he's made his first appearance in the senior side.

On his performance, there's not much to report – a mis-kick that goes high, some good control to get round the direct-minded opposition, and good passing. The critics were generous, stressing that the youngster seemed intimi-dated at the start. He wasn't the centre of attention as he usually was when playing for Atlético, and they also under-lined the lack of interaction with his team-mates. That's nor-mal, it's the first time. The try-out, however, is sufficiently convincing, at least for Iñaki, that at Elche in Spain, in the home match against Ukraine, he will be a definite starter. And this time it's going to be serious. Qualification is in the balance. In the 51st minute, Dymitrulin up-ends Etxeberría in the area. Penalty. Fernando Torres takes the ball and calmly places it on the spot. Before the match, Sáez asked who was ready to take a penalty. El Niño raised his hand. He wants to show that now he's arrived in the national side, he wants to stay. For a long time. He's not nervous or overawed as he steps back from the spot. To score is crucial. Spain aren't playing well and Andriy Voronin (a future team-mate of Torres at Liverpool) has already sent a message of intent to Spain keeper, Iker Casillas. Fernando makes his run-up and sends a slow, limp, average shot to the left of the keeper. Shovkovskyy guesses right and grabs the ball. Torres can't do anything more than kick the air in frustration. Fortunately, this failure doesn't turn out to be decisive (Spain, thanks to Raúl, win 2-1), but next day, criticism of the youngster's error doesn't make for light reading.

And what's more, all the commentators ask why it was up to him to take responsibility for the penalty when, in the national team, there are others with more experience of spot-kicks, like Reyes or Xavi. Iñaki Sáez calms the waters and explains: 'I think you have to go through this sort of experience in order to be successful. But there's nothing to worry about. This will help him become a better player.' Prophetic words. Because that's certainly what he becomes. He applies himself to the task, as well as Gregorio Manzano, his trainer at Atlético, who, for several days, is photographed explaining to his player exactly how to take a penalty and get it right. 'It was just an exercise in how to visualise,' explains Manzano today, 'so that he would take other penalties, with the thought that your first idea is what you have to stick with and not change it at the last moment. I wanted to help him. He was starting to grow in the national team and to demonstrate his skills in spite of the failure against Ukraine.'

Also of interest at Elche is that Milan sporting director, Ariedo Braida, is amongst the spectators. He wants to see in the flesh the new jewel of Spanish football. Information that he's received from his observers is very good. They're thinking seriously of making an offer to Atlético. But Torres, who has spoken to his team-mates and ex-Milan players Demetrio Albertini and José Mari, rules out for the moment any move to Italy. It's better to be older for Italian football. There's the risk of getting burned ...

But we return to the national side and redemption. It takes place seven months later by complete coincidence in Italy, in Genova, against the Italian national side on 28 April 2004. An important friendly. For Italy, it's a homage to 37-year-old Roberto Baggio, the great improviser of Vicenza, Fiorentina, Juventus, Milan, Inter, Brescia and of the national team, from which he will retire at the end of the season. The European Footballer of the Year 1993 returns to the national team after five years' absence for one last game in the blue shirt. For Spain, it's the last test before Euro 2004. The Spanish manager sends out the same team as for the game with Portugal. He decides to try out two strike pairings, Raúl with Morientes and Valerón plus Fernando Torres. El Niño comes on at the beginning of the second half wearing his lucky Number 14. His team-mates have given him permission to choose it because fourteen, he says, has always brought him luck. And these things in football are no laughing matter. Fernando wants to score. He feels that this time it's right. After four matches with the national side, he needs to get rid of his psychological block. One knows that the first goal for a striker is crucial. Eight minutes after the break, Albelda wins the ball in midfield, passes it directly upfield to Valerón who waits for the right moment – the Italian defenders come out – before giving it to Torres, who shoots across the goal towards the far post, which is out of Peruzzi's reach. It's his first goal with the senior squad. A celebration that is rained on three minutes later by Bobo Vieri who, by chance, is an ex-Atlético Madrid player. Torres is also left with the sensation that he could have scored again. This time, however, everyone praises El Niño's impressive performance.

He gets the OK for Euro 2004 in Portugal. Iñaki Sáez explains Torres' call-up like this: 'He is youth personified. What he has shown in the national side is his character. He has two essential qualities – competitiveness and speed. He is growing and no one knows his limit.'

In spite of all the praise, the manager, once on Portuguese soil, doesn't count on him at the beginning. In the first match against Russia, he comes on as a 77th minute substitute for an unlucky Raúl. It's the same story in the second encounter against Greece, with barely a quarter of an hour on the pitch, once again replacing the team captain.

The 10,000 Spanish fans who have arrived in Porto to see the match that could give them qualification to the quarter-finals are encouraged to see him on the pitch. But the 'little prince' of Atlético hardly touches the ball. He can't turn the draw into a win and the resulting stalemate now requires Spain to put everything on a win against the host side, Portugal.

Lisbon, 20 June 2004, 8.45pm, the José Alvalade stadium, the third and final match day in Group A and this time, El Niño is in the starting line-up. It's what he was hoping for. He doesn't want to go home without ever being in the initial eleven, he wants to respond to the expectations that his call-up generated after his eye-catching performance against Italy. 'I've also put a lot into this European competition,' he says, 'and we all have great expectations for this tournament. Not to reach the quarter-finals would be a failure,' and adds: 'We can't go into history as another national side that has achieved nothing.' He's convinced that 'if we do things well we shouldn't have any problems against Portugal.' After all, Spain had beaten them easily on 6 September of the previous year, on his debut. Of course, this isn't a friendly, but the idea of getting eliminated doesn't enter the head of the twenty-year-old with five matches wearing the shirt of Spain. He's changed his look for the occasion, getting rid of his long locks with a crew-cut down to almost zero. In the absence of his trusted Madrid stylist, he asked Juanito del Betis to shave it off, setting the cutter at Number 1. But the new look doesn't do much good.

At the end of the first half, the result is still 0-0. Fernando has hardly been in the game. The person who has been, and who has become a nightmare for the Spanish defence, is Cristiano Ronaldo. His performance is tremendous. The Manchester United winger has lots of opportunites to score but fails, either sending shots wide or through the efforts of Spanish keeper, Iker Casillas. The good news for Spain comes from the other game where Greece are losing 1-2 to Russia. With this scenario, it would be Spain and Greece going through. But with the second half barely under way, it's clear that the host nation has no intention of being kicked out of its tournament. A great strike by Nuño Gomes puts them 1-0 up in the 56th minute. Saint Iker (Casillas) can't get to it. Like this, Portugal go through. Five minutes later, Fernando has a chance for the equaliser. A splendid assist from Xabi Alonso, but as keeper Ricardo comes out of his goal, El Niño puts it onto the post. He despairs, he cannot believe it. He puts his head in his hands, his mouth open. Iñaki Sáez still remembers that failed attempt by Fernando: 'A draw would have been enough and we would have got to the quarter-finals. Instead, we came back home. It was another failure by the national side. To think we'd set off with so much hope. It was a young team with players like Torres, Xavi, Alonso and Reyes, together with very experienced players like Raúl, Baraja and Albelda. But in the end, my plans didn't work.' And Iñaki's adventure ended.

On 1 July 2004, the Real Federación Española de Fútbol (Royal Spanish Football Federation) named 66-year-old Luis Aragonés as the new manager, with 30 years' experience across Spain and an old acquaintance of Fernando Torres. His debut is set for 18 August in Las Palmas in a friendly against Venezuela, ahead of qualification for the 2006 World Cup in Germany. Fernando is there. He will be a fixture in the call-ups of the Aragonés era. He will be left out only once, for a friendly in Tenerife on 10 November 2006, against Romania, because of the Atlético captain's poor league form with only two goals in eight games – his worst results since playing in the first division. Aragonés maintains that there are four strikers who are in better form than El Niño. He says he's leaving him at home 'so that he learns'. The match ends in a defeat for Spain. From that moment on, apart from when circumstances are beyond his control, the manager will not leave Fernando out of the side and Spain will not lose again with him on the side. At the beginning, however, things aren't easy between Torres and Aragonés. The Atlético Number 9 is always the first to be substituted. Something that doesn't make him at all happy. On 7 September 2005, Spain play Serbia in a qualifying game for the Germany World Cup in Atlético's Vicente Calderón stadium. Torres comes onto the pitch in the starting line-up because Fernando Morientes – then a player at Liverpool – is injured. For El Niño to play in his home stadium in the national side is something very special. A big moment in his career.

But in the 56th minute, he's substituted. On in his place goes Tamudo. In the papers the following day, he reads that he's played without composure, not knowing how to use his skills, speed or strength. In other words, that in the national side he's not able to establish himself, to prove his worth or demonstrate his gifts. The encounter ends in a draw. The qualification process is getting bogged down. They need to win against Belgium. And it's typical that Aragonés puts him to the test in a difficult match like the one in the Heysel stadium in Brussels on 10 October 2005. He listens to El Niño's complaints about his repeated substitutions and takes a gamble on him. He puts him on the pitch in a complicated match. And it's there that he finally gets a big thorn out of his side. Two superb passes from José Antonio Reyes (then a player with Arsenal and a former team-mate of Torres from the junior national sides) and two goals that re-energise the team's drive for qualification. The first, in the 56th minute, is a wonderful strike. Reyes sends a long ball upfield, Torres gets behind the Belgian defence and takes off to thump the ball exactly in the space between the opposite post and crossbar.

Finally, El Niño does what everyone expects of a centre forward – finally he silences the doubts that his play was generating.

Spain qualify through the play-offs, without too many worries, beating Slovakia 5-1 in the first leg (including a penalty from Torres) and a one-all draw in the second to put them into the World Cup.

'I've dreamed loads of times about being in the World Cup,' says Fernando, adding with a smile, 'I want to be in the final and be champion of the world.' It won't be like that. Let's see what really happens …

In Leipzig's Zentralstadion on 14 June, 2006, the first match in Group H. Spain 4 Ukraine 1 – a victory, a perfect game and an 81st minute goal for Fernando is the icing on the cake. A move that starts with Puyol, the Barcelona defender getting free of the Ukrainian defence by making a *Rocastle Manoeuvre* (named after former Arsenal player David Rocastle) or *Marseille Turn* (after the version of the move used by French player, Zinedine Zidane), involving a 360-degree spin or turn with the ball, while on the move. He gives the ball to Arsenal midfielder, Cesc, who looks around and returns it to the sender, who heads it on and into the path of the Number 9. A great strike taken in mid-air and the Spanish media brand it goal of the tournament. Overcoming the team of Andriy Shevchenko (the 2004 European Footballer of the Year and Chelsea's then new signing) in such fashion sparks World Cup fever in Spain. The road to the final looks an easy downhill ride from here. Torres, who has scored his first goal in a World Cup final, insists: 'We are playing well. We're going step-by-step. We're going to get people talking. But we aren't the favourites – the favourites are those who've already won a World Cup and those who have more experience than us. They are the ones under pressure. Us, no. Because Spain hasn't won a World Cup, nor been in a final.'

Five days later it's Tunisia. Losing by a goal, Spain fight back. Against the rain and the North Africans' defence, Torres is decisive. He scores twice, to make it 2-1 and then a third to make sure. The first is typical Torres – an inviting long ball from Cesc and off he goes running, beating the Tunisian defenders on pace, then tricking the keeper to score before celebrating like an archer in homage to his former Atlético team-mate and idol, Kiko. The second is a cleanly executed penalty. He's brought down while about to fire in a header. He converts the spot-kick with a powerful shot. The keeper guesses correctly but the ball flashes between arm and leg. Torres is top-scorer for the tournament with three goals and Spain is through to the last sixteen.

But waiting there on 27 June is the France of Zinedine Zidane. The ex-Real Madrid player has already announced his retirement from football at the end of the World Cup. Three days before the game, Spanish sport daily, *Marca*, decides to stoke up the prematch atmosphere by running a front page headline: 'We are going to retire Zidane'. An attempt at humour that doesn't please the French captain, prompting him to comment: 'There's no need to talk before the match. It's a pity. There are people who talk who would be better off keeping quiet, like *Marca*. What they've written has hurt me.'

Fernando Torres doesn't take the same line as *Marca* and sends this message: 'It's important to see Zidane in this World Cup. We will try to beat them but I hope he doesn't retire and that we enjoy having him around for a lot longer and we hope it isn't his last match.' But even he is confident of the final result: 'France is a great team,' he says, 'but we believe in our football and in victory.' Spain reaching the last sixteen is one of the pleasant surprises of the competition. The players are young (24 is the average age compared with 29 for France), they have a squad bursting with upcoming talent playing abroad (Cesc Fabregas for example), they're hungry for victory and they want to surprise. They know how to play the ball and they never want to give up. All in all, they get so much out of playing that they have proudly come to symbolise the New Spain, which has achieved the top spots in Europe and across the world. From gastronomy (Ferran Adriá), sport (Fernando Alonso, Rafa Nadal), art (Miquel Barceló) and architecture (Santiago Calatrava). A country that doesn't feel itself inferior to anyone and a new footballing generation that doesn't carry the weight on its shoulders of endless failures. It can dream of overcoming its World Cup quarter-final taboo, always seen as an insurmountable obstacle.

The favourites by miles. They all say it. Even Spanish Prime Minister Luis Rodríguez Zapatero is convinced that against the French his fellow-countrymen will do it. The morning of the match, he calls Luis Aragonés to tell him: 'You have my support and my confidence.' An awful lot of confidence because on the other side is a France that is sad and depressed. They are a group of stars on the wane, so much so that someone has compared them to the Rolling Stones. They qualified as the second team in Group G (two draws and a victory), as a divided squad, overwhelmed with doubts and criticism. A group that found it difficult to get to Germany and continues down the same road. One recognises that they have skill and much experience but opposite the youthful attractions of Torres and his team-mates, these qualities don't count for much. More or less everyone thinks like this in Spain.

It's a pity that things don't turn out differently. Going a goal up via a David Villa penalty won't help them at all. Franck Ribéry, former Arsenal player Patrick Viera and Zidane – that old player destined for early retirement – will bury the Spanish dream. Once more they leave empty-handed. And there is even someone who reports that the defeat – or the crucial second French goal scored with a header from Viera – is the fault of Torres. 'I told one of them: "You, what you have to do is learn three words in French and when there is a free-kick, get close to Viera and distract him",' relates Luis Aragonés. It's a shame that at the crucial moment Torres, with the responsibility of keeping an eye on Viera, forgets the advice of his manager. When he gets near the dugout, Luis shouts at him: 'But didn't I tell you? What happened?' 'Boss, Viera had already learned Spanish.' An urban myth, one of the many jokes doing the rounds. What is certain is that Fernando hasn't forgotten the defeat against France. He remembers the Germany World Cup and because of this, damps down the euphoria after the resounding victory in the first match of Euro 2008.

Chapter 21
Sweden 1 Spain 2

14 June 2008

Oddly enough, the day after the hammering of the Russians and in the seclusion of Neustift, a charming Tyrolean village, there are long faces all round. What has happened? Luis Aragonés doesn't like Torres' reaction one little bit after he substituted him in the 54th minute. What had El Niño done? Nothing that might be on a par with Egyptian Ahmed Hossam Hussein Abdelhamid, better known as 'Mido', the Wigan Athletic striker previously with Tottenham and Middlesbrough. In the semi-final of the 2006 African Nations Cup, Mido lost his cool as he made his way to the bench, insulted the trainer, Hassam Shehata, by calling him a donkey and it almost came to a punch-up. He got himself a six-month suspension. No, the Liverpool striker hadn't gone that far, he hadn't made a big scene. It was just that, eight minutes into the second half, the electronic panel announcing the change had appeared and he had walked over to the bench with a seemingly peeved expression on his face. But what's all this? We're winning. I'm playing all right. I can really get stuck in too and score on the counter-attack and the gaffer takes me off – always me, it's always me who has to come off first. The change has really upset him. So much so, that when Luis offers him his hand to greet him off, Torres looks the other way and hurls the tracksuit top the kit-man passes him onto the ground. He sits on the bench looking miffed. It seems like history has rewound back to his first year at Atlético Madrid, when the Wise Man of Hortaleza would substitute him time and again. And at a press conference everyone imagines should be a happy event, Aragonés doesn't pass up the chance to tell all and sundry:

'I can understand it when a player gets annoyed, and I'm on Torres' side, but then a bit of decorum is important. This isn't the last of this. I agree with footballers getting angry when they're replaced, and it's happened to me, but these are special circumstances and the ones that play are just as important as those that don't. Those that don't play should be pissed off, sure. Otherwise, why would we have brought them here? But first let them be annoyed with themselves and then with whoever. Manners though, and I say this again, are what is most important.'

And to finish off he aims a very clear message at Torres: 'This isn't the last of this; one shouldn't let things like this go.'

A pretty harsh reproach, which leaves the journalists nonplussed. For example, Enrique Ortego, writing for *ABC*, thinks that 'Luis could have just said nothing and had a quiet word alone with the player, as he has already done.' But Ortego, like a lot of other commentators, understands why he did it: 'He wanted to show public opinion that he's not going to take any cheek from any players. He doesn't want a repeat of what happened in the World Cup in Germany, when some who weren't in the starting line-up for the first match didn't contribute towards a good atmosphere.'

And what does El Niño say? He plays the whole thing down: 'There's no big deal. I've had a chat with the boss and it's just another change, there's really no problem. I've never had any problems with trainers. I just think it's a shame that these things are being singled out so much when Spain has just beaten Russia 4-1.' And in front of the Tele 5 cameras he adds: 'It's always the same. The code of conduct in the dressing room that Luis has taught me since I was sixteen is the one that should apply to me in all this. What happens in the dressing room is straightened out in the dressing room. I would never snub the boss. All of us players are with our national trainer right up to the very end.' The controversy ends there. So much so, that Luis says: 'And I'm not angry, not bothered at all. What happened with Torres doesn't matter in the slightest. I had a chat with him in training, but that's nothing new. I had him as a player at Atlético since he was a kid. He's almost like my son and I've always given him what I believe to be useful little tips.'

After the explanations the gaffer confirms that Fernando is set to start in the Sweden match at Innsbruck: 'He's key to my plans,' he says. That's a certainty, but the national coach asks Fernando to do a job he doesn't do at Liverpool. He asks him to do what he used to do at Atlético, which is to drop wide to create spaces and make runs to draw people in, which can make life hard in front of goal. So much so that, with the national team, Fernando has only scored two goals in 33 outings – a paltry haul for the striker who, in the season just ended, caused a furore in the Premier League.

And so the Sweden match has become a do-or-die affair for Fernando. Will he manage to do what has been asked of him? Will he score? Will he, after all, be at ease as part of the *Roja*? Everyone is waiting on Torres as though he were Godot. But this time Godot arrives on time. It's Fernando who gets the scoreboard moving. An emphatic reply to the doubts sparked by his replacement and the subsequent statements from the gaffer. It's fifteen minutes into the first half and Luis' prepared plan to topple the towering Swedes swings into action. Because Torres' goal is pure strategy, somebody has dubbed it a 'laboratory goal'. Corner: Xavi, from the corner to the Swedish goalkeeper's right, kicks it short for Villa, who comes in to receive the ball along the touchline and draws in a central defender. David nudges it back, where another David comes in – Silva, the Canary Islands man. From the corner of the penalty area the Valencia midfield linkman with the strikers knocks in a waist-high cross-shot with a lot of swerve. Three Spaniards (Capdevilla, Ramos and Torres) are waiting to pounce on goal. The quickest is El Niño, who gets in ahead of his marker Hansson, sticks out his leg, and with the tip of his boot – or rather the studs – taps the ball into Isaksson's goal. Fernando is back among the goals. He hadn't scored with the *Roja* since 12 September, against Latvia. He's satisfied because the set pieces and tactical plays practiced in training sessions have worked. He won't score another goal until the final, against Germany, but his contribution against the yellow-shirts is vital.

El Niño is finally a star, his elusive runs cause pandemonium among central defenders, his ability to shake people off opens up space, he battles for every ball and he puts in the teamwork by dropping back to defend. And he also acts as a peacemaker between the referee and his team-mates when they claim a penalty against Silva that wasn't blown. And one shouldn't forget his contribution when Villa made it 2-1 in a last-gasp attempt when a draw seemed certain (the Swedes had drawn level through Zlatan Ibrahimovic, thanks to a mistake from Sergio Ramos). The miracle happened courtesy of *Villa Maravilla* (Villa the Wonder-worker), yet Fernando assisted with a monster pass (over 50 metres) from Capdevilla by jumping up, bamboozling an opponent, and allowing the ball to reach the Spanish Number 7, 'El Guaje' Villa, who sees the *Roja* through to the quarter-finals. On 15 June the talk is all about 'the finest pairing in

Europe' – Torres and Villa, with 51 goals this season they are the most lethal duo. Everyone concurs, admitting that they admire and envy the Number 7 and Number 9, who have put together five goals and two assists in two games. No one in the European Football Championship has done a better job. There is a shower of praise. The first to step up is Aragonés himself: 'They have a perfect rapport because they have unique qualities and an amazing turn of speed. They are a major bonus for the team. They can get goals out of nothing.' Pepe, a central defender with Portugal and Real Madrid, says: 'With this brace of strikers Spain can really go places in the European Championship.' And Ruud Van Nistelrooy, the Netherlands and Real Madrid striker, observes that: 'Villa and Torres are at a spectacular level, can score a hell of a lot of goals and Fernando is playing as well as he does in the Premier League.'

The protagonists fit together well and cannot stop complimenting each other. El Niño says good things about Villa: 'I think he is the best goal-scorer in Europe. And he is bound to top-score in this tournament.' And Villa waxes lyrical about Torres. Rumours that they were at loggerheads have been quashed. Pepe Reina, the Liverpool and Spain goalkeeper, being a mutual friend, has helped bring them together. To celebrate getting through to the quarter-finals the three get together with their families for a *fabada* (an Asturian bean stew) in a Neustift restaurant.

The third game against Greece is a formality and Aragonés can rest 9 members of his usual starting line-up. Torres and Villa don't play. Greece starts by getting ahead but Rubén de la Red and Dani Güiza put that right. In the quarter-finals on 22 June, in Vienna's Ernst Happel stadium, the world champions, the *azzurri*, await.

Monday, pizza. We'll polish it off like we did Italy on Sunday. That is the view of many Iberian people and their media as they tip a wink at the gallery. They all say they are certain that Cannavaro and company won't be any trouble at all. They are really confident about *Villa Maravilla* and 'the Kid' Torres, the big players, and about the old guy on the bench. They are certain that this time, thanks to Spain's better crop of young players coming through, they will lift the curse of the quarter-finals – the customary burial ground of the *Roja*'s dreams of ultimate triumph. They swear that this time they will break their jinx with Italy: 88 years of defeat in official competitions. With one stroke they will avenge the slight of being knocked out in the quarter-finals of USA 94 – Luis Enrique ending up with a bloody nose after being elbowed by Mauro Tassotti.

But it doesn't end there. For the eleven wearing the red shirt, Italy is the icing on the cake. Having sent the European champions (Greece) home, it's all-out for the world champs. But these musings hide the fact that the Spaniards are scared that, once again, their great adventure might come a cropper. It will prove otherwise. After 120 minutes nobody has scored. Torres makes no odds in the 84 minutes he plays before being substituted by Güiza, and neither does Villa. Fate will be decided from the penalty spot. Saint Casillas keeps two out and Cesc Fabregas – the 21-year-old who had never taken one in his entire sporting career – makes no mistake. He nets for the final 4-3 scoreline. 'That's where we won the European Championship,' Torres recalls months afterwards. 'I think we celebrated more that day than in the final.' A final that would come around after a resounding 3-0 win against Guus Hiddink's Russia. Torres tries everything and more to find the goal, but to no avail. He is replaced by Güiza, who keeps his rendezvous with the net.

On Sunday, 29 June, Spain will play their third final after 24 years out in the cold. David Villa won't be in the game. In the 30th minute of the semi-final, while lining up a free-kick he feels a stabbing pain from behind and five minutes later he drops to the ground, head between his legs, in floods of tears. His European Championship is over. Fernando Torres will play as a lone striker against Germany.

Chapter 22
Germany 0 Spain 1

29 June 2008

When the players walk onto the stage of the Ernst Happel stadium in Vienna and Iker Casillas, captain of the *Roja*, receives from Michel Platini the European Championship cup, King Juan Carlos asks Fernando Torres what they give him to eat in England to make him so strong.

Earlier, three hours earlier, another old man, Luis Aragonés, gives Torres a kiss. On the eve of the final, Aragonés had said: 'I must tell El Niño something. Tomorrow, after the meeting [with the players], I will have a private talk with him and I will explain it to him then.' he says. The manager knows that the boy from Fuenlabrada isn't happy with his performances, so before the match he makes a prediction: 'Today you are going to score two goals,' he says, then he touches his forehead as if to banish bad omens and then gives him a kiss like you might kiss a favourite son who makes you furious but whom you forgive everything.

It's the same gesture that he made many years earlier when Torres was a youngster at Atlético Madrid. Then, he scored. And ever since then, the Number 9 has stuck to the same ritual. He gets on the team bus listening to very loud music through the earphones of his iPod, and he gets off the bus in the same way. And he recalls a meeting with another old man, in May at Las Rozas, La Ciudad del Fútbol, where the Spanish national side was preparing for Euro 2008: 'Are you the one who scored that goal?' Torres asks. Marcelino Martínez, the Zaragoza forward who clinched the European Championship victory for Spain at home in 1964 against the USSR – the first and last major win for Spain in 100 – looks at him and responds: 'Yes, I am. Let's hope you can do the same and achieve something really great in Austria.' Fernando thinks about this for days – he wants to be the new Marcelino.

In the dressing room, he knows that the Championship is slipping from his grasp. There are only 90 minutes left and he still hasn't managed to make his mark in the tournament. He's certainly played well, but he's only scored one goal, whereas Villa – who will win the Golden Boot – has scored four and Güiza, a substitute, has notched up two. Yet again, despite an outstanding season at Liverpool, Torres has not become the national hero he longs to be. But there's still the final to come – the most important game. He leaves the dressing room and, as always, stands behind Sergio Ramos with a face that indicates he wants to be left alone. Don't touch me. But the Wise Man of Hortaleza is ready for a joke, as Torres recounts a year later:

'For several days before the final match with Germany, the gaffer didn't stop talking about Wallace. At the beginning we were all looking at each other not knowing who was he talking about. Until we realised he was talking about Michael Ballack. Then he told us that he knew his name but that he called him Wallace because that's what he felt like calling him. But if you know Luis, you can imagine the actual expression he used. It didn't stop there, though. When we were in the tunnel leading to the pitch, Aragonés went on in front of us, winked in our direction, and went to Ballack. He said to him, in Spanish, "Good afternoon, Mr Wallace", and went on speaking to him for a while. The German didn't understand a word and Aragonés didn't understand what Ballack was saying to him, either. We couldn't help it, but we were laughing our heads off as we went out to play the final.'

A nice way to start the most important game of your life …

And then, in the first fifteen minutes of the game, Spain stutter. They're uptight and can't reproduce the form they've shown up to this point. On the pitch, in the stadium and across the country – for once crazy about its team – they fear the worst, that the giants in white shirts will slot home a couple of goals without even trying and finish the game before it's started. But Spain get their act together with the help of Torres. In the 23rd minute Sergio Ramos crosses the ball from the right and Torres leaps up for a header, hitting the ball full-on. He doesn't know how he manages to do it, given that Mertesacker is two heads taller than him, but El Niño manages all the same and the ball hits the post. It could have been the first goal – it will be just the beginning of Spain's recovery. The clock in the Happel stadium shows the time as eighteen minutes past nine and on the pitch, 33 minutes have been played. Marcos Senna, the man from Sao Paolo, steals the ball in midfield. He looks around and sees Xavi through a crowd of German players. He's far from Mertesacker and next to Frings. The Barça player sends a pass into space, where, from behind, Fernando is arriving at speed. Good control and past Philipp Lahm. The Number 16 looked to have had it under control. 'Xavi's pass was spectacular but Lahm was already in a good position,' Torres will explain later: 'If he had gone a bit to the right the ball would have been for the keeper, but I think that maybe he doesn't have a good understanding with Lehmann. He gets too confident, he relaxes … This gives me a fraction of a second in which I am able to move to the other side and seize the opportunity to shoot. Maybe if the pitch had been dry I could have tried bending it but the ball skates across and enters just inside the post. I knew it was going to go in.' It's the goal he's been dreaming about. Fernando Torres puts his thumb in his mouth like a dummy. It's dedicated to his nephew, Hugo, the son of Israel, born little more than a month ago, then he dives across the Viennese grass. He shouts his head off and is lost in a sea of hugs from his team-mates. He doesn't forget Villa, who's not playing in the final. He reciprocates the dedication that El Guaje had made to him in the first match of the tournament. 'This victory is for David, who has been suffering on the bench like one of the fans,' he says.

Germany are nowhere. Michael Ballack, whose eyebrow is split open after a clash of heads, is doing all he can to motivate his side. He gets furious and takes it out on everyone, the referee included, but he is a symbol of his team's impotence.

In the second half there are chances for Ramos and Dani Güiza, but for the Spanish it's hard work. In the 78th minute Torres is taken off, but then comes the final, liberating whistle of Roberto Rossetti. And the Spanish party starts. Everyone goes mad on the pitch and across the country, where, after 44 years, they can finally shout: 'Champions! Champions!'

'When you are a boy, and see these matches on TV, you dream of being there. Now that I am here I find it difficult to realise what I've achieved. At last justice has been done and this team has recovered its due place in Europe,' says Fernando Torres as he walks off the field, the Spanish flag wrapped around him. At a press conference, having been chosen best player of the game – as he was twice in previous junior European Championships – he makes an intelligent and concise speech for the world's media: 'I am happy because Spanish football needed a success like this one after so many years. Besides, this triumph is really going to help football in general because it has been the best team that has won the European Championship, a team that's had a great tournament, and that doesn't always happen. We are proud that we have promoted the idea of attractive football, which is enjoyable to watch, even for a neutral spectator. We are a team that knows how to use the ball. This has been a success for both the manager, who persevered with the idea, and for the players, who knew how to take the concept on board and apply it. The group is the main weapon of this team. All of us – the players who have been on the pitch a lot, and those who have been on the pitch less, as well as the technicians and the rest of the staff – have to feel just as happy. It is the victory of being together. To win is always good, but to do it like this is even better. We have kept the style, our way of playing throughout the whole tournament. And we've won. That shows that it is possible to play well and get results at the same time.' Almost a masterclass in the art of football and the Beautiful Game – traditionally the territory of Brazilians. Torres lays claim to a certain style. His goal matches this philosophy and it's a sign of how the mentality of the national side has changed. 'Yes, it's another indication that this national side has known how to mature. Maybe before, we've lacked those elements, like continuing to chase loose balls or the quality of the team's defending. Now we are champions and we have more experience to go after more trophies. Let's hope this is just the beginning.' He's just won but already El Niño is looking to the future, but he's clearly one of those people in life who are never satisfied. As he waits for his future to unfold, he knows he has scored the goal of a lifetime; he is aware that he has had a profound influence – just like Marcelino – and he knows that he's entered 'in people's hearts and in the history of Spain for ever'.

Next day the headlines in the Spanish press pay homage to this sensation:

'Torres, the Golden Kid, scores a goal for history' – *El Mundo*

'A goal from 'The Kid' Fernando Torres gives birth to the first champion team after waiting 44 years for the delivery' – *La Vanguardia*

'Thank you, *Niño*, you are a legend' – *AS*

'El Niño has become a man' – *Sport*

'Marcelino's heir' – *Público*

'Torres goal reaches mythical heights' – *Marca*

And it is not only the Spanish press that praises him. Newspapers from *The Times*, to the *New York Times*, from *La Gazzetta dello Sport* to *L'Équipe*, from the *Guardian* to *Clarín*, Torres is the unquestionable hero. He's the King, agree both *The Times* and *La Gazzetta dello Sport*. After being hidden from the rest of Europe he has taken the sceptre and crown and assumed the throne of Europe. Journalists from around the world recount his life and his performance as if talking about Orlando. Even his tattoos are talked about, such as the Number 9 in Gothic letters on his right arm, his name in the *tengwar* alphabet as created by J.R.R. Tolkien in the *Lord of the Rings*, and on one of his legs, in Roman numerals, the date 7 July 2001, which is said to be the date of his first kiss with Olalla. The ratings given to the Little Prince by journalists are exceptional. *The Times*, ungenerously, gives him an 8, saying: 'Magnificent. Did it time and again with Liverpool last season and did it time and again last night. No one could stop him.' And the picture on so many front pages is that of his arms outstretched like a red angel, Lehmann beaten and on the floor and the ball with its chequered panels rolling towards the net.

The next day it's back home for the parade with the cup through the streets of Madrid and a 24-hour party. At 19.55 on 1 July, the team plane lands at Madrid Barajas airport. The faces of the players betray fatigue – they haven't slept much because of all the celebrations, first in Vienna and then in Neustift, where the squad trained. But no one wants to stop the fun at the moment. An open-top bus takes two hours to make its way to the Plaza de Colón, where, waiting for their heroes, are one million fans and a big stage, where Pepe Reina will be the master of ceremonies. Fernando Torres places himself at the front corner with the cup in his hands and his red shirt. From the crowd a boy calls out and hands him flags of Spain and Atlético Madrid. He holds them and waves them aloft.

Chapter 23
Ambitious

*Conversation with Liverpool and Spain
goalkeeper, Pepe Reina*

'I gave my son two bits of advice: to be a good team-mate and, during the match, keep your eye solely on the ball. He's a great goalkeeper and I don't say that as a father but as someone who knows about these things,' declared Miguel Reina during Euro 2008.

And he is right to say that he knows about these things because Miguel, the father of José Manuel Reina Páez – better known as Pepe – was also a leading goalkeeper. He played 312 matches in the Primera Liga with Córdoba, Barcelona and Atlético Madrid – the club where he ended his career in 1980. He won one league title, two Spanish Cup trophies, one Copa de Ferias cup, an Intercontinental Cup and two Zamora Trophies for the best Spanish League goalkeeper. His worst moment was losing the 1974 European Cup final against Bayern Munich. His son, who he admits is 'better than me', went through the same bitter experience in Athens in 2006, losing the Champions League final against Milan but, two years later, got the satisfaction of winning the big continental title, Euro 2008, with Spain.

And it is his son, who, as a child, wanted to be a winger but instead – thanks to his support – became the goalkeeper for Liverpool. Pepe arrived in the city of The Beatles in July 2005 and Rafa Benítez described him as the best Spanish goalkeeper. He came from Villarreal, where he was on loan from Barcelona, the club where he had worked his way up from the junior ranks to the senior squad. He won two Intertoto Cups and was renowned as a penalty-stopper.

In his last season with Villarreal, he saved seven out of nine. Within a short time at Liverpool he managed to push out Jerzy Dudek, the hero of the winning side in the Champions League final in Istanbul, gradually gaining the confidence of manager, team-mates, fans, and increasing his reputation. For three years running (2006–08) he won the Golden Glove award for the highest number of clean sheets in the Premier League, only just missing out (by one) on a fourth consecutive title in 2009 to Manchester United's Edwin Van Sar. The goalkeeping son of a goalkeeper has become more famous than his father because, explained Miguel, 'He is a very safe, all-round keeper, who dominates his area and who is also very good with his feet.' But Pepe is not only a great player, he is a charming character, the ideal dressing room companion who can give you a boost when things are going badly or when someone is feeling down. And that's not all, the Number 25 of Liverpool (Number 23 in the national side) is also very funny and a bit of a performer. Few Spaniards have forgotten his display on the podium in Madrid's Plaza de Colón, the day after the Euro 2008 victory. With microphone in hand he introduced all his team-mates, inventing a few humorous lines for each of them, and then almost lost his voice during a six-minute audience participation routine, which made a million people go wild with delight: 'It was an unforgettable moment for everyone, for them and for me. It was a moment of celebration and affection for my team-mates. We were all on a high and it just came out like that. Nothing was prepared, everything was improvised. The truth is I'm proud of having done it and that people have fond memories of it.'

And what are your memories of the winning goal?
'I remember this huge suspense, as the ball kind of swept its way into the goal, floating through the air before brushing the net next to the post. Once we saw it was actually inside, there was an explosion of joy. We had put ourselves in front in a European Championship final after so many years and having suffered so much in qualifying. It was the best moment of those two years and the deserved result of a hard campaign.'

What was the hardest moment of Euro 2008?
'The match against Italy was difficult. We suffered because we were up against a team that fought really well, typically Italian, but above all because there was a psychological barrier. The quarter-finals were where Spain always lost. It was the tensest moment but I think the football, in the end, was where we won it. If someone deserved it over the 120 minutes, it was Spain. We wanted to win the match, the Italians wanted a draw. We went to penalties and we went through in the way that Italy is used to going through and we arrived in the semi-finals on merit.'

Most countries envied Spain's striker duo of Villa and Torres. Is it true that it was you who got them to understand each other better over a 'fabada' (an Asturian bean stew)?
'I get on well with El Guaje and Fernando, I've known them both for some time. We met up with the families and they got to know each other a bit better as well. In the end the friends of my friends get on well with each other. It's a source of pride for me, but I don't want to give myself the credit – it's normal that two good people get on well together. And the story about the *fabada* is true. El Guaje's mother made it and we ate it after the match against Sweden and I can assure you we all enjoyed it.'

Talking of food, it seems that your wife's tortilla (Spanish omelette) has helped Torres adapt to Liverpool?
'I'm lucky to have a wife, Yolanda, who is a fantastic cook and a very good hostess. Fernando and Olalla live about 50 metres away. We like to meet up with them and other team-mates to have lunch, dinner, or just have a good time together. When you're outside your own country, it's nice to be with people from your own culture and to enjoy oneself as much as possible. We are a very homely family, we have two daughters, Grecia and Alma, and when friends come round we like to have a barbecue or watch a film. We also go out as a group and in Liverpool there are places that aren't at all bad.'

What advice did you give Fernando to help him when he arrived?
'Fernando is very good at getting his head round different situations and that's why he's adapted to Liverpool so quickly and so well. He knows exactly where things stand and is extremely mature for his age. He very quickly felt comfortable here, so much so that now it's Fernando who's giving me advice and not the other way round. When I arrived at Liverpool, it was Fernando Morientes who helped me a lot and I try to do the same with whoever comes, making an open invitation to visit me at my home, giving advice and making myself available for whatever they need.'

Did you ever imagine that Fernando would do what he did in his first season with the Reds?
'I think that not even he expected it. To be truthful, no one expected it because he had some serious difficulties – a new league, new team-mates and a different way of playing. For those reasons, you have to give him a lot of credit for his 33 goals and I think that Fernando can feel proud of what he did.'

But this last season hasn't been fantastic …
'No, it hasn't. Because first, to repeat what he did in the 2007–08 season was almost impossible and second, injuries haven't been too much help for poor Fernando. I hope the next season will again be brilliant. I'm sure it will be.'

How do you rate the 2008–09 season?
'Well, I think we've improved as a team but if we're not winning titles one can't say that it's been a good season. We always have to try to win trophies and this year that hasn't been the case, but what we have done is beat the club points record and we've only lost two league games. We've achieved a lot and we have fought right to the end to try to win the Premier League. We can be proud of what we've done but we're still one rung below Manchester United. We have a Champions League place but no titles and we're not happy about this. Nevertheless, the atmosphere in the dressing room is good and we have the feeling we have improved. I think that big things will be happening to us in the coming years.'

How is Torres seen from the perspective of the Liverpool goal?
'He's a player that makes all of us a little better. He has skill, speed and directness, which all help the team. For those who play around him, he makes their passing easier and he can turn a bad ball to his advantage. For me, from behind, the counter-attacks that we have practised are a lot easier when I can take advantage of his speed. It's something we have talked about, we know each other well and we know when to do it in a match. In a given moment, I can find him with a ball behind the opponents' defence.'

And as an adversary?

'Let's just say I have suffered considerably. While I was at Villarreal, he scored against me on various occasions. It's strange because the people who've scored most against me are him and Villa and now they two are good friends. They are footballers who, when you play against them, you always suspect that something bad's going to happen and Fernando is one of those. I don't know exactly how to explain it but it's a feeling of danger. When he has the ball, your goal isn't safe.'

Since when have you known each other?

'I got to know Fernando in the national Under-21 side, we were both there but it's really been in Liverpool where I've had the pleasure to really get to know him, as a person, and a close friend.'

What is the quality that strikes you most about Fernando?

'His ambition. Yes, he is a very ambitious player, and for that reason he comes out on top. He's never content to sit back with what he has, he's always trying to improve himself. At all moments, in each match, he looks for the things that haven't worked out, he studies errors he's made and works very hard to do it better the next time.'

Torres is a star of the team?

'Yes, Steve and Fernando are our stars and that's how it should be because they really are the two players who make the difference. Fernando has created a place for himself amongst the Liverpool greats because he's very charismatic, a good guy, a warm guy, a worker and that's how the people of Liverpool see him and they really appreciate him.'

And he's also the 'pin-up boy' of the team …

'That's not how he appears to me. Men are not my thing but I understand that Fernando has that attraction. He's tall, strong, handsome and he's got hair – what's more it's blond – not like me!'

Chapter 24

Atlético de Madrid 1 Liverpool 1

22 October 2008

No, El Niño isn't here tonight. Not on the pitch and not in the stands of the Vicente Calderón stadium. The previous week in Brussels, at the King Baudouin stadium, against Belgium, his luck runs out. Twelve minutes into the game the Number 9 of Spain's national side feels an intense pain in his thigh. He pulls up and asks to go off. At the end of the game (1-2 in Spain's favour) Fernando leaves, head bowed, without speaking to the journalists waiting for him. His return home to Atlético the following week for a Champions League tie is now in doubt. The verdict, which comes the next day, leaves no room for appeal: a small tear in his right hamstring. The same problem he suffered back in August. The prognosis: three weeks out.

Enrique Cerezo, the president of Atlético, invites him anyhow through Rafael Benítez. His manager gives the green light but Fernando says he won't be able to be there. The insignia of gold and diamonds that his ex-team-mates have wanted to give him to recognise his years of service to the club will have to wait for another time. On his website he expresses his gratitude and apologises to the fans of his former club, saying: 'After meeting with the manager, the doctor and the physiotherapists, we have decided that the best thing is for me to stay in Liverpool because I would lose two days of recuperation. At this stage in the season, we cannot permit that kind of luxury. As the fans of Atlético are already more than aware, I want to play again as soon as possible and I'm working to get myself ready.' He adds that, for him, not being able to play at the Calderón is very upsetting. He doesn't use these words lightly, because ever since Atlético and Liverpool were drawn together in Group D, he's been longing for 22 October with the expectation of a child anticipating the visit of Father Christmas: 'I really can't wait for the match at the Calderón to arrive. I feel curious about what my return will be like and how the fans will greet me, although I'm convinced they have good memories, as do I.'

At first, the game's venue seems in doubt: after police clashes with Marseille fans and racist abuse was targeted at Marseille's black players, UEFA decides to sanction Atlético by moving the club's next two scheduled home games. But the punishment is suspended, and the game will be played at the Calderón. Torres will be back after sixteen months' absence and is already imagining what he will do. He'll arrive at the stadium and greet many friends, then get changed – something strange – in the visitors' dressing room. He'll run onto the field acknowledging the cheers of the fans, he'll be there in the official photo with the ballboys he knows so well. If he scores, he won't celebrate – it would be silly, a lack of respect for the place, and for the people who watched him grow as a footballer. But he's sure to play the best he can. He wants to put in an unforgettable performance and help his Liverpool team to victory. But all these ideas and dreams are put to one side. However, even if Fernando Torres doesn't set foot on the pitch at the Calderón, no one's going to forget about him – no one among the 3,000 Reds travelling from Liverpool and no one among the 50,000 Atlético fans. The two groups of fans merge together and arrive at the stadium together peacefully. Once inside, they all invoke the name of their idol. The Atlético fans sing out to Fernando as they always have, to the tune of 'Can't take my eyes off of you'. The Anfield faithful respond with 'Liverpool's Number Nine'. And then, at the end of the game, the visitors sing out 'You'll Never Walk Alone', and the whole stadium erupts in applause. A great evening for the supporters, who head home happy with a draw that does both sides justice.

For the return leg at Anfield, Torres looks to have recovered. Rafa Benítez gives him a 70 per cent chance of playing. It's not clear if he'll make the starting line-up, or if he'll be on the bench, but everyone's counting on the Number 9. They know he's desperate to play. He himself hopes he'll pull through, but on the morning of the game he fails a fitness test. There's nothing he can do: 'It seems I'm cursed,' he says. Unfortunately, during the first half of the season, injuries among the forwards are a regular problem for the Reds. These injuries prevent Liverpool from unleashing the torrent of goals of the previous season. Fernando scores again on 1 February (twice against Chelsea) – it's eight months since his last home goal and 119 days since his last Premiership goal (5 October against Manchester City). Even if he's unlucky on the evening of Tuesday, 4 November, Fernando Torres is still at Anfield. An hour before kick-off, accompanied by Olalla, he walks onto the field to respond to the Atlético fans gathered in the Century Stand. 'Fernando Torres! Fernando Torres!' they shout enthusiastically. And then, inside the stadium, many reunions with people he's known for much of his life. The game begins and the TV cameras pick him up. The Kop starts to sing. Maxi, his Argentine ex-team-mate, disappoints him by putting the *rojiblancos* one up.

Fernando closes his eyes and bites his lip, but when he sees the joy of the Atlético players his irritation passes.

Liverpool push forward, creating chances, but can't make the breakthrough. The Number 9 despairs. He throws up an arm as Liverpool claim a penalty after Perea handles. He seems to press his team-mates to play more efficiently. He swears as a chance goes begging. The clock shows 93 minutes and 43 seconds – the game looks to be over, but then the referee blows for a penalty that leaves the visitors fuming. To them, nothing happened. Robbery, plain and simple. At first, Torres does not react, but then applauds the decision. Gerrard steps up. As usual, El Niño doesn't want to watch his team taking a penalty. This time he doesn't know what to do. He buries his face in his hands and hardly dares look. A goal. He waves his fists and celebrates his captain's goal, a gesture that earns the reproach of one of the visitors from Madrid. El Niño can't understand why. For him it's logical to celebrate. No treachery, no mistake. It's a view shared by the members of the *Peña Atlética Fernando Torres* fan club from Fuenlabrada. That Tuesday in November they're at Anfield, together with 2,600 other *rojiblancos*. They're surprised by the affection in which their hero is held by Liverpool fans. They swap scarves, flags, handshakes, addresses and pictures of El Niño (2009 calendars printed by the *Peña* with a photo of Fernando as a youngster or celebrating Spain's Euro 2008 victory). They've even managed to hang their scarves around the mannequin sporting Torres' shirt in the Liverpool Club Store, in Williamson Square in the heart of the city.

The night when Spain play in Seville against Fabio Capello's England, they turn up at Tommy's Café in Calle Ferrocarril street in Fuenlabrada. It's just down the road from the station underpass where Moroccan immigrants are drinking mint tea, eating kebabs and anxiously watching their national side playing a friendly in Casablanca against the Czech Republic. Spain's game, however, has not yet kicked off.

It's nine o'clock and there's time, over a beer and a plate of well-cut cured loin of pork, for Pasqual Blázquez, José Antonio Camacho and Tony Roldán to swap stories. They are three of the members of the *Peña*, which has some 150 members and continues to keep its full name, even though El Niño has long since left Atlético. They've known Fernando since he was a child and followed his progress from the juniors to the first team. On the wall, a newspaper cutting recalls Fernando's first call-up to the national side under Iñaki Sáez. A signed Liverpool shirt is a symbol of the present. There are photos of the blond, freckled lad with the president, the secretary and the treasurer, which show a mutual respect. Fernando, a traitor? Not at all. 'There are no recriminations against him. He's gone because the club didn't respond with the signing he wanted. They didn't know how to build a competitive team that could fight in Europe. Fernando has done an awful lot for Atlético. There's nothing to reproach him for,' says Roldán. 'He's been our flag-bearer – one of the greatest in our footballing history. He's at the same level as Gárate, the most effective Number 9 we've ever had (José Eulogio Gárate, an Argentinian from Sarandi who played eleven seasons with Atlético, scoring a total of 123 goals) and at the same level of Adelardo (Adelardo Rodríguez Sánchez, seventeen seasons between 1959 and 1976, and 112 goals) or even Aragonés himself,' explains Camacho.

'Real Madrid had Raúl and we had El Niño,' adds Pascual. 'His departure was necessary, above all because he needed to measure himself against the great European players and so, signing for Liverpool has been good for him. But his transfer has also been beneficial for the club, which has been able to sign Simao, Luis García and Diego Forlán and one has to say that the Uruguayan is doing very well. We will see if they also sell him.'

Roldán interrupts the thoughts of Camacho: 'Have you seen the last interview with El Niño, saying that he will never go to Real Madrid. He's a player who feels the club colours, which is a difficult thing in this era of millions.'

The three of them chat about values, about feelings for Atlético. They tell their guest that, to be a *rojiblanco* is almost like a religious calling. 'You believe and you go on believing, even if miracles don't happen. It's important not to lose faith.' They recall that Chamartín (the Bernabéu, the stadium of their main rivals) is like an opera, with everyone seemingly reluctant to get involved in the game. The Calderón, on the other hand, is where to find passion for real football. 'Indeed, it is almost the same atmosphere as it is in Anfield. The fans are similar and absolutely in love with Fernando. We have met him recently and he's very happy there. His father told me that as well,' confirms Camacho. And he explains: 'I was sure he was going to be successful because there they play in the same style as Fernando.'

They remember the time of Jesús Gil, someone points out that, with him, Torres never had problems and that, in fact, he was always protected by Gil. And he was opposed to the sale of his crown jewel against the opinion of many who thought that the player was at the top of his game and therefore should be sold before his value declined. Camacho goes back in time to remember the shy boy, who, when playing with *Mario's Holanda*, succeeded in filling the stadium. He talks about Torres' family in complimentary terms.

Roldán comes back to the present, to 29 June 2008, when the bar was packed to the rafters and nobody from the *Peña* or from the neighbourhood wanted to miss El Niño's final: 'We were all convinced that he was going to score that day. It's a shame', adds Pasqual, 'that he never got to play at the

Calderón, but we're confident that he'll come back one day to finish his career here, where he started, where people still think so much of him.' The conversation ends. The television is showing the start of Spain v England and El Niño is on the pitch.

Chapter 25

A danger

Conversation with Liverpool and Spain defender, Álvaro Arbeloa

The shirt is red, but over the part which covers the heart is the badge of the Spanish national team, the Real Federación Española de Fútbol (Royal Spanish Football Federation). Sitting on the steps that lead to the residential area of the Federation's Ciudad del Fútbol de Las Rozas training complex, 12 miles from the centre of Madrid, the former Real Madrid and Deportivo La Coruña player – currently Liverpool's Number 17 – chats away happily. The weather is wonderful – a deep-blue sky without a cloud in sight, and on the horizon, the tops of the Sierra mountains still covered with a light sprinkling of snow, while the sun beats down with almost summer-like strength.

'At Liverpool, we dream of weather like this. It only happens a few times a year,' laughs Spain's Number 26 from the western city of Salamanca. The training session for the national side is scheduled to take place in the late afternoon. Before that there is time to ask a few questions.

Does the team feel different when Torres isn't there, like in the match with Atlético?
'Yes, a lot. It's normal because we don't have a squad like Manchester United. If they don't have Rooney, they can bring on Tévez, if they don't have Tévez, they can use

Berbatov. We have Fernando, who is the best in the world and when he is missing, it shows. When he's there, upfront, you know that he is going to 'create danger' at any moment because his presence alone creates insecurity and Kuyt, Riera and Steve take advantage of that. When he's on the pitch, he gives us total confidence.'

You were in the team for the Liverpool-Chelsea match on 1 February 2009. How do you remember that game?
'It was very important, above all because we'd just come from four consecutive draws. We weren't in a good situation; we'd lost the league leadership and second place as well. If we didn't beat the Blues we'd be several points adrift of Manchester United. We were better than them but the ball just wasn't hitting the back of the net. Luckily, in the end, came the two goals from Torres.'

It was an important match for him as well, wasn't it?
'Fernando was coming back from injury. It had been months since he'd scored and, with just a few minutes remaining, he scored the first and then, in extra time, got the second. Well, everyone knows that for us, Fernando is hugely important.'

How would you describe Torres, seen from behind, from the Reds' defence?
'A danger, absolutely. I was lucky to play against him with Deportivo a few weeks before I left for Anfield. Fernando and I were talking about it just the other day.'

Lucky or unlucky?
'I think that one is always lucky to play against great players. Well, OK, as long as they don't make it too bad for you. But the truth is that Fernando is a spectacular striker – he never

gives a ball up for lost; physically, he is a phenomenon, he has incredible power and, above all, enormous confidence in himself, which makes him one of the best in the world, if not the best.'

Liverpool has helped you get into the national side and turned Torres into one of the best players in the world. How did it happen?
'Well, I think it's very important to play at a club like Liverpool, which is in the Champions League and competing for the Premier League title. It's an international shop window – it's clear that a player's value increases. But one can't ignore the fact that, in order to get there and to play at Anfield, you have to show your worth. And it's no easy feat to be there. Fernando, apart from the fact that English football, because of its characteristics, suits him better, he doesn't have the pressure that he had here (in Spain), he doesn't have all the media on top of him. He's been able to dedicate his time to training, improving his play and to enjoying his football, and that's been really important. You could say he's been let off the leash.'

And in two years he's already an idol …
'There, he's a legend like Ian Rush or Kenny Dalglish – players that spent years at Liverpool and won a lot of trophies. Fernando's been compared to them and he has been put on the same level.'

Of course you, together with Fernando Torres and Pepe Reina, have met Dalglish, Souness and Sammy Lee in person. What were your impressions?
'It was a bit like going back to your childhood and reviving your idols. Once you are a footballer you forget when you were a kid and the excitement of seeing those players.

The day we had dinner with them, for Michael Robinson's (Spanish TV) programme, it was like reliving those childhood years. They told stories about the matches and the victories of that Liverpool side and us three with our mouths open listening as if it was a fairy tale.'

How does a new player get to understand the values of a club like Liverpool?
'Rafa Benítez has always wanted to get those values across, right from the start. He's reorganised Melwood (Liverpool's training ground), covering the walls with club legends, photos of the most distinguished players and the trophies which Liverpool has won. And later, this is passed on to you by people in the street or in Anfield and you realise that you've come to a club that's very special. And right from the first day, you want to absorb its history.'

What advice did they give you when you arrived in January 2007 and what advice did you give to Fernando?
'I don't usually give much advice. It's Pepe (Reina) and Xabi (Alonso) who do that. The first thing they make you understand is that it's different in England. You don't complain, you don't throw yourself on the ground, you don't try to engineer a free-kick. They encourage you to get yourself acclimatised on the pitch and give you help off it.'

You grew up in the 'white factory', as Don Alfredo Di Stefano calls it and then, aged 24, you arrived at Liverpool. What do you think have been the main differences?
'Differences? A lot. To go from one country to another, you change language and habits, but above all you come across a footballing culture that's completely different. You see it in a different way, you play a different way and the atmosphere is something else.'

Tell us about this different culture …
'English football is very physical. Much more contact is allowed. Sneaky or 'smart alec' behaviour doesn't exist as it does in Spain and it's very much looked down on. There's also the difference in the crowd's attitude to football. You could see this in the first knockout round of the Champions League. My ex-team-mates at Real Madrid were surprised because, following the half-time break, when they came back out on to the pitch – and they were losing – the Anfield fans applauded them. In the Bernabéu, when we came onto the field, we were greeted with whistles and insults.'

It was a job well done, the Anfield game against Real Madrid?
'It was a victory to savour. It's a good feeling to beat a big side like Real Madrid but it also hurts to see team-mates who've been your friends so dispirited by the defeat. But if I had to choose, I'd go for the Champions League knock-out round against Barcelona. I have great memories of that match in the Camp Nou. It was my European debut with Liverpool and we won 1-2.'

What's life like in the Spanish Liverpool?
'Life's good, calm. Above all, I appreciate the relaxed atti-tude with regards to the media. You don't have to worry if this person has said that or another something else. You can just concentrate on playing football. Everything is very homely. Sometimes, with Fernando and Pepe, we meet up for dinner, but not much. We train, we have lunch and at home, I relax with my partner Carlota, or have a siesta. What you really appreciate is the incredibly warm wel-come we've received, because very often in Spain, when a group of Dutch players arrive at Barcelona or Brazilians at Madrid, maybe they don't get the same kind of welcome. Why? I don't know. Maybe the people of Liverpool are very

welcoming and we are less so in Spain. At Anfield you see how the fans sing to Rafa, while here you very rarely hear a stadium sing to its manager.'

Speaking of Benítez, what kind of a person is he?
'Rafa is very much on top of you, correcting your positions, studying your every movement on the pitch. For me, for example, when it's my turn to play on his side of the pitch, I always listen to him. It's as if he has a joystick to move me around – forwards, stay still, back. It's true he gives a lot of orders but he improves all his players.'

A survey by (the Italian newspaper) La Gazzetta dello Sport *elected him as the best trainer, ahead of Sir Alex Ferguson, José Mourinho and Fabio Capello …*
'I haven't worked with the others but I'm sure that Rafa is one of the best, especially because of the constant dedication he gives to his work. I think there are few managers that spend so many hours studying football like he does.'

'See you, it's been a pleasure,' says Álvaro Aberloa as he moves off towards the training complex accommodation.

Chapter 26

Third Place

2 December 2008

'What the hell is wrong with you? Fernando Torres is your candidate for the *Ballon d'Or* (European Footballer of the Year) – 33 league goals, the best foreign debutant ever in the Premier League, the scorer of the winning goal in the European championships, the most important in 44 years of Spanish football history and yet he's not your candidate. Why not? Why, in Catalunya, their candidate was Lionel Messi and then Xavi Hernández? Why in Madrid their candidate was Iker Casillas?'

The strongly voiced thoughts of an imaginary Englishman, who, in autumn 2008, is desperately trying to understand why the Spanish never unite behind El Niño. Liverpool's Number 9 is a strong candidate amongst the 30 nominations for the *Ballon d'Or* prize awarded by *France Football* magazine, thanks to his goals for the Merseyside club and his winning strike in the final of Euro 2008. Nevertheless, for him, his nomination seems incredible: 'When I saw that Kaká, Ronaldino and Zidane had won the *Ballon d'Or*,' he says in an interview with *Eurosport*, 'I thought they were players from a different planet and I could never get to their level. And then after Euro 2008, they talked about me alongside other great footballers. For me, that's incredible. I can't say that it was a dream because I never considered the possibility. I never thought I would even be near. Even today, I still see it as something that is a long way off.'

And yet Torres is on the list and forms part of a strong Spanish presence: Iker Casillas, Sergio Ramos, Marcos Senna, Xavi Hernández, Cesc Fabregas and David Villa. An explanation from El Niño: 'The trophy (Euro 2008) has catapulted us into a position from which we can compete for individual recognition.' However, for Torres, Cristiano – the overwhelming favourite to win the top prize – has been 'the best, the most consistent. He's played at a very high level. He's won the Premier League, he's won the Champions League and scored in the final. He's been the top scorer in all competitions and he won the Golden Boot. I think it's very rare that a player has achieved so much to win. Let's hope I get near. Let's hope I'm in the first three. For me, that would be sufficient,' explains Torres.

Cristiano Ronaldo, the Manchester United Number 7, is certainly the strongest candidate and the sure-fire winner of the *France Football* prize – no debate. The Portuguese from Madeira has played the perfect season and 2008 has been his year. He has bagged an impressive total of 42 goals (31 in the Premier League and eleven in the Champions League). At Euro 2008, he was disappointing. His Portugal were eliminated in the quarter-finals but the European tournaments have rarely been a determining factor in the *Ballon d'Or* award.

Meanwhile, the Spanish newspapers have very different ideas as to who should win the competition. Take *Sport*, one of the two dailies based in Barcelona that covers news about football. It began collecting signatures from celebrities and fans all over the world to support the nomination of Leo Messi. An initiative that reaches a total of 60,000 within a few days – and this in spite of the 2007–08 season, which has not been the best for the little Argentinian. Apart from the gold medal with the national team at the Beijing Olympics, Lionel has won nothing with Barcelona. His year has been ruined by injuries and, in addition, he lost the direct clash with Ronaldo's Manchester United in the semi-final of the Champions League. From last September, under the guidance of Pep Guardiola, he has once again returned to the top level, performing well and scoring goals. A bit late, though. Staying in Barcelona: *Mundo Deportivo*, the other daily of the city, champions Xavi – also a Barça player – undoubtedly the leading participant at Euro 2008 in Austria and Switzerland, as well as being elected the best player of the tournament. Moving to the Spanish capital, one discovers that *Marca* is campaigning for Iker Casillas, the keeper whose saves and cool-headedness in the penalty roulette against Italy got the national side past the taboo of the quarter-finals.

To sum up, everyone has their axe to grind, but the situation in Spain is such that the weight of the two historic clubs is more than the national team. Real Madrid and Barcelona rule the roost, as always. Nevertheless, the fact remains that it's all very irksome. Even to Fernando. In an interview with French sport daily, *L'Équipe*, on the eve of the World Cup qualifying match between Estonia and Spain last October, El Niño said: 'You'd have to be blind not to see the huge campaign in favour of Iker. I'm the first to recognise that he deserves it, but so does Villa, Xavi or me. But no one is saying so. According to where you are geographically, you are rated more highly. I don't like this difference in treatment.' A controversy that is immediately hushed-up. The different voices from one side or the other tone themselves down and there's less discussion on the issue. Xavi Hernández makes light of the quarrelling and draws a line between the personal jealousies: 'The individual prizes', he says, 'are a reflection of the collective success. I don't think that I have much chance. I would certainly like a Spaniard to win. If not then Messi, my Barça team-mate.' But that is not to be.

On the cover of the 2 December edition of *France Football*, there is Cristiano Ronaldo. With 446 points, he is European Footballer of the Year (winner of the *Ballon d'Or*) 2008. Second, on 281, is Lionel Messi and Fernando Torres third with 179. Following-up behind are Iker Casillas, who just misses out on the podium, Xavi in fifth and David Villa seventh. Steven Gerrard, the Liverpool captain, comes in tenth. To complete the Spanish Armada, midfielder Marcos Senna, of Brazilian origin, is also there, finishing in 11th, Cesc Fabregas 20th and Sergio Ramos 22nd.

The result is expected – at least for the top place. Messi keeps second place, the same as the previous year. Torres mounts the podium for the first time. Fernando was nominated in 2006, the year of the Germany World Cup, the year in which Fabio Cannavaro, the Italy captain, took home the award. El Niño ended up in the body of the group, 26th, equal to lots of other good players. This time, things go very differently. Despite the vote in favour of the Manchester United winger, five judges on the award panel made Torres their top candidate. Their opinions make for interesting reading: 'Torres for me is the best-performing player of the year,' writes Franks Van Den Nieuwenhof of the Dutch *Eindhovens Dagblad*. 'Torres is the best over the last 30 metres,' from Paché Andrade, *Canal RCN*, in Colombia. 'Fernando Torres, in his first season with Liverpool, has achieved the incredible total of 24 goals and got the crowning goal for Spain. For all these reasons, I put him ahead of Cristiano Ronaldo,' comments Luo Minn, *Titan Sport*, China. 'Torres is a strong character and has immense talent,' from Dafrallah Mouadhen, MBC TV, Dubai. 'His outstanding season with Liverpool and his enormous contribution to the Spanish national side persuade me to vote for Fernando, who this year has become the complete footballer,' argues Francisco Rivas García, *El Heraldo*, Honduras. Who did the English representatives, Max Marquis and Henry Winter, of the *Daily Telegraph*, vote for? For Cristiano. In their order of preference, Torres is second. Paco Aguilar, of Spain's *Mundo Deportivo*, chose Xavi. A confirmation of what has been said before.

And what does Fernando Torres think of his 'bronze *ballon*?' 'The prize is an important recognition, which comes just as I'm recovering from an injury (picked up on 26 November, during the Champions League game against Marseille. The prognosis is that he should be fit again within about four weeks). It'll give me a boost to get back to playing again as soon as possible.'

He is proud to have made the third spot and expresses his gratitude to his team-mates at Liverpool and in the national side: 'Their support has been both significant and essential and their contribution is one of the reasons that I can enjoy this event today.' He knows that 2008 has been a fantastic year. 'This has been my best year as a professional player, different from what I was used to. I arrived at a great club,' he explained, 'that gave me the opportunity to play at the highest level, to play in the Champions League and to learn from some of the best in the world.' As a smart pupil who went on to get good marks at school, he says the prize is simply a motivation to do better.

On 12 January, 2009, the story repeats itself. On the stage of the Zurich Opera House there are five people seated in the front row, waiting for Pelé to open the envelope containing the name of the successor to Kaká, FIFA World Player of the Year 2007. Brazil's former Number 10 is more emotional than the candidates themselves. He has some difficulty in opening the secret envelope. Once he has succeeded – and before revealing the winner's name to the television cameras – he remembers that, when he presented the prize the previous year to his compatriot, Ricardo Izecson Dos Santos Leite (aka Kaká), he assured Ronaldo in Portuguese, 'Next year, you will be the winner.'

And, sure enough, Cristiano Ronaldo is FIFA World Player 2008, picking up his fifth crown of the season. In-between one trophy and another, the Number 7 was also in the Manchester United side that won the FIFA Club World Cup on 21 December in Yokohama, Japan, beating Ecuadorian side, Quito (holders of the 2008 Copa Libertadores) 1-0. Cristiano, according to the votes cast by 155 national team managers and captains, got 935 votes. Since the previous year, he has gone from third to top spot. Runner-up for the second year in succession is Lionel Messi with 678 votes. Third is Fernando Torres on 203 points. El Niño confirms his *Ballon d'Or* position in front of Kaká (183 votes) and Xavi (155). Casillas is eighth. 'It's really important to be here,' declares Torres, formally dressed in white shirt, black jacket and tie. 'I wasn't expecting it. I had just changed my team and country but I adapted to English football really quickly. After that, I began to score goals and that made it all much easier. After not winning a trophy with Liverpool, which was what I really wanted – because they have given me so much and I wanted to give them something back in return – the trophy arrived with the national side. Something probably even more unexpected. After a long time, Spain is once again one of the best. And me scoring in the final. I'm here because of that. But without all the efforts of my team-mates, I wouldn't have this recognition,' says the modest blond lad. And for the Spanish fans, he adds: 'It's really good that two players from our country are amongst the finalists. Let's hope it's the beginning of a phase in which our footballers are always present.' A great night, he says, the first in his career in Zurich. To him, his third place behind two world stars seems fair because 'Messi is the best in the world and Cristiano Ronaldo is the one who's had the best year. But my aim is to improve season on season. I don't look back. I want to do things well so that when the 2009 (awards) come round I can once again be one of the candidates.' He is asked if one day he will win one of these two trophies and he modestly replies: 'To win one it's clear that there've got to be a lot of favourable circumstances. There are times when a player has a great season but doesn't win any trophies and that affects him. What's important is to be one of the candidates for many years. Look at Gerrard, he's always been in the top ten but has never won the prize and he deserves it. But he goes on giving his best.'

Chapter 27

A Hartung

Conversation with England manager
Fabio Capello

His name is on the entry phone. After pressing the button you are let into the hallway of a nineteenth-century villa, where a lift takes you to the fourth floor. The narrow compartment door slides open and there on the other side is Fabio Capello, sporting a geometrically patterned sweater, blue shirt and designer glasses. The England manager invites the visitor into his sitting room. At the end is a huge window looking out on a beautiful private garden with ancient trees and, shining through the mist, an immaculate lawn and tennis court – a silent, tranquil and elegant location right in the centre of London. A computer and various documents sit on top of a long table – the ex-manager of Milan, Roma, Juventus and Real Madrid had brought work home from his FA office.

During the next two days he will be performing a spectator marathon, watching all four games involving Liverpool, Chelsea, Manchester United and Arsenal, ahead of their appearances in the quarter-finals of the (2008–09) Champions League. There is still some time before the 2010 World Cup in South Africa, but the England coach must always keep a close eye on the European tournaments and the Premier League, as well as the players who will make up the basic structure of the team that will probably represent his last campaign in the dugout. This is a manager who doesn't beat about the bush, so it's best to get straight to the point.

Cristiano Ronaldo, Messi and Torres: European Footballer of the Year, one, two and three and the same order for the FIFA World Player of the year. What do you think?
'Cristiano Ronaldo is a very good, very dangerous and very technical player with great pace. Messi is a genius, no one in the world today has his talent. He can do extraordinary things. As for Torres, let's say that last year he burst onto the scene and did very well. The 2007–08 season was his coming-of-age. Here in England he's succeeded in doing what he failed to do in La Liga – score goals. In Spain, everyone acknowledged his tremendous skills and pace but in front of goal he lacked coolness and ability. Obviously the change of climate has served him well – and how! Here, he's become a truly impressive goal-scorer via his ability to put the ball in the back of the net by every means possible.'

How is such a major transformation possible?
'That's something I've asked myself too. Probably he needed to leave Madrid. He needed more responsibility.'

But he had responsibility at Atlético – he was captain and was just eighteen at the time …
'Here he's feeling more responsibility because of what they paid for him. And perhaps this has produced the step-up in quality. Psychologically, it's helped him. At least that's what I believe.'

Maybe English football is well suited to his style of play?
'Yes, Torres has the sort of speed and pace that often wrong-foots English central defenders – they are a bit slower and

have more experience in coping with high balls than a passing game. And one should also say that here, like all the other foreign players, he's learned to play with few interruptions and with more physical contact. So to sum up, it's not only his technique but also his running, understanding and physical condition.'

Have Liverpool and Rafa Benítez had an important role in this transformation?
'Undoubtedly. For him to be playing alongside Gerrard, the standard-bearer of Liverpool, has given him a real enthusiasm.'

What has Torres brought to Liverpool?
'The certain knowledge of having someone up front that can create alarm. You know that, at any moment, with even just a half-chance, he can create a goal. He's got great pace, he's not afraid, he has good technique, is strong and smart. These are the skills of a good striker.'

Liverpool almost always use Torres as a lone striker …
'That's right but it's not just Liverpool that plays like that. Now when I hear people talking about formations, it makes me laugh. I say that the modern formation is 9 + 1. There are nine who defend, leaving just one upfront. Then you need to see how many of them have the technical ability to move up into attack. That's the true game plan. Everything else is just baloney.'

Let's talk about how well Torres and the other Spanish players have settled in at this historic club …
'Yes, Torres and the Spanish players are very well integrated. First, because there is a Spanish manager and second, the players all play for the national side. They are top-class.

Reina is a great goalkeeper and now he's been there four years, having been signed when he was 23. Arbeloa is a superb player. Riera – I had thought about as a possible signing for Madrid (when manager of Real Madrid). And with Xabi Alonso there's no debate. They are all footballers with great technical ability, which, in league matches where pressurising, running and strength are crucial, allows them to shine.'

It's impressive to see how Torres has become an idol for the fans at Liverpool …
'He and Gerrard are indisputably the Reds' two heroes. In my opinion, that has given Torres self-confidence, which he didn't have 100 per cent in a team like Atlético Madrid because he was born there, he grew up there and was pampered by the club. In short, at Madrid he felt young, with no responsibility, while at Liverpool the responsibility has made him mature rapidly.'

It seems that El Niño *understood straightaway the values of the club. How is that possible?*
'I don't know. I believe that all the great teams have a special chemistry. You feel it, you breathe it, and they can transmit it to you. You live it. And in a club like Liverpool there is a "passing on of the baton". The older players hand it on to the younger ones and make sure they understand how this process works. Another important and attractive element of the game is the crowd and the support they give you throughout the match. At Anfield, the fans are very generous with players who give their all. When you come onto the pitch and you hear them singing "You'll Never Walk Alone", you feel something extra and a special responsibility on your shoulders towards all these people who really do, in effect, never leave you alone.'

*Would you be pleased to have Torres at your disposal for the
England side?*
'Let's not talk about that. We have excellent English strik-
ers. I don't want to talk about England.'

*OK let's talk instead about the past, Euro 2008 and the influence
of Torres in the Spanish national side …*
'As I was saying, at Liverpool he's matured and he's brought
this maturity into the national side where he's achieved a lot
and, above all, scored the winning goal in the final. After
the fantastic season he'd enjoyed with the Reds and the
spate of goals he'd scored, it was certain he was going to be
one of the stars of Euro 2008. And for me Spain were, on
paper, the team with the best players and one of the four
favourites, together with Germany, France and Italy.

*The strike pairing of Torres and Villa at Euro 2008 had all the
commentators drooling and the Liverpool fans dreaming of seeing
the two playing together in red shirts. How do you see them?*
'They play together really well. Torres is the centre forward,
while Villa moves off him. He has very good movement off
the ball, with excellent technical and shooting skills.'

*As he demonstrated in the friendly against England last
February?*
'Yes but we don't talk about that.'

*Let's go back a bit to your last period as manager of Real Madrid.
What was your impression then of Torres?*
'His potential was obvious but it was still a work in progress.
He hadn't yet transformed from the chrysalis into a
butterfly.'

Nevertheless, in the away match of the 2006–07 season with your Real Madrid team, it was he who scored the first goal, while in the home match there was controversy following your comments on an incident involving Torres ...

'Ah, *el tramposo*, the "cheat" controversy – I remember it well. In the second half, after making contact with Sergio Ramos, Torres fell in the penalty area and rolled around as if he'd been elbowed – so much so that the referee sent off my defender. For me, I don't like it when a player goes in for diving in order to deceive the referee and gain an advantage for his team. At the press conference after the match, I wanted to make a point about this but I didn't know exactly which word to use. My press officer suggested *tramposo* ("cheat") and the whole thing became a soap opera in the Spanish media. Here, I wouldn't have had any hesitation in saying "diver". Anyway, it's an old controversy and closed in the best possible way.'

You have played with and managed champion players in Italy, Spain and England. Who does Fernando Torres remind you of?
'In one way, he reminds me a lot of Altafini.' (José João Altafini, a Brazilian-Italian striker who burst onto the international stage at the 1958 World Cup in Sweden, scoring three goals in two matches. He then moved to Italy, playing for Milan, Napoli and Juventus, before finishing his career in Switzerland with Chiasso and Mendrisiostar. He also played for the Italian national team in the 1962 World Cup).

Why?
'Because José had this speed and this ability of not being in a game and then playing a crucial role. I would say that Altafini was smarter with his shooting. In front of the posts, when he took up a particular position, it was a certain goal.

It meant the ball was, effectively, already back in the middle of the pitch for the kick-off. But I'm talking about an Altafini who was by then 30 years old. Torres is still very young – so we must wait.'

Many have compared him to Marco Van Basten, a player who you managed for several seasons at Milan …
'No, no. Van Basten moved differently, he had other technical skills, another way of reading the game. Torres is quicker than Van Basten, he likes playing deep, while Van Basten was looking more to link-up with the midfield. No, they're two different players.'

We now come to the 2008–09 season, which, for Torres, has been full of injuries with one problem after another …
'As always after the European and World Cup tournaments, players are injured. Everyone pays for it and the after-effects drag on for months. There's nothing you can do about it and in the end you pay the price for all that euphoria. After such an important victory, it's often the mental approach that suffers. What's certain is that this year he's not the same and hasn't been able to do what he was doing before.'

At this point in the conversation 'Don Fabio' (as he is known in Spain) went off on a tangent, analysing the Champions League and the headlines of the Spanish sporting press, which portrayed him as the solution to crisis situations when results were negative and difficult to manage. Later, there was time to look at and appreciate the eye-catching paintings and sculptures that decorated the sitting room. Fabio Capello is an enthusiastic art collector. Perhaps the final question was somewhat prosaic but it was impossible to resist.

How would you describe – pictorially – the playing style of Torres?
[He gave the question much more thought than any other during the entire interview. Then he said decisively:]
'A Hartung.'

The Encyclopaedia Britannica describes Hans Hartung (born 21 September 1904, at Leipzig in Germany, died 7 December 1989, at Antibes in France) as: 'a French painter of German origins, one of the leading European exponents of a completely abstract style of painting. He became particularly well known for his carefully composed, almost calligraphic arrangements of black lines on coloured backgrounds.'

The catalogue of one of his recent exhibitions is entitled 'In the Beginning There Was Lightning'.

Chapter 28

Liverpool 4 Real Madrid 0

10 March 2009

Do you remember *An American Werewolf in London,* a 1981 film directed by John Landis? The landlady of the Scottish pub warns Jack and David, two American lads on holiday, not to go wandering off into the mist, never to leave the road and, above all, to be extra-vigilant whenever there was a full moon. But the pair ignore that good advice and the werewolf makes its savage entrance.

It's Tuesday evening at Liverpool and a full moon, bright, radiant, mysterious and threatening, looms over Anfield. But no one has warned the players of Real Madrid. No one has told them they will be meeting the werewolf dressed in red. No one has told them that Fernando Torres, together with Steven Gerrard, will be attacking them right from the first minute. They have not been vigilant. They are ripe for being taken apart without mercy. But before seeing how The Kid gets stuck into them, we take a step back … Twenty days before the first leg of the knockout tie with Real Madrid in the Champions League, Torres explains:

'To play against them is nothing special for me. It would be special if the other team is Atlético. Still, I'm looking forward to it because it will be a way of going back to Madrid, to play in a stadium where I've never won and against a big team. But I'm sure we'll win the tie.'

Declarations that were repeated in the sport dailies of Madrid with front-page headlines like 'We're going to eliminate Madrid' from *Marca*, all of them picking holes in El Niño, because what he was saying was true – in seven matches at the Santiago Bernabéu (Real Madrid's ground) he had never scored.

The first occasion was during the 2002–03 season. The game hadn't even started when Fernando Hierro, the Real Madrid captain, made him understand how certain things were done. He went up to the eighteen-year-old in the red-and-white striped shirt, then Atlético's bright new hope, and asked him: 'What's up, son? Didn't you sleep well last night?' Torres didn't score and the match finished in a 2-2 draw. The following year, Madrid won 2-0. In 2004–05 it was a scoreless draw and in the next season's fixture, the white shirts of Madrid chalked up a 2-1 victory. A year later, in Fernando's final season in Spain, it was another draw, this time 1-1. He achieved a goal only once, on 2 January 2002, when he got past reserve keeper, Carlos Sánchez García. But it was only a friendly.

Maybe, for Torres, it was a case of 'stage fright' – a condition referred to by the former Argentina player (and former Real Madrid player, manager and then Sporting Director), Jorge Valdano, to describe the apprehension that seems to grip visiting team members when they play in a famous stadium. But it didn't stop with the stadium: in the 10 league encounters that El Niño played against Real Madrid wearing the shirt of Atlético, he never won. He scored just once against his great city rivals, at home in the Vicente Calderón stadium, on 24 February 2007, in an encounter that the Atlético side dominated (against a Real Madrid side managed by Fabio Capello, which that year went on to win the league). Torres scored in the 11th minute, then various opportunities and disallowed goals followed. But, as on so many other occasions, they let victory slip from their grasp, this time by allowing Real to equalise through Gonzalo Higuaín. To sum up, Real Madrid is Fernando's *bête noire*. A typical view is that he was a jinxed striker against Real. But this time, things would be different …

Álvaro Aberloa maintains there is no need to remind him about his goal drought in the Bernabéu: 'Fernando says he's fired up enough on his own. There's no one more keen to score in the Bernabéu, to have a good game and to win the tie than him. Even Rafa Benítez is confident, saying Torres would score. Why? 'Because there's always a first time.'

But how does Fernando himself view the encounter? He is convinced that 'small details or an individual action will decide who goes through to the next round'. He knows that Madrid will be coming out in 'better footballing shape than they have been'.

And that was the main topic of all the debates. But when, on 19 December 2008, at Nyon in Switzerland, UEFA drew Real Madrid and Liverpool against each other, the situation was very different. Bernd Schuster, the German manager of Real Madrid at the time – who'd won the 2007–08 league title – had just been driven out of the job because of a run of bad results, including the team's elimination from the Copa del Rey (King's Cup) by Real Unión de Irún of the Second Division. Taking Schuster's place in the dugout was Juande Ramos, ex-manager of Sevilla and, more recently, Tottenham Hotspur. His first task was to take on Barcelona away in the league at the Camp Nou, where they were beaten 2-0. This meant that, after fifteen games and halfway through the season, Real were in sixth position, twelve points behind the leaders, Barcelona.

The atmosphere was very different in Liverpool, where the Reds were top of the table with a two-point advantage over Chelsea, and with Manchester United even further behind. After nineteen years of abstinence, it really looked like this would be the year they would win the Premier League. Everything was going extremely well and the book-makers were offering short odds on a Liverpool title. If that wasn't enough, Madrid were immersed in an institutional crisis of unprecedented dimensions. On 16 January, following three days of high-profile accusations, Real president Ramón Calderón was forced to resign because of what the press christened 'Nanigate' – allegations of vote-rigging during an official assembly the previous December to confirm the club's 400-million Euro budget. Vicente Boluda, a 53-year-old shipowner and president of the third-biggest tugboat company in Europe, would take the helm until new elections in the spring of 2009.

In February, Madrid's future was still uncertain but on the sporting front, things were improving. Since the Barça defeat, Juande Ramos had notched up nine consecutive victories and reduced the distance with Barcelona to seven points. The league title was once again up for grabs. Hope in the white half of Madrid was reborn. The opposite was the case in Liverpool, where, on 19 January, they lost the top spot in a 1-1 draw against city neighbours Everton, which the next day allowed Manchester United to stretch their lead at the top of the table. On 4 February at Goodison Park, against The Toffees, Liverpool said goodbye to the FA Cup after they were beaten 1-0 in the 118th minute, thanks to a goal from young substitute Dan Gosling. It was the Reds' first defeat since 12 November 2008, when they fell to Tottenham in the Carling Cup. Furthermore, there was the unwelcome news of a 16th-minute injury to captain, Steven Gerrard, the team's leading scorer with nine goals in 21 league games and the driving force in midfield. Replaced by Benayoun, he left the field with an injury later diagnosed as a torn left hamstring. Benítez didn't play him in the league game against Manchester City (1-1) and his presence at the Bernabéu was in doubt.

In short, the first leg of the tie arrived at the best possible moment for Real Madrid. It's true that the team's style of play had not won many plaudits. It had been criticised repeatedly for being safe, even boring, but results talked. The defensive shortcomings of the Schuster era had been replaced with order and precision. The midfield, with Gago and new acquisition 'Lass' Diara (from Premier League side Portsmouth), had recovered its solidity. Robben was intimidating – to such an extent that Torres observed: 'He is a key player. If we give him space he could damage us because he can decide a match in an instant. We'll take all the necessary steps to keep him under wraps and reduce his effectiveness.' Higuaín had grown in stature and the front line had begun to function again – so much so that, in the last game before the Champions League tie, it had inflicted a six-goal defeat on an unfortunate Betis. Raúl, the captain, increased his club goal tally to 308, beating that of the legendary Don Alfredo Di Stefano. Those were some of the factors that augured well for Real Madrid in a competition on which they'd placed so much importance. Since the Portuguese, Carlos Queiroz (ex-assistant manager at Manchester United and then manager of the Portuguese national side), was manager in spring 2004, Real Madrid hadn't got past the first knockout round of the competition and for a club that likes to define itself as the biggest in the world, not to triumph in Europe is a disaster. But as Juande explained: 'In the Champions' League we rely solely on ourselves, in La Liga we are reliant on others' (implying that it was Barcelona who would have to make a stumble in order for them to be caught).

'White pride' and a good run of results emboldened interim president Vicente Boluda to declare: 'Here (in Madrid) we will win 3-0 and over there we'll score a load of goals.' The colloquial verb he used at the end to indicate a 'flow' or 'flood' of goals ('chorrear' in Spanish) can have other, less refined, interpretations, which were understood by everyone in Spain and, of course, by the Spanish Army at Liverpool, where it provoked unfriendly reactions.

The last time Liverpool and Real had met was on 27 May 1981, in the European Cup final in Paris. It is strange that the two big powers in terms of European titles (Real has nine European Cups, two UEFA cups and one European Super Cup against Liverpool's five European Cups, three UEFA cups and three European Super Cups) have not had more face-to-face encounters. At the Parc des Princes in Paris in 1981, it finished 1-0 to the Liverpool of Bob Paisley, in front of more than 48,000 spectators. Seven minutes from time, the left-footed left-back, Alan Kennedy, made the winning strike – a goal that 'Barney Rubble' (the nickname given to him by the Kop, after the character in the TV cartoon series, *The Flintstones*), remembers it like this: 'There was a throw-in and the Madrid players thought that Ray (Kennedy) would give it to Sammy Lee or to Dalglish. I started a run from behind. No one was expecting me. I chested the ball down and slipped into the penalty area. García Cortés came for the challenge but failed to clear. He was afraid of giving away a penalty and so didn't touch me and I ended up in front of Augustín. He thought I was going to pass and opened himself up a bit. Because of that I decided to shoot close to the left-hand post.' A perfect angle and it brought them their third European Cup in five years.

Other times, other stories. That Liverpool side was made up of Clemence, Neal, Thompson, Hansen (Alan), Kennedy,

Lee, McDermott, Souness, Kennedy (Ray), Dalglish and Johnson. The one that comes out on to the pitch in Madrid at 8.45pm on 25 February 2009, lines up as Reina, Aberloa, Carragher, Skrtel, Fabio Aurelio, Mascherano, Xabi Alonso, Benayoun, Riera, Kuyt and Torres. Gerrard does not even make the warm-up, going straight to the bench. The Bernabéu is not the pressure cooker that their captain has asked for but there is a lot of noise from the crowd, with constant whistles for the Reds. The Real Madrid fans and the *Ultras Sur* (the most radical and extreme supporters) pick on Torres because of his Atlético past. They can't bear the fact that the player, according to a list compiled for *The Times* just twelve days before the Bernabéu game, is now one of the 50 Greatest Liverpool players of all time. On the pitch, however, the players are wary of him. This is what Raúl says when asked about Torres' goal drought in the Bernabéu:

'Since Torres went to Liverpool he's got rid of the pressure he had at Atlético and is displaying all his qualities as a footballer. He feels very supported and he does what he knows best, which is to upset his opponents with his power and his goal-scoring instincts. He is one of the most formidable strikers in the world.'

Torres responds to this flattery in the 20th minute, just when the Bernabéu crowd was shouting '*Arriba Madrid*' in a bid to encourage their team not to be so timid and to go on the attack. Pepe Reina makes one of his trademark cannon-like clearances, Dirk Kuyt glances the ball further forward and El Niño runs onto it in typical style. Real's defence, Cannavaro and Pepe, stay firm. Nevertheless, Fernando gets round the back of the Portuguese defender, ending up with just Iker Casillas to beat. He makes an angled shot but the keeper just gets a glove to it and deflects it. It was a good opportunity to break the jinx – and it proved to be the last. Torres had been playing with an injury since the end of the first minute – as Rafa Bénitez would explain later – and is quite clearly limping in pain from his left ankle. He comes off just before the half-hour and sits down on the turf, while the club physios check him over. Bénitez comes over to assess the situation. Several minutes go by and, after bandaging the ankle, he puts his boot back on and returns to the pitch. But by then he's like a loose buoy floating between the white lines. He doesn't move off the ball, he can't run to receive the passes from the midfield. He stays there, hoping for the chance of a loose ball resulting from some kind of error. It's obvious to everyone that he's injured. And yet at the beginning of the second half, he comes back on. When questioned later, Bénitez explains that the doctors had assured him 'it's not a serious injury and he could continue'. In addition, Torres himself wants to play and asks Bénitez if he can carry on. But he can't play properly and starts getting annoyed – so much so that, in the 55th minute, after an argument with Pepe, he is booked. Six minutes later, with his ankle swollen, he gives in. He raises his hands to salute the Liverpool fans up in the third tier, which provokes insults from the south corner. Choruses of '*Hijo de puta, hijo de puta!*' ('son of a whore!'), echo round the stadium until Torres disappears into the dugout.

He leaves the stadium 50 minutes later with a grim face and a brace round his ankle. The Liverpool striker, who should have been the key man of the match – the one who'd scored at Stamford Bridge and in the Emirates Stadium, who'd dominated Chelsea in the closing minutes – isn't able to meet expectations. He's not the Reds' extra weapon. The kid from Fuenlabrada, who should have taken his revenge in the Bernabéu, is thwarted. But at least he returns to England with the first victory of his career against his eternal rivals – thanks to the diminutive Israeli, Heinze, who, in the 80th minute, pulls down Liverpool's Kuyt and is punished with a free-kick on the right. Fabio Aurelio takes responsibility, places the ball, surveys the options and puts in a dipping cross. Yossi Benayoun arrives from behind, completely unmarked, and with all the time in the world, leaps up to head the ball under the crossbar, leaving Casillas clutching thin air. The 6,000 travelling fans are delirious. The Bernabéu is struck dumb while the *Ultras Sur* end up, as usual, fighting amongst themselves.

Liverpool had won by putting a perfect plan into action. As Mascherano and Arbeloa explained, the match went according to the prepared script: 'We subdued Higuaín and Robben, the only two with speed and the ability to overlap. Now we've done the hard part,' said the Argentinian.

'We knew the match could be decided with a corner or a penalty or a counter-attack and that's what we were able to do. This is how we've played knockout ties for years,' explained the Spaniard. Rafa Benítez could put on a relaxed face at the press conference. Before anything else, the ex-manager of Real Madrid B denied the rumours circulating before the game that he had already handed in his resignation to the Liverpool club owners. William Hill and Sky Bet had been forced to suspend all wagers on Benítez, after too many punters had put their money on the manager no longer being in charge from the following Monday. He calmed the waters saying that his lawyers had been negotiating and that he would be talking personally with Tom Hincks and George Gillett. Once that subject was cleared up, the Liverpool manager went on to explain: 'We had in mind to play a very defensive game and to come out on the counter-attack. This we did and it worked for us with the goal from Benayoun. We have a very important win, although the tie isn't over. There are still 90 very difficult minutes left and we will have to concentrate at all times.' Benítez could also derive personal satisfaction – both as a Spaniard and as a manager – for sending out a team in the Bernabéu with five more Spanish players than Madrid: 'chorreo? (referring to the word 'chorrear', used by Real Madrid president Vicente Boluda). Experience suggests that one should talk on the pitch and my players have done that very well in the name of Liverpool. I am very proud.' Of Torres, he added: 'He was very affected by his ankle and we decided to take him off when he couldn't go on. I don't think he'll be able to play on Saturday either.'

From there, it went like this: against second-from-bottom Middlesbrough, The Kid didn't play and the Reds lost 2-0, which allowed Chelsea into second place and they went six points behind Manchester United. Torres still wasn't fit, even for the game on 3 March at Anfield against Sunderland (2-0 for Liverpool). The injury wasn't improving as rapidly as everyone had been expecting. The ankle continued to cause problems but the Number 9 was optimistic he'd be there for the return against Real. He was certain it would be a difficult match, despite the away-goal advantage. You have to beware of Real, he said, they'll want to come out and kill off the game as quickly as possible to secure their passage to the next round. He said he wasn't surprised at the welcome he got in the Bernabéu and had been expecting it. 'They've always been like that to me when I've played there. They even whistled at me in a friendly when I was playing in a World XI. In England, they're not so hard on you. There are rivalries there as well but the fans are more respectful. There are different ways of understanding football,' he explained and added that whatever the atmosphere at the Bernabéu, 'it's nothing compared to Anfield. I don't think there's a stadium like ours anywhere else in the world'.

He was right. The 3,000 followers of Madrid that fill the Anfield Road Stand on 10 March at 7.45pm realise it too as the teams come out onto the pitch. They understand what it is, the atmosphere one breathes in at this 'fortress', this temple of football. The 20,000-strong Kop are all on their feet, singing 'You'll Never Walk Alone' and holding their red-and-white scarves above their heads. They wave flags carrying images of Bill Shankly with open arms, of Bob Paisley, of Rafa Benítez with the inscription (in Spanish), 'Siempre se puede' ('It's always possible'), and a silhouette of Fernando Torres celebrating a goal. The Kid is on the field, the physios have fixed him up, even though – as we will know later – he is playing with a bandage and plaster on his ankle. Three minutes later he shows why the Liverpool fans adore him. A long ball arrives and with a backheel he gets past Fabio Cannavaro to put himself one-on-one with Casillas. He hits it hard towards the near post but the keeper denies him once more with the tip of his foot. It is the first indication of what The Kid and Company will do and it is the perfect example of the class, elegance, movement and speed of a player who has magic and, above all, who wants to play a central role and win.

In the subsequent minutes, Torres and his team-mates seem possessed, moving at top speed, laying siege to the Madrid goal from all possible angles. Mascherano powers a shot and Casillas is saved by the crossbar. All long balls from Reina are a problem. Any run from Torres sows panic in the Madrid defence. Liverpool is like a pneumatic drill, breaking down its opponents. The Reds are following Ian Rush's advice in the *Liverpool Echo*. The headline of his weekly column before the game reads: 'Attack is best form of defence for the Reds. We can't afford to sit back in Anfield clash.' Rafa Benítez surprises his adversaries with the same strategy he had used years before with Juventus. Juande, who, like so many others, was expecting a team that would gamble on keeping its one goal advantage from the first leg, is completely wrong-footed. His side are seeing nothing of the ball. When they do get hold of it they find themselves encircled like the Seventh Cavalry of General Custer at Little Big Horn. They barely have time to look up before the enemy has once again robbed them of the ball. In addition, no one gives up chasing, not even Torres who drops back into his own half to take the ball off Sergio Ramos (to a great roar from the crowd), to take on Lars Diarra, to tackle Gago, to fight for every high ball with Pepe, to harass ex-Manchester United defender, Heinze (who will become the villain of the night, picked on by the crowd every time he touches the ball).

In the 16th minute, Anfield explodes. Reina clears to Carragher, who sends the ball high and long. The bounce catches Cannavaro by surprise and he tries to clear with an overhead kick but fails. Torres heads the ball, puts Pepe under pressure, the Portuguese falls to the ground and Kuyt, who's moved up outside on the right, picks up the ball. Casillas comes out of his goal, El Niño moves to the centre and calls for the Dutchman to give him the ball. A killer move and Torres puts it in the net. Referee Frank De Bleeckere confirms the goal and the lad from Fuenlabrada celebrates by parading his Number 9 under the eyes of the Spanish fans and leaps up high to punch the air. His goal has opened the floodgates. Real are reeling, like a punch-drunk boxer, who in the 10th round still hasn't understood that the contest is over. In the 47th minute it's a knockout. Steven Gerrard, with a penalty and then a goal of textbook quality, completes the demolition of the clay-footed giant. At Anfield, Fernando Torres has many things to be satisfied about apart from his goal. Going back to the centre spot after making it 1-0, he turns to the executives' box containing Real president, Vicente Boluda – who had said that his team would 'score loads' in Liverpool – and made the same gesture that Spanish Formula One driver Fernando Alonso made famous on the Grand Prix winners' podium: 'You talk a lot' was the clear message. The other thorn out of his side was Pepe. The Portuguese defender had declared that it was a pleasure to play against such a powerful striker as Torres and that he knew exactly how to close him down. In the first leg it was clear the duel had begun. In the return, the two end up face-to-face on several occasions and Pepe reminds Torres that Madrid had won nine European Cups. 'Yes but you, zero,' replies El Niño, accompanied by an unmistakable zero-shaped hand gesture, similar to what José Mourinho used in Italy when he told Juventus: 'You have zero titles'.

In the 84th minute, Fernando Torres is replaced by the Italian, Andrea Dossena, who would still find time to score a fourth goal. The *Ultras Sur* took aim but this time the insults are overpowered by the Kop, which belts out the Torres Song full blast.

'This is Anfield,' said Fernando in front of the microphones, notebooks and television cameras. 'A very difficult ground. It's not just any team that wins here. The fans have given us a real lift.' And, remembering the controversy of the past, when he played in the red-and-white stripes of Atlético, he went on to explain: 'As a Liverpool player, I'm happy, but if we've also given enjoyment to the fans of Atlético, then so much the better.'

Chapter 29

A horse that needs to run

*Conversation with Juventus defender and Italy
captain, Fabio Cannavaro*

Green lawns, white goals in the middle of the pitch, low-flying swallows and empty stands with seats marking out the words 'Real Madrid'. In the background, an ever-expanding housing development and four new towers of glass and steel, which disappear into the low clouds and darkness of a leaden sky. Real's training session has finished a short time ago. Behind the huge windows of the press room, on the second floor of the Ciudad Deportiva di Valdebebas sports complex (about 10 miles north of Madrid city centre) journalists are waiting patiently for the appearance, behind the microphones and in front of the red and black sponsor's background, of the Argentinian, Gonzalo Higuaín.

On the first floor, Fabio Cannavaro, in black leather bomber jacket, blue striped shirt and torn jeans is smiling – a smile that, for about three years, has also won over Madrid. 'How are you?' – 'Well, thanks and you?' With his piercing blue eyes, the street kid who was a ballboy at the Napoli team's San Paolo stadium in Naples (in order to see at close hand his idol, Diego Maradona) has come a long way. After Naples, he went to Parma, Inter and Juventus and on into the Italian national side.

Then, in 2006, in Germany, the biggest, most exciting football experience – the World Cup. And as captain of Italy, raising the trophy aloft in Berlin. Six months later came the European Footballer of the Year trophy (the *Ballon d'Or*) and then the FIFA World Player of the year – an honour in recognition of the defensive skills that only Franz Beckenbauer could previously claim. A prize that showed what is meant by tackling, anticipation, a sliding interception and maximum concentration in an area of the pitch where errors are costly. And in that World Cup summer of 2006, Cannavaro arrived at Real Madrid to don the Number 5 shirt (formerly of Zinédine Zidane) and went on to win two consecutive league titles and a Spanish Supercopa. Good memories of a city and a country, Spain, to which he is now saying farewell in order to return to Turin and Juventus – first as a player and then maybe as a director. These are the last days here in Valdebebas of the central defender, who, the day after the second leg of the knockout Champions League tie against Liverpool at Anfield, was not feeling too great.

The Daily Mirror *writes that Torres, in the first chance of the match, goes round you as if you were 'a Sunday league player, not one of the most decorated men in the game …'*

'Regardless of what the *Mirror* writes, it was a difficult match because they started superbly and we are a team in which, when we don't play like a team, our errors stand out. And with those spaces, with those strikers, to defend well becomes impossible.'

With you, and above all with Pepe, Torres had quite a lot to smile about …

'For Torres to play against Real Madrid was something special – a derby. But except in my first year at Madrid, when I was sent off for two yellow cards against him (I never did anything to him but he just started to scream), I never had any problems. He is a striker who takes it and gives it. I've given him some. That's normal. The only thing I can say is that, in Spain, he had these theatrical habits. Fortunately, in England, he's got rid of them. The English don't accept that kind of thing.'

Is it difficult to mark Torres?
'I've marked Fernando both in Spain, when he was playing with Atlético, and with the national team and also with Liverpool. If I'm really honest, when he was playing here, I didn't like him very much.'

Why?
'One could see that he had great potential but he was … a bit soft. He was a player without any "bite" – sporting-wise, you understand? He was a player who worked well with the ball but he went through patches, he wasn't always at the heart of the game, he wasn't involved, he wasn't talking with his team-mates. When I came up against him again in the national team, in the friendly with Spain in March 2008, one could already see the difference. Then with Liverpool, in both the home and away legs, I saw a completely different player.'

In what sense?
'Mentally, in the way he attacked defenders, in the way he spoke with team-mates. He's a much stronger player. Before, when you knocked against him, he gave way. Now, that's difficult, because mentally he's got much stronger.'

How do you explain this change?
'It happened to me. I was at Inter and I wasn't able to train any more or find the right kind of enjoyment or motivation to go out and play. I went to Juve and within two days I changed completely. I met up again with my friends, my

team-mates, in a more family-like atmosphere. I changed
the chip – so much so, that in my first year with the *bian-
coneri* (Juventus) I played 38 games out of 38 and only
picked up one yellow card. These are things that happen
to a player … Click – you regain your confidence and that
of your team-mates and the fans chant your name. I think
the same thing has happened to Torres. At Atlético he had
all the weight of the team on him, knowing that if he made
a mistake and they lost the match, he would be blamed.
Going to Liverpool, he is a foreigner, he's more relaxed, he
scores one goal, two, then three … The fans go crazy about
him and everything becomes easy. Yes, going to Liverpool
has really done him a lot of good.'

He's benefited from the Benítez system …
'He's benefited, for sure, because for Torres it's much better to play as a lone striker – he can play in various positions
along the line of attack. He suffers when he has another
striker playing up high alongside him. He's not a footballer
who likes one-twos much. He should play on his own upfront,
with Gerrard behind and Kuyt on the right. For him that's
the ideal. But of course English football for him is definitely
more rewarding. Here in Spain, it works as one against
one, little touches, possession. Torres on the other hand, is
a horse that needs space, that needs to run. The more he
runs the happier he is and the more his skills come to the
fore. The same thing is happening in the national side. We
talk a lot about Spain playing an attractive kind of football,
putting great value on possession of the ball, it's true. That's
because the midfield has people like Iniesta, Xavi and Senna
– all top-quality players. But if we look again at the goals
they scored in Euro 2008, a lot of them were made on the
counter-attack – two against Russia, one against Sweden and
not forgetting that one of Torres in the final. When I saw the

two German defenders, Lahm and Metzelder, covering the whole pitch – well, quite honestly, I could see what would happen, because when there is space, Torres is going to have a field day. Maybe in a tight area, he's going to have some difficulty but when he can run and use his strength and speed to its maximum potential, you're in trouble.'

Since we're on the subject of Italy-Spain, the quarter-final of Euro 2008 was decisive in determining Spain's destiny …
'It was a strange match with a peculiar atmosphere. I remember saying "Be careful", that whoever goes through from this tie will win the championship. Because of the two teams' mental strengths and their skills on the pitch, it was the most finely balanced of the quarter-finals. It was an encounter where we let them take the game, as always, because we are a team that gives the ball to the opposition. But the best chances fell to us. As for them, yes, they had plenty of possession and they made lots of attempts on goal but they were all off-target. Torres and Villa were invisible in that game. Why? Because we conceded very little space to the strikers and with a pair like Torres and Villa, who are good on the counter-attack, if you limit the depth of area in which they can operate, it makes it much more difficult for them.'

Apart from not conceding too much space, what would a coach's advice be to a defender who needs to close down a striker like Fernando Torres?
'Nowadays, it's no longer like it once was when you attached yourself to a striker and didn't let him breathe throughout the whole game. I would play a one-against-one but try to minimise it. Today, no. Today one talks of units, and the defensive unit should work in the best possible way, it should be perfectly synchronised like a precision timepiece to close down strikers like Torres.'

In a list of the world's best strikers, where would you put Torres?
'Amongst the top ones, amongst those who cause panic, such as Drogba, Berbatov and Ruud (Van Nistelrooy). Torres is definitely one of the strongest strikers in Europe – he's young, he plays in a set-up like Liverpool, he's in the Spanish national team, and he's still got so many areas in which to improve.'

Which areas?
'He should improve his technique in the one-against-one. Torres relies on his speed but when you have a defender in front of you, you have to go past him and not through speed alone. Take Cristiano Ronaldo, Messi or Ronaldo in his better moments. They home in on you, skip past and they're away. This is still missing in Torres, even if he has the quality and the skills to be able to do it. His best weapons? His bursts of speed, those 10 to 15 metres in which he launches himself at the back of the defender and his overwhelming physical power. Even when he makes a mistake, he gets to the ball ahead of everyone else. Another thing he does that I like is that he doesn't give up when his opponents have the ball. In the match with Liverpool, for example, I will always remember two recoveries of the ball he made – one from Sergio Ramos and the other from Heinze. There, you really saw the strength of a striker. You saw that he wanted to win. But beyond the goals and the games, it's an important message to the whole team. He shows the spirit of the centre forward. As a defender, I would like my strikers to be doing that.'

Who does Torres resemble?
'Perhaps Ruud Gullit for his running abilities and his strength. I remember Ruud had fantastic acceleration. He

was a player who would start from a long way off and could
play at various points along the line of attack.'

*Torres said some time ago that in a few years, to complete his
career, he would like to play in Italy and try Serie A. What do you
think of that?*
'After his English experience, I think he'd have some difficulties, because of how football is lived in England, because
of how it is organised. We (in Italy) are the opposite (to
England) – ugly grounds, lots of disputes and fans with little
sporting culture. And there they don't go away from home
on training camps. With us, you hardly need to start losing
before everyone has to go off to a training camp. Things go
badly and immediately they sack the manager. That's typical Italian-style. I'm Italian, I'm proud of my country and
of our football but I have to admit that, today, the English
teams have an undeniable superior physical strength, technique and financial backing. The Premier League is the
best league in Europe, even if the Italy manager, Marcello
Lippi, says that the maximum expression of football is not
the (domestic) league, or the Champions League but the
national side and, at the moment, the most important
national side is Spain.'

*Talking of national sides, how do you view the chances of
champions Torres & Co. in the next World Cup?*
'One can't deny that they are favourites. They are champions
of Europe, they have a generation of fantastic young footballers. But the tournament is outside Europe and the favourites
almost never get to the final. The World Cup is another thing
altogether, where so many factors depend on the luck of the
draw. But certainly, to achieve the run of victories they've
had, with qualification already in the bag, allows you to have,
as they say here, "mas confianza" ("more confidence").'

Chapter 30

Manchester United 1 Liverpool 4

14 March 2008

Good afternoon and welcome to Old Trafford ...

The stadium is full and we have just been informed that there is a crowd of 75,569. This match tops the bill for the 29th day of action in the Premier League. The meeting is due to kick off shortly, at 12.45pm. Top of the table Manchester United are playing host to the Reds, who are joint third in the overall standings along with Guus Hiddink's Chelsea on 58 points, seven adrift of United, who have a game in hand (Portsmouth). If Sir Alex Ferguson's men win today, they move ten points ahead of Liverpool and could wrap up the league, or almost. They are clear favourites. They have had a run of eleven wins on the trot, let in only two goals in the last sixteen games and have booked their place in the semi-finals of the Champions League without too much trouble by seeing off Inter Milan in the quarter-finals. The Reds come into this vital match with their morale running very high following a convincing Champions League victory on Tuesday against Real Madrid. Here their last chances for a tilt at the league are at stake. If they manage to cut the distance from the leaders they could open up the fight for the title again. Will the effort from the match against the men in white weigh against them? It may well do, but Benítez's wards will give it their best shot to come out on top at a ground where Liverpool has not won since 2004, when Gérard Houllier was on the bench. Rafa has never walked away as the winner from the Theatre of Dreams.

The bad news for the Merseyside team is the absence of Xabi Alonso, who won't be able to lay down the law in midfield. He is replaced by Lucas Leiva. For the other side Dimitar Berbatov settles into the dugout, while 'The Apache' Tévez starts. Let's have a look at the line-ups announced:

Manchester United: Van der Sar, O'Shea, Ferdinand, Vidic, Evra, Ronaldo, Carrick, Anderson, Park, Rooney, Tévez. Subs: Foster, Berbatov, Giggs, Nani, Scholes, Evans, Fletcher.

Liverpool: Reina, Arbeloa, Carragher, Skrtel, Aurelio, Mascherano, Lucas, Kuyt, Gerrard, Riera, Torres. Subs: Cavalieri, Dossena, Hyypia, Babel, Insúa, Ngog, El Zhar.

Referee: Alan Wiley

The players are coming out onto the pitch now, Manchester in their traditional red shirts and Liverpool in grey.

Álvaro Aberloa isn't there among the Reds. He has had physical problems in the warm-up. Sami Hyypia takes his position and Carragher will play in the right back berth. A position he doesn't really take to, if the truth be told.

The game gets underway.

2nd minute

Wayne Rooney seems to be all fired up. He is dangerous in the Red Devils' first couple of attacks. Carragher looks uneasy opposite 'Bad Boy'.

3rd minute

From over on the right Cristiano Ronaldo feeds a ball in for Ji-Sung Park but the Korean's shot is cut out by Carragher – corner. Manchester United is producing some good football and playing well.

6th minute

Liverpool make inroads for the first time, Torres chasing up an extremely long ball. Rio Ferdinand checks on the edge of Manchester's box.

21st minute

Torres swerves brilliantly with one touch and gets away from Ferdinand on the edge of the penalty area – a touch of genius. For a moment it looks like a goal, but Vidic and O'Shea don't let him finish off the move.

22nd minute

A penalty to Manchester. Park chases a ball down the inside-left channel and into the box. Reina races out and slides towards Park's feet. Park runs into the prone keeper and tumbles over.

23rd minute

GOAL, CRISTIANO RONALDO! MANCHESTER UNITED 1 LIVERPOOL 0

The man from Portugal is unforgiving from the spot. He shoots right-footed and low, just inside the left post. Reina guesses right but doesn't get there.

28th minute

GOAL, TORRES! MANCHESTER UNITED 1 LIVERPOOL 1

Liverpool seem punch-drunk after the goal and unable to respond to the moves made by the Red Devils. It would be fair to say they haven't put a foot right for five minutes and then the most amazing thing happens. Martin Skrtel frees things up in his area and hits a really long ball forward. Vidic scampers towards his goalmouth, allows the ball to bounce, and lets Fernando steal it off him – El Niño is off. Van der Sar rushes out to close up the angle but Torres keeps an extremely cool head and beats him on the run with an accurate finish into the left-hand corner of the Dutchman's goal. Fantastic work from The Kid. Game on.

31st minute

Torres once more against the unfortunate Vidic, who appears not to have a clue how to handle the fair-haired Spanish striker. First he forces him to clear for a corner and next up he heads past him (cross from Fabio Aurelio), slips into the penalty area and the Serbian defender stops him by stretching the rule-book to the limit.

34th minute

Cristiano Ronaldo blasts a free-kick from miles out and Reina almost makes a howler. He manages to get his hands round the ball after fumbling, just before Tévez arrives …

36th minute

Yellow card for Jamie Carragher for going in dangerously.

37th minute

Rio Ferdinand goes yellow for a dangerous tackle.

41st minute

Torres releases Riera on the left into the Manchester 6-yard box. Ferdinand gets there in the nick of time to sweep clear.

43rd minute

Penalty to Liverpool. The Kid takes the ball outside the penalty area and when the United central defenders come out to get him he does a half-turn and slides in a perfect pass between the lines for Gerrard who is in the area. It is all Evra can do to stop the captain by fouling him.

44th minute

Yellow card for Edwin Van der Sar for protesting.

44th minute

GOAL, GERRARD! MANCHESTER UNITED 1 LIVERPOOL 2
Van der Sar just manages to touch the ball but the shot from the Reds' captain is well-placed and struck hard.

45th minute +3

Gerrard again. His thunderbolt is cleared by O'Shea. Manchester United reply in the shape of Tévez, who wins a corner. Nothing actually happens as the referee blows for half-time.

Half-time

An exciting game with no let up in play. Liverpool are deservedly ahead and have read the game well.

The second half gets under way.

48th minute

Cross by Ronaldo and the ball squirms away from Reina and hits the post.

49th minute

Torres collides with Tévez and has damaged his already injured ankle, but he seems able to play on.

59th minute
United dominate play and buzz the Liverpool penalty area, but they aren't creating too much danger.

60th minute
A yellow for Javier Mascherano.

64th minute
Yellow card for Skrtel for fouling Tévez.

66th minute
Gerrard leads the first attacking move from Liverpool in the second half. It ends with a shot by Leiva from the edge of the box. Van der Sar fields it.

68th minute
A Liverpool change – Andrea Dossena comes on for Albert Riera.

71st minute
Great chance for United – Tévez almost manufactures a goal out of a dead ball in the area.

73rd minute
Triple substitution by Manchester United. Anderson, Ji-Sung Park and Michael Carrick are replaced by Ryan Giggs, Paul Scholes and Dimitar Berbatov.

76th minute
Vidic is red-carded. As with the Torres goal, the United defender is beaten by the ball. Gerrard breaks away on his own and the Serbian has no choice but to grab him and throw him to the ground. There's no arguing about the referee's decision.

77th minute
GOAL, AURELIO! MANCHESTER UNITED 1 LIVERPOOL 3
A sweet shot from Fabio Aurelio that goes right in the block-hole. That's how to shoot free-kicks! The Brazilian master-fully converts the foul given away by Vidic for pulling.

78th minute
Torres tries a deep pass to his skipper. But Gerrard is caught offside.

79th minute
Torres tries to catch Van der Sar out from the centre of the pitch, but the shot strays very high and to the left.

81st minute
Second change by Liverpool. Fernando Torres goes off and Ryan Babel comes on.

Nine minutes later, Fernando smiles and celebrates Liverpool's fourth on the bench – a masterly effort by Andrea Dossena. As he did against Madrid, the Italian brings the Reds' cracking game to a close. The score-line is 1-4. Amazing – the statistics say as much.

The last time United let in four goals at home was New Year's Day 1992 against Queens Park Rangers. Liverpool's 4-1 win is the second biggest since November 1936, when the Reds won 5-2. And while we're on the subject of statistics, it should be remembered that this is Rafa Benítez's 100th win since he arrived in the Premier. But the main thing is that the league is still open.

'They think it's all over … it isn't now' runs the headline in the *Sunday Times*, above a huge photo of Torres battling it out with Vidic. Torres, together with Gerrard, is the hero of Old Trafford – the star of Liverpool's big week. Two wins and eight goals scored in five days. The Reds' captain pays tribute to his team-mate: 'He's magic. He's the world's greatest striker and a lot of people probably agree with me.' And he's right. Plaudits from all sides are fantastic. Let's leave the English and the Spanish to one side, as they are too closely involved here, and see what Giancarlo Galavotti writes in *La Gazzetta dello Sport*: 'The lethal weapon is always the same: Fernando Torres. Simply wonderful, El Niño surprises and wipes out the opposition with an undeniable show of class and power. After Madrid he also humiliates Manchester. The panel of the Golden Ball should be alert to this.' Nothing more to say. Steve Gerrard, though, does chime in with something: 'Liverpool can win the Premier League. If we carry on like this from now on, we've got a chance to walk away with the title, and Fernando Torres is the key to doing it.'

It wouldn't be the first time. March 1998 – United has an eleven-point lead over Blackburn and twelve over Arsenal and Liverpool. It seems they've got the League title in the bag. Final standings: Arsenal 78, Manchester United 77. The Gunners win ten games on the trot and crown themselves champions with two games in hand. This time there are nine games to go, but it seems there's a chance. Even more so when, a week on, United lose to Fulham. Two defeats in a row – something that hasn't happened since 2005. At Liverpool, who have just given Aston Villa a 5-0 thrashing, they are convinced the Red Devils are feeling the heat. But after their two routs, Ferguson's men hit the accelerator and don't let up right to the end.

On Saturday, 16 May, United win their third League in a row, their 18th. They draw level with Liverpool in number of trophies won and leave the Merseyside team with a bad taste in their mouths. They've lost fewer times than the Red Devils (two versus four times), have netted more goals

(72 versus 67), but in the end they are second in the overall standings, and four points adrift of the champions. Their high draw-rate has cost them dear. It is nineteen years since the Reds have lifted the league trophy. Another season over without silverware. In the Champions League Liverpool came up against Chelsea in the semis, in a duel that, in England over the last few years, has become as much a custom as tea or rain. They were eliminated in a night to remember, an eight-goal thriller – an unbelievable game, as the English press wrote, following the 4-4 *dénouement* at Stamford Bridge. They praised the pluck and pride of the Reds, one step away from changing history, one step away from turning round a 1-3 result from the home match, one step away from winning the mother of all battles, as the *Guardian* wrote. But in the end the Champions' dream faded away.

Fernando has scored two goals in Europe's team championship. In the league he has netted fourteen goals, five less than top-scorer Nicolas Anelka of Chelsea. Whenever on the pitch he has been decisive. It's just a shame that bad luck hasn't given him a better strike-rate. This is something Gerrard also sees as an unhappy circumstance: 'The frustrating thing for both of us is that we haven't been together more times on the pitch this season.' It's true. The awesome partnership (28 goals) has only been together on the pitch for twelve out of 36 Premier matches. 'Let's hope,' says Stevie G. on the club's official web-site, 'that next season we are ready to give Liverpool the best chance of success. We both feel that if we are both clicking, we can cause defences loads of problems. We both enjoy playing with each other and we can both either score goals or set them up for each other.' Fernando is also hopeful about next season: 'Winning the Premier League will be our big objective again. We will fight for the title again by looking to win at home more regularly against the teams that are more winnable in theory. As we have seen this season, they choked us. I reckon Manchester United and Chelsea will be our main rivals, though we can't rule out Arsenal either, or Manchester City. I hope that this year we will achieve what all the fans expect from us'.

Chapter 31

You'd be happy if your daughter brought him home

Conversation with former Liverpool player and manager, Graeme Souness

He's hardly arrived in the United States before he's already on his way to Rome. The ex-Liverpool captain is going back to the Eternal City, where, on 30 May 1984, he held aloft Liverpool's fourth European Cup. The final trophy of an impressive season, which also saw them win the league championship and the League Cup and the first under manager, Joe Fagan, who had replaced Bob Paisley.

Souness, the Number 11 in the red shirt, remembers that final well. The Roma side of Bruno Conti, Paulo Roberto Falcao, Ciccio Graziani, Roberto Pruzzo and a young Carlo Ancelotti (now manager of Chelsea) were regarded as odds-on favourites. Playing at home, with the fans behind them, they had already proved their ability (through convincing and impressive football) to win the previous year's Scudetto. It was a zonal style of playing, which was put into practice very effectively under the guidance of Swedish manager, 'Il Barone' Nils Liedholm – a renowned midfielder from the 1950s, who went on to manage a host of Italian sides over a 30-year period. And yet, despite being favourites, the score was 1-1 after 90 minutes (goals from Phil Neal and Pruzzo). After extra time, they finally bowed out to the English side

4-2 on penalties. Graeme Souness didn't fail with his kick, the third in the sequence, high towards the angle of post and crossbar to the left of Roma keeper Franco Tancredi. Bruce Grobbelaar, the South African who came up with his 'spaghetti legs' routine (never forgotten by the Liverpool fans and successfully reprised by Jerzy Dudek 21 years later in the final against Ancelotti's Milan) unnerved the unfortunate Graziani so much that he ended up shooting over the bar. The big-handled Cup was Liverpool's. Michael Robinson – to whom the trophy had been entrusted – left it in a shop at Fiumicino Airport. Fortunately, he remembered it at the last moment and managed to get it back.

It's 25 years since that day. Souness is now 56, returning to the Stadio Olimpico – minus his distinctive moustache and thick curly hair – via the Sky Sports commentator's box.

He'll be asked for his opinions on the Manchester United of Cristiano Ronaldo and the Barcelona of Lionel Messi, the teams contesting the Champions League title. Because of his intelligence and experience, Souness is someone well qualified to talk about Fernando Torres. And yet he says that he doesn't have much in-depth knowledge about football. This admission leads to a chuckle from the Scot and the interview begins …

Let's start with last season's big Premier League clash between Manchester United and Liverpool. What do you think of the performance of Liverpool and particularly of Torres?
'I have played in many games like that and we were the best team but we never had a result like that. For me, the turning point was when Torres outpaced Vidic (Manchester United defender, Nemanja Vidic). Vidic thought he was quite comfortable in his defensive position but Torres, with his electric pace, got there before him and from that moment on,

Manchester United found it very difficult and Vidic, especially, was frightened to death by Torres' pace.'

Despite this result, Manchester and Alex Ferguson went on to win the league again. It's nineteen years since Liverpool won it. What more does Liverpool need to do to win it?
'They've got closer this time but they rely too heavily on Steven Gerrard and Torres for goals. Manchester United have five or six very special players. Liverpool have two very special players. I think it's all about quality at the end of the day. I think for any Liverpool player the concern is that Manchester United have a good group of young players coming through, where that is not the case at Liverpool. Liverpool will have to buy and I'm not sure they have the money. They will have to go out and buy another two or three very special players. But I'm not sure at Liverpool because they have to spend their money on a bigger stadium.

'We'll have to get a new stadium because we'll just keep dropping further and further behind Manchester United and Arsenal. But a new stadium obviously costs a lot of money and that will mean we'll not be buying new players. As a Liverpool supporter, looking forward, I'm still worried about that. Because the two people who now own Liverpool, what have they done? All they did was go to the bank and borrow money to buy Liverpool. The previous chairman, David Moores, could have done the same thing. The previous board could have done the same thing. Liverpool are no further forward now for me than they were before these two Americans came in.'

What is the main difference between your Liverpool, the 'glorious' Liverpool, and the current Liverpool?
'Well, I just think we had better players. There's no secret in football. I think this group of players is very good. The

supporters are the best supporters in the country because they allow you to play football the right way, they are patient with you. In my day we were a solid group of seven or eight very, very good players and we had the support, like this group have, of the supporters. But when things aren't going well, we were all in it together. This group of players understand that but I don't think they've got six or seven very good players. They've got two very, very special players and another three or four that are good players but not special players.'

As a manager and former captain of Liverpool, what's your technical judgement of Fernando Torres?
'He's an exceptional talent. He's explosive. I think he's like all the top strikers. He can be having a quiet game but if you're playing against him you're always aware that you can keep him quiet for 89 minutes and in that 90th minute he can kill you. His pace is his obvious attribute. But as well as that, he is a good finisher, he's brave and he works hard.'

What is his contribution to Liverpool?
'It's enormous. There are the two very obvious threats of him and Gerrard. Gerrard's not a midfield player, he's like a central striker. And I believe those two strikers are the best out there. For me, Steven Gerrard is not a midfield player. He's behind Torres. Torres can make the little, quick runs in behind defenders and Gerrard will find him. Those two are the best front two out there today.'

When Liverpool and Rafa Benítez chose Fernando Torres, many commentators said it was a risk for the amount of money they paid. How then, did he score 33 goals in his first season? This was explosive and a revelation, no?

He was young and he'd never played outside Spain before, so there was always an element of risk. I think that, in his first season, he very quickly understood that he was playing for a special football club and the relationship between the players and the supporters is a special one. But I reckon you can analyse it and analyse it but he's just a very, very good footballer and he felt at home immediately when he went to Liverpool because Liverpool supporters appreciate players who give 100 per cent, who score goals. There's no acting with him, he's not throwing himself to the ground, he's not looking for fouls in the box all the time. He is a Liverpool player and I believe that very quickly he won the hearts of the Liverpool supporters.

It isn't easy to enter into the history and spirit of a club, particularly a club like Liverpool. How did he manage to do this so quickly?
'Because he's good! All clubs like a star in the team, a goalscorer. He's following on from people like Ian Rush, Robbie Fowler, Michael Owen. They were all great goalscorers. He's built up their hopes. He's now their new hero and I always think that getting off to a good start helped him. But I come back to him being young, when he arrived nobody really knowing him and everybody took to him immediately, all the supporters liked him immediately and he would have realised that, they would have got that message across to him and from that point on the Kop was won over, he feels loved and the rest was history.'

And you met him, in the programme that Michael Robinson made last year. What was your impression of him?
'He seems a very modest, humble young lad.'

He doesn't speak a lot but he knows how to play ...
'Exactly, he does his talking on the pitch. When I met him, that time, he was very respectful. He's the sort of boy you knew you'd be happy if your daughter brought home. During the two hours that I spent with him, that was the image I got from him.'

How do you see Torres' future at Liverpool?
'I think he'll be happy to stay there as long as they want him because he feels loved by the crowd and I think the only way he'd leave Liverpool would be if Liverpool dropped out of the Champions League and then they couldn't afford to keep him. But I think that as long as Liverpool play in the Champions League, he will stay there. The fans would not allow the board of directors to sell him.'

What for you are Torres' best moments, best goal or best moves during his two years at Liverpool?
'I think he's scored some fantastic goals but beating Manchester United so convincingly at Old Trafford, I can never remember that happening before. I think his goal set them on the way to win that game – it would have to be that one because it meant so much to every Liverpool supporter. It was a very special day.'

Finally, one more question. It's out of curiosity more than anything. Was it Michael Robinson who called you 'The Cat', or you who called him 'The Cat'?
'I called him 'The Cat'. He thinks he is a goalkeeper!'

Bon voyage Mr Souness, and enjoy the final in Rome ...

Chapter 32
The same as always

*Conversation with Julián Hernández and
Ángel Sánchez*

Both of them are wearing their work clothes. A red-and-white-striped shirt and a red tie – the colours of Atlético Madrid. They work as receptionists at the Vicente Calderón stadium. You see them as soon as you enter the old stadium, after the glass door that leads to the management offices. Julián, 24, from Carabanchel Bajo, a neighbourhood of Madrid, has worked here for four years. Ángel, a 25-year-old and also from Madrid, arrived a bit later. They're both close friends of El Niño. They got to know him by chance. Ángel, who used to play as a striker for Roma Club de Futbol, a junior team based in Ventas near the Plaza de Toros in Madrid, first found himself facing Torres as an opponent but then, thanks to Oscar (who played with him and knew Fer from when they were juniors), joined their group. Julián was a friend of Hugo, who knew Torres through football and ended up being inseparable from his group. They've known each other for eight years. And even though Fernando plays in England they have not lost contact. Julián spent two weeks in Liverpool and London, the two weeks in which the Reds played in the Champions League semi-final against Chelsea, so that he could watch both games and be with Fer. Ángel wasn't able to go ... otherwise, who would answer the phones at Atlético Madrid? But he's promised himself that he'll go over just as soon as he gets a few days' holiday. Neither find it difficult to talk about having such a famous friend, who has appeared on the front pages of newspapers around the world. But they're careful not to say anything that could show him in a bad light. That's normal, it's the way close friends are. Seated in the office of Manuel Briñas, they chat about their famous friend's past and present.

OK, so how has he changed, the boy who began playing for Atlético Madrid and has now conquered the world?

J.H. 'He hasn't changed, he carries on being just like he was before. He hangs around with the same people and the same friends as ever. And he continues being very close to his mates. I've heard people say he's a show-off, arrogant and even conceited because he's successful at Liverpool. But it's all lies what people say, people who know nothing about him. Fernando is a modest guy and not at all conceited and with us he's really good company, amusing and has a great sense of humour. He's always had his head well screwed-on, with a good family behind him, people who look after him well in every sense, and good friends who for a long time have been genuine mates. Not like those who suck up to you when everything's fine but disappear if things go badly. And I'm not talking only about the two of us.'

A.S. 'With us, he's the same blond, freckly bloke. A really straightforward and compassionate guy. A true friend. We can go for months without talking and then, when we do, it's as if we'd just seen each other five minutes earlier. Neither the fact that he's one of the best strikers in the world, nor the money that he earns, have made him behave differently. Fame hasn't gone to his head either, not like it has with a lot of footballers, who change the people they mix with and their social circle. He's got the same girlfriend that he had when he was seventeen and the same friends.'

'It's true,' says Manolo Briñas, joining in the conversation, 'when Fernando was here and already an exceptional player, he didn't go to Los Angeles or Miami on holiday but instead, here in Spain with his fifteen mates. Ángel, you explain …'

A.S. 'Yes, every summer we went on holiday for a week or two. I remember we went to Gandía and five years ago to Las Palmas in the Canary Islands. Between World Cups and European championships it wasn't easy to find a gap. We had such a good time and I still remember the smaller kids, who, when they saw that El Niño was part of our group, couldn't believe it and started swarming around us like flies.'

And Julián, how does he seem to you now, in Liverpool?
J.H. 'He's got accustomed really quickly to life in England. Also, because he's a very home-loving guy and he likes the quiet life. Sometimes he goes out at night but most of the time he stays in with Olalla watching films or programmes on Spanish TV. And sometimes they go to Pepe Reina's house or Pepe and Yolanda go to his house. Olalla and Yolanda have become great friends. And with Riera as well. They meet up whenever they can.'

What does he really love doing?
J.H. 'He still likes the Playstation and Pro Evolution Soccer. He listens to music, all the favourites, El Canto del Loco, Andrés Calamaro, Joaquín Sabina, Nirvana, Duncan Du. And later, he likes it when he can go walking with his dogs. When he's got a free day, he'll go off on a trip to explore the country. I don't think he's changed his life much in England. Apart from one thing, which, to be honest, really shook me. Fernando has always eaten everything but now, in the morning, he also likes sausages and beans for breakfast with a coffee. They give it him in Melwood and he's got used to it.'

Is he calmer and more relaxed than he was in Madrid?

J.H. 'He seems like that to me because there the media don't hassle you, nothing like the extent to which that happens here. There the paparazzi don't go after you. You can get on with your life without any hassle. He and Olalla go out walking, they go shopping at the supermarket and it's no problem. The people, the fans are very respectful. I was out walking with him and I was surprised because before they even asked Fernando, they always asked me if they could take a picture of him.'

What do you talk about now when you meet up?

J.H. 'We don't talk much about football, which might seem strange, but that's how it is. We don't want to bore him with that and besides, there's much more to talk about than just football.'

OK then, what do you think of his success in England?

J.H. 'When I was there, it surprised me how much the people really love him.'

Why?

'I don't know really … He's fallen on his feet because he's a really nice guy.'

A.S. 'And one has to say that he's a great football professional. He hasn't got to be almost as popular as Gerrard just because he's got a pretty face. No, Fernando has worked hard and one's got to say that he deserves what he's now got. No one has put him up there.'

Do you envy him for his money, fame and success?

J.H. 'No, he deserves it all.'

A.S. 'Me, yes! As a striker I've always envied his liveliness and power.'

Chapter 33

The Kid

29 May 2009
Conversation with Fernando Torres

Here is The Kid – who's not such a kid any more. Last
20 March he turned 25. On 26 May, when Rome was hogging
the limelight in the footballing world for the Champions
League final between Barcelona and Manchester United,
Fernando José Torres Sanz got married to Olalla Domínguez
Liste, his lifelong girlfriend. A registry office wedding at the
town hall in El Escorial (a town some 50 km outside Madrid
and a tourist attraction due to its monastery). Olalla, who
has lived with Fernando since 2004, is seven months preg-
nant. Yes, the kid is going to be a father. But he will never
manage to shake off the nickname he was given when he
got into the Atléti first team. A kid who has signed a new
contract with Liverpool up to 2014. A kid who is the only
crack player to own all of his own image rights. His earnings
have soared in the last few months. He has lent his name
to advertising campaigns by Banco Gallego, El Corte Inglés
and Nike. Together with Leo Messi he will be the face of Pro
Evolution Soccer 2010. A star – and he is welcomed as such
at the Hotel Meliá Avenida de América in Madrid.

It's twelve in the morning and 700 people await his
arrival. They are friends, Atléti and Liverpool fans, boys
and girls; fifteen-year-olds who are crazy about the blond
angel. His entrance is worthy of a rock star – hysterical

screaming included. Hair as fair as could be, immaculate white shirt, black jacket, faded jeans, black trainers with white laces. Fernando sits down at the table of the Marca Sports Forum. He greets everyone and listens to the brief words from Eduardo Inda, the director of the Madrid sports paper, from José Antonio 'Petón' Martín, someone who has known him ever since he was a small boy, and José Antonio Abellán.

Afterwards it's his turn to speak: 'I'm not surprised by the loyalty the fans are showing me. I was born an Atlético person, I've spent virtually all my life at this club, and I know what Atléti folk are like. I know that when I left some people didn't understand it, but luckily, two years down the line, most people can understand it. I can see Atlético shirts here and some from Liverpool. Being united like that is the best possible news as far as I'm concerned. When I watch Atlético games on television and I see Liverpool shirts, it gives me an amazing sense of pride. It's like when I see a lot of Atléti shirts at Anfield and it's something I love. I have to say, I feel a part of both clubs, and that is the biggest and best thing I've ever had'.

The questions start ...

How would you define the Atlético feeling?
'It's hard to put your finger on. I think you are born an Atlético person. There aren't very many people who become fans of the red-and-whites on the way. Kids see Real Madrid winning and it's one of the giants, so they become fans of the whites. In my class I was the only Atlético supporter out of 30 children. They were all Real Madrid fans. How did I handle it? Well, I had to put up with the jokes every weekend, but I felt more and more proud. I used to go to the ground to watch my team play and when we lost I thought, "oh well, we'll win next week" ... and when we won I was

happy for the whole week afterwards. More important than the results there is the desire to support your team in the hope that one day they'll get back up where they belong. I experienced the double as a fan, and when we went down as a fan, and as a player. Good things and bad things, and that's what Atlético Madrid is like. But the main thing is that the ground is packed and the fans are devoted to their team. That's what makes it different.'

Will you come back to Atlético?
'Seriously, that's not just down to me. Sure, I'd love to finish my career with Atlético, but you never know what strange turns events might take in football. But I intend to – let's see after 2014 …'

Do you think your departure from Atléti has already been worth it or won't this be true until you win some silverware?
'I've achieved the two goals I set myself. I've seen Atlético grow in stature. They've played Champions League football, signed up some really good players, and are now a team that's recognised in Europe – my team-mates at Liverpool talk about Atléti. That's what I wanted when I left. Personally speaking, I think I've come on a great deal over these two years. In my first season at Liverpool I managed to score more goals than any other foreign player in the Premier League and I came third in the Golden Ball and the FIFA World Player awards. I've developed in footballing terms and it's been Liverpool that has let me do that, because it's a team that always plays at the highest level. That's why I'm very happy with the decision I took.'

Do you get on better with the club people at Liverpool than with those at Atléti?
'At Atlético there were people I had known since I was a kid, players who I was with in the junior levels and afterwards in the first team, and I knew the people at the club, the people working at the Vicente Calderón. Now, at Anfield, I've started from scratch and get on well with everyone. I'm not a person who has had or caused problems in the dressing room. I've always tried to be as consistent as possible because I know that it's your team-mates who are going to make you a big name or not. I know that, in this sense, I've been lucky to be in two great dressing rooms.'

Who do you feel more at home playing with, Mascherano and Xabi Alonso or Xavi and Iniesta?
'Luckily all four are really good. It's very different though. English football is a lot faster … there's hardly any play among the defenders and the midfielders before you're upfield, and within two or three touches and moving really fast you're suddenly in front of the other side's keeper. With my playing style this has really suited me, but that doesn't mean playing alongside Xavi and Iniesta isn't a luxury. You just know they're going to have the ball and you know you're going to be more relaxed when it comes to finishing because you don't have to worry. It's a joy to know that the ball is safe at their feet. You know that you can send them a shocker of a ball and they'll manage to keep it under control. If you get the chance to have Xavi and Iniesta in one place and Xabi Alonso and Mascherano in another, it's just the best thing.'

How are things with Gerrard?
'I wish I could play alongside him my whole life. He's a player I admired from before, but from being on the pitch

with him you realise that he's even better and greater than you ever thought. When he's on the pitch there's nothing to be afraid of and you know he's always going to be there, lift the team when the going gets tough, and always give you a hand. And in the dressing room he gets 10 out of 10 because he always makes himself available and always has a word of encouragement for you. I remember first coming to Liverpool and after having my medical I landed in Madrid to say goodbye to the fans. The first message I got was from him. It said, 'welcome to the club', and he hoped I could help the team bag some silverware. I wasn't even a Liverpool player at that point. I had gone through the medical but I still had to put pen to paper, and here he was welcoming me on board. It's a nice touch that makes you see what a great captain he is. I never managed to transmit that to my team-mates at Atlético when I was wearing the skipper's armband because I wasn't experienced enough ...'

How did you know it was him? Did you notice his number?
'Not his number or what he was saying either!' (laughter and applause from the audience). I was with Jorge, who had to translate for me, because there was no way I was going to understand.'

Can you tell us how you felt the first time you went through underneath the shield that says 'This Is Anfield' and came out onto the pitch?
'The fact is that Liverpool is a club with nice touches, which really looks after its history, and in that sense it's very similar to Atléti. It remembers its legends and the greats who made it a big club and that little sign, which isn't much more than a picture in the tunnel, means so much for a lot of people and has ended up as something special. On the day when I was presented, when there weren't any people in

the ground, I saw it when I walked past it but it didn't mean much to me. But on my debut at Anfield against Chelsea … while the crowd was singing "You'll Never Walk Alone" … boy, that's when it sinks in that you are in a special place and that the sign is special too.'

Who has given you more as a trainer, Rafa Benítez or Luis Aragonés?
'I think both of them have. I've been with Luis for a long time. Since I was very young and starting out he's taught me the fundamentals, both on and off the pitch. I was seventeen and he had seen everything as a player and as a trainer, he had a lot to teach me and I had a lot to learn. Those were the days when I had to listen, learn and keep my mouth shut. And then with Luis I've won the national team's biggest trophy in the last 44 years. With Rafa I've made a big leap forward in terms of quality. He's taught me a lot of things and made me improve areas where I was lacking, and he still does that because he's a person who doesn't stop in his everyday life, even for one minute, and tries to improve you in every detail and every move, while trying to explain to you why. He's obsessed with you doing things because you understand why, because you understand the reason he asks you to do them. He doesn't say to you, 'Do this because I'm telling you to.' That's Benítez. I hope I'm with him many more years so that he can keep teaching me and I can win silverware with him.'

If Rafa Benítez were to be chosen as trainer of Real Madrid, would you go with him as a player?
'Nooooo! Nooooo!' Murmur the fans.
 'Rafa's got a contract, like I have, that runs up until 2014 and I honestly hope that scenario doesn't come about and

that he doesn't leave, but if he did, I wouldn't follow suit.'
(*Hearty applause from the seating area.*)

*If Barcelona and Real Madrid made the same offer for you, which
one would you go for?*
'I'd stay at Liverpool.' (*Applause*)

*Which striker from the Spanish Liga would you take with you to
Liverpool as a partner in the attack?*
'I'd say Diego Forlán but no … because then I'd be taking
him off Atléti. (*Laughter again*)
    'No … David Villa or David Silva. I wish they could come,
it would be a great asset for our team.'

What would it take for Liverpool to win the Premier League?
'We need match-winners like Rooney or Tévez, footballers
who break the deadlock in matches. In fact, Liverpool is
losing the Premier League in home games against average
teams.'

What was your first press conference in English like?
'I've never been so scared in all my life.'

By the media pressure?
'No. In England there's no pressure from the media. There's
no daily coverage of the team. There are no sports papers
and the tabloids give it two or three pages, which is what
the major informative papers do too. Training sessions are
behind closed doors and supporters and journalists can't
attend. There are no interviews or press conferences, only
when we played in the Champions' League because UEFA
makes us. Everything's a lot calmer but the first time I did a
press conference in front of dozens of journalists I had a lot

on my plate. If you don't understand a question … but I got through it okay. More or less.'

How did you feel when it turned out that Liverpool would face Atlético?
'When I got injured in Brussels the first thing that went through my head was the Atléti match in the Calderón. There were only a few days to go and I already knew I wouldn't be able to make it. It was really frustrating not to be able to be there and see people again. But then you learn to live with it, the match comes round and when I saw the two sets of supporters on television swapping shirts it was the best thing since sliced bread from my standpoint – imagine! There were a lot of people there that I thought would be upset with me for leaving but that wasn't the case. After hearing my name chanted in the Calderón it became the best moment all season besides all the awards.'

What went through your mind when you scored against Real Madrid at Anfield?
'It was a special moment for me because I hadn't trained for the 10 days leading up to it. I was playing in a lot of pain and I had to cut a bit off my boot because my foot wouldn't fit in it with all the strapping on. I was on the verge of not playing but I was really dying to. In the end I managed to play and imagine what it was like when I made it to the game and I scored … the knock-out game wasn't decided because it's Real Madrid we're talking about and anything could have happened. But the feeling … it was incredible. It was worth the risk.'

How did you feel when you netted the winning goal in the European Championship against Germany?

'It's the sort of feeling you spend your whole life looking for. You dream of being a player when you are younger, you dream of playing in the first division, and when you are there, you want more, you want to play for your country, you want to play in a European Championship, in a World Cup, but they are such far-fetched dreams that you think they'll never come true ... and when that ball went in ... you realise that all the dreams you ever had have come true. A feeling we did have was that we knew that Spain was united around us. I was in the street and to be responsible for that goal, for the feeling of unity the country experienced after so many years without lifting a trophy, is incredible ...'

And now, having realised that dream, it doesn't seem so hard to make others come true: to become world champions ...

'We're going to go all out for the World Cup, obviously. In our situation we can allow ourselves to imagine that happening. While remaining wary and humble, like the national team always has been, I believe it'll be virtually the same team from the European championship, but with two years' more experience. We can learn from the few mistakes we made, get stronger and go for it at the World Cup. And hopefully in South Africa we can repeat our success.'

What do you need to be the same Fernando Torres for the national side as you are at Liverpool?

'I suppose I'd have to get used to the style of football that they play in the Spain team much more quickly. It's more elaborate than how they play at Liverpool and there's more touching the ball. Plus changing your mindset isn't easy when, like in the World Cup qualifiers, you only have two or three days to train. Switching from the mentality in the

English system to the one in the Spanish Liga is something I still have to sort out.'

What is Vicente del Bosque like?
'He's very approachable and like another team-mate. He's brought in a much more relaxed atmosphere.'

What would give you the bigger thrill, winning the World cup or the Champions League?
'I don't think I could decide. A World Cup is something that's in every footballer's mind, even more so now that it seems achievable and it's just round the corner, but winning the Champions with my team would be really great. Either way then.'

What's the best league in the world, the English or the Spanish?
'It's hard to say. I think that, as things stand, the English league is the most competitive in the world because it's got four great teams that can go all the way in Europe's biggest tournament. In the Liga this year there's been one team like Barcelona, which has been better than the English ones, but that's been one team and the other three semi-finalists were English teams, and we also lost to an English team. I think the Premier is stronger at the moment. It's a league where Spanish players can fit in, as can others from all over the world. Each one has its moments though, and there have been seasons where the Italian League has been the best and now it's the English, but things can change.'

Who is the best player in the world for you?
'For me it would obviously be Gerrard, because I see him every day, though I think Leo Messi deserves the honour more than anyone else. He's been the best this year. He's won everything.'

And it comes to the last question ... Torres, can I have my picture taken with you?

The request comes from Rubén Calvo, a ten-year-old lad with fair hair and big green eyes, clutching a Liverpool shirt. Fernando has no problem agreeing to this. He hasn't forgotten the promise he made years back to Flori, his mother. That day, after watching the Spanish national side train in Boadilla del Monte, Torres went up to the internationals to get their autographs along with some other boys. No joy. He got into such a stew about it that he promised his mother that, if he should ever make it into their boots, he would never deny anyone a photo or an autograph. Now that he has arrived, El Niño does not forget, and *el niño*, with fair hair and big green eyes, smiles.

Career record

Personal summary
Full name: Fernando José Torres Sanz
Place and Date of Birth: Madrid, 20 March 1984
Parents: Flori and José. Sister: Mari Paz. Brother: Israel
Married: 27 May 2009
Wife: Olalla Domínguez Liste
Height: 186 cm
Weight: 78 kg

Early career
As a junior, played for Parque 84, Mario's Holanda and Rayo 13
At eleven years old, scouted to Atlético de Madrid

Atlético de Madrid
Debut: 27 May 2001 v Leganés (home) Second Division
First goal: 4 June 2001 v Albacete (away) Second Division

Appearances
Liga 174 Goals 82
Copa del Rey 25 Goals 7
Became Atlético de Madrid captain in 2003 aged eighteen.

Liverpool

Debut: 11 August 2007 v Aston Villa (away) Premier League
First goal: 18 August 2007 v Chelsea (home) Premier League

Appearances
League: 57 Goals 38
F.A. Cup 4 Goals 1
League Cup 3 Goals 3
Europe 20 Goals 8

Spain

Debut: 6 September 2003 v Portugal (away)
First goal: 28 April 2004 v Italy (away)
Caps 67 Goals 22

Tournaments played:
European Championship 2004
World Cup 2006
European Championship 2008
Confederations Cup 2009

Honours won

European Championship 2008
European Championship Under-19, 2002
European Championship Under-16, 2001

Individual Honours

MVP for the Final of the 2008 European Championships
Premier League Silver Boot Winner (2007–2008)
MVP for the European Under-19s (2002) and Golden Ball
winner
MVP for the Euro Under-16 (2001) and Golden Ball winner

Bibliography

Cruise, Ian, *Fernando Torres, Liverpool's Glorious Number 9*, 2009 John Blake Publishing

Hughes, Simon, *Fernando Torres: a year in the life, 2008*, Trinity MirrorSport Media

Miguélez José and Matallanas Javier G., *Sentimiento Atlético: cien años de sueños, alegrías y desencantos*, 2003 Plaza Y Janés

Manolete, *Soy del Atléti,¡y qué!* 2008, Now Books

Newspapers
Spain
EL País
El Mundo
ABC
Público
La Vanguardia
El Periódico de Catalunya
La Razón
Marca
As
Mundo deportivo
Sport

UK
The Times
Independent
Guardian
Sun
Daily Mirror
Daily Mail
Liverpool Echo

Italy
Corriere della Sera
La Repubblica
La Gazzetta dello Sport

France
L'Équipe

Websites
www.fernando9torres.com
www.thekidtorres.com/
www.liverpoolfc.tv
www.clubatleticodemadrid.com
www.rfef.es
www.uefa.com
www.fifa.com

Acknowledgements

To Elvira, Olmo, Lorenzo, Alda and Tullio.

Thanks to Fernando Torres for his football

Thanks to the Liverpool fans

Thank as well to the Atléti fans

Thanks to Laure Merle d'Aubigné, Oliver Pugh, Geoffrey Goff, Yolanda Vega, Stephen Jones, Simon Cranston-Smith, Filippo Ricci, Carlos Carpio, Juan Castro, Sid Lowe, Guillem Balagué, Michael Robinson, Abraham García, Fabio Capello, Franco Baldini, Fabio Cannavaro, Álvaro Arbeloa, Paloma Antoranz, Javier Camacho, José Antonio Camacho, Pascual Blázquez, Tony Roldán, Maria Teresa Chiriví, Manolo Rangel, Pedro Calvo, Vicente del Bosque, Andrés Perales, Juan Gómez, Alexis Gómez, Iñaki Sáez, Rafa Benítez, Javier Aguirre, Manolo Briñas, Pepe Reina, Kiko, Andrés Iniesta, Sergi Noguera, Nacho Aznar, Gregorio Manzano, Héctor Romero, Graeme Souness, Kenny Dalglish, Juan Francisco Sánchez Argüello, Manolo Robles, Miguel Ángel Gómez, Julián Hernández, Ángel Sánchez, Javier Tamames.

In memory of Paul Marsh, West Ham fan and founder of The Marsh Agency.